What people are saying about City Dog...

"I highly recommend *City Dog* to everyone who either lives with a dog or is thinking about doing so, in the city or the country."—**Marc Bekoff**, author, *Strolling with our Kin, Minding Animals*, and (with Jane Goodall) *The Ten Trusts*

"A well-written, informative, and carefully researched book that will help many dogs adapt more easily to city life, along with their human companions....With this book, urban parents will have a much easier time bringing a dog into the family and enhancing the quality of life for all concerned."
—**Michael W. Fox**, author, *Understanding Your Dog*

"How did we ever get along without this invaluable guide? There's no way I would adopt a dog without having it within arm's reach. Its use will certainly make a lot of dogs and their owners a lot happier."—**Rue McClanahan**, actress and animal advocate

Trowser, a capital dog

CITY DOG

Choosing and Living Well With a Dog in Town

Patricia Curtis

Lantern Books • New York
A Division of Booklight Inc.

Lantern Books
One Union Square West, Suite 201
New York, NY 10003

Copyright © Patricia Curtis 2002

Cover photographs: Robin Holland
Front cover design: Wendy Palitz
Book design: Erin K. MacLean

Printed in the United States of America

TABLE OF CONTENTS

Acknowledgments

B efore I thank the people who helped me with this book, I want to pay homage to the dogs I have had over my lifetime—Laddie, Benjy, Dandy, Sally, Lucy, and Susannah—two males and four females, all of them mixed-breed, sweet-tempered, beautiful, and lovable. If they hadn't taught me so much about themselves, I couldn't have written this book.

I am extremely grateful to my daughter, Wendy Palitz, for the cover design; to Lily Horan, who cooperated fully by posing with her favorite dog, my docile Susannah, for the cover photo; and to the photographer Robin Holland, for her patience as well as her skill.

A special thank you goes to Dr. JoAnne Greenberg, a competent and caring veterinarian, who read and advised me on the medical and diet information in several chapters. And I am indebted to Dr. Audrey Hayes, who served as the expert reader on the previous edition of this book.

My appreciation also goes to Josephine Gassner and Linda Thompson, professional dog walkers in my Brooklyn neighborhood; Dr. Susan Phillips Cohen, counselor at the Animal Medical Center in New York City; photographer Jane Sapinsky; photographer Charles Debold, who took some of the photographs under difficult conditions; Paul Glassner, editor of *Our Animals*, the magazine of the San Francisco SPCA, for his kindness and help; Jonathan Pearl, who generously lent me his photos of his dog Trowser; Dennis

Knebel and Ken Burgess, for the photos of Elmo and Louie; and my friends who contributed photos of their own dogs: Margery, Claire, Donna, Lynn, Robin, Judy—I owe you.

And finally, my deep gratitude to Sarah Gallogly for her superb editing.

Preface

When you read this book, you'll notice that I use the pronoun "it" when referring to a dog. Of course, no dog is an "it." My use of this word stems from the failure of the English language to provide a singular pronoun that applies to both genders, as the plural pronouns "they," "them," and so on do very nicely. To avoid the tiresome repetition of "he and she," "him and her," and "his and hers," I had to fall back on it, or its. My apologies to all dogs and their owners for this.

I also wish there were a word other than "owner" to use when referring to the person who lives with and is responsible for a dog. The law still considers our dogs property, even though we all know they are much more than that. "Parent" is certainly too coy, though in a way we do parent our pets. "Guardian" is better, though we do more than guard our pets.

As yet, there is no satisfactory word that covers our relationship with our dogs. Perhaps one will evolve as the animal's meaning to us becomes fully recognized and established in common language. Meanwhile, for referring to their people as their owners, my apologies to dogs.

Louie and Elmo believe this book will show that, with adequate training, humans can make excellect city companions

1. YOUR CITY DOG
Choosing the Best for You

Dog: a four-legged carnivorous animal whose natural habitat, in most parts of the world, is the human home. The creature comes in various sizes and may be beloved, mistreated, or simply taken for granted.

The early canids evolved in such close association with the first human beings that nobody knows for certain just when or how the relationship began. Presumably, wild dogs hung around prehistoric caves or campsites and scavenged for the remains of meals. According to early cave paintings, primitive people trained these wild dogs to hunt with them; the animals' keen hearing, sense of smell, and speed were no doubt useful.

But those humans took from their environment only what they needed for survival and were gatherers as much as hunters, so dogs must have performed other functions as well. They probably gave warning when strangers approached. Perhaps their pups were playmates for the children. They also may have filled a need for companionship, as they most definitely do today.

The way I imagine it, one cold, wet day when a cave man (or woman) returned from a successful hunt, the dog stopped as usual at the entrance of the warm cave and looked in hopefully.

"Oh, all right, come on in," the man (or woman) said, and made a gesture inviting the animal in out of the bad weather.

When the dog walked warily across the threshold, it took a giant step that affected the lives of all dogs thereafter. It cast its lot with us and became domesticated. It may have had cause to regret it many times since. When people were little more than barbarians, they probably treated dogs worse than they did each other. Eventually, certain fortunate dogs were upgraded to the status of pets and fared better, though in some societies they were still looked upon as little more than vermin. Certainly, references to dogs in the Bible are contemptuous.

I will spare you the details of the brutal general treatment of dogs from the Middle Ages until the first anticruelty laws of the nineteenth century. Even today, dogs endure monstrous cruelty in many places, and not just in poor and backward countries. They may be abused and neglected even in the genteel neighborhoods of modern America.

Nevertheless, over seventy million dogs live with us in our modern, urban caves. Over half of all American households have dogs or cats, or both. The animals have adapted to our ways and made themselves indispensable to us. And, though there are a few remaining species of wild dogs, the domestic canine cannot survive without us.

Let me tell you how I got my first city dog.

One Sunday afternoon many years ago I was walking with some friends in Central Park in New York City, where I live, when we met a little brown dog running loose. Heartless people who want to get rid of dogs frequently use Central Park as a dumping ground. It's said that packs of feral dogs (former pets that are now homeless and have more or less reverted to a wild state) exist there, though I have never seen any such packs, and lack of food and other problems of homelessness ensure that the survival rate among them, like that of most abandoned dogs, can't be very high.

Many other dog owners simply let their dogs run off the leash in the park, in spite of the city ordinance against it. So we looked

Benjy, an excellent city dog

around for any possible owner of the brown dog and did not encourage him to follow us, especially since he didn't look particularly starved or unkempt.

But follow us he did. His behavior was extremely anxious and humble—a telltale sign of an abandoned dog.

Two little boys materialized; the dog seemed to know them. "He used to be our dog," one replied to our question. "But our father got a German Shepherd he likes better."

So that was it—the kids had been told to lose the dog in the park. One child picked up the dog in his arms. "Here, lady," he said to me.

Just like that, I became a dog owner. I borrowed the drawstring from a companion's parka and put it around the dog's neck as a makeshift leash. He acted willing, even relieved, to come along with us. When I got him home, my family's two cats eyed him suspiciously, though without fear. He sized them up and, realizing that they lived there, he apparently discerned that if he wanted to live there, too, he'd have to keep his distance. From then on, his behavior toward them was the height of decorum.

I named the Central Park dog Benjy. He looked rather like a small deer—short brown coat, big eyes, big ears, and slender, longish legs. His ancestry must have included some Basenji, though unlike the true Basenji he had a loud bark.

Benjy was our good dog for nine years, and when he died, I missed him terribly. I could see him lying in all his favorite spots; I could hear the tick-tack of his nails across the floor. Unconsciously, I expected to find him waiting inside the door each time I returned home.

Ten days later, I couldn't stand being dogless any longer, so I answered an ad in the newspaper. A young couple living in a garden apartment with a whole passel of dogs and cats wanted to pare down.

Poor two-year-old Dandy was the dog fingered for giveaway, and suddenly, as I was sitting in the apartment talking to the couple, she knew. She crawled into a corner under the bed. Her former owner had to pull her out, drag her from the house, and stuff her into a taxicab with me.

Dandy was subdued for a few days, but settled in bravely. She became a beloved pet and for her sixteen-year lifetime was one of the great delights of my life, friend to my family, cats, friends, and the entire neighborhood.

Dandy illustrates another time-honored way of acquiring a pet. Perhaps it was just marvelous luck that both she and Benjy, though I didn't go out and choose them, turned out to be perfect city dogs.

My next dog, Sally, I adopted from the Humane Society of New York, and with her I enjoyed fifteen years of pleasure and companionship. All three dogs were tough acts to follow, but Susannah, whom I adopted from her previous owner and who is lying by my chair this minute, is equal to her predecessors in every doggy way.

Dogs, like people, owe their temperaments and intelligence to a complex combination of their genes and their individual life experiences. And there's one additional factor in dogs: They have a strong desire to please the people they love, so they are amazingly flexible.

If you already have a dog—have taken in a stray, adopted from an animal shelter or private home, or gone out and bought one—you may have found a winner and are reading this book just for additional information and, I hope, pleasure. I'll try to provide you with ideas for steps you can take to make living with your pet in the city more comfortable and rewarding for both of you.

Or, if you are about to choose a dog and wish to do it in a clear-eyed and well-informed way, this book is here to help you make that commitment a permanent and mutually happy one.

YOUR LIFESTYLE

There should be nothing tentative about acquiring a dog—it ought to be almost like adopting a child. You wouldn't keep in the back of your mind the notion that you could always return the baby to the adoption agency if it got too big, or you had to move, or it turned out to be too much of a bother.

Having a dog is a privilege and a joy, if you do it right. If you aren't prepared to put up with the hassles, take the responsibility, and be the animal's friend for life, you should forgo the pleasure.

But once you've decided you really, really want a dog and are prepared to do right by it, the first thing to consider, obviously, is how having a dog would fit into your lifestyle. I have so often heard people say that they would love to have a dog but aren't home enough to take proper care of it. They know a dog needs a minimum of three outdoor walks a day, for example, and they simply can't manage it. So if you travel a lot, work long hours, or have a busy social life, and no one else is home, you must come up with good solutions to these problems.

You can avail yourself of the services of a professional dog walker—those hardy souls you see on the street with a whole covey of assorted dogs trotting along on leashes. And in some towns, there are doggy day care businesses—places that keep dogs while their owners

Charles Debold

Professional dog walker Josephine Gassner at work

are away during the day. Both cost money, of course, but many city dog lovers swear by these options.

Hiring a regular dog walker or enrolling your dog in day care not only solves the problem of your dog's loneliness, lack of care, and possible misbehavior but can really be fun for the dog: most dogs, in their race memory, are pack animals anyway and like nothing more than hanging out with their own kind. It will also give you peace of mind.

In general, it's best to use real professionals as dog walkers and day care providers, and to check their references. If it's a day care place, visit it yourself. Some day care places are homes, but some are elaborate businesses and offer all sorts of amenities, such as pools, gyms, and grooming services.

It is not a good idea to rely on the high school kid next door to care for your dog on a regular basis, unless the boy or girl is that rare child who is not only totally, completely dependable but never, never has soccer practice or music lessons after school. Hire the high school boy or girl on occasion, but on a regular basis, an established, professional person or place is a better choice.

Even if you have a yard, don't even think about leaving a dog tied up or fenced in all day long. Not only is that cruel, but there is a real danger that the animal will escape or, more likely, be stolen. A dog can be stolen by someone who wants it, or hopes to sell it, or just for mischief. It can also be stolen by someone who sells dogs to experimental laboratories (see Chapter 7).

If you own your own home, there is probably no legal reason you can't have a dog. And I'm assuming that if you live in an apartment, the building allows dogs. (For more on this, see Chapter 11.) Some apartment building managers, or co-op or condominium boards, may allow dogs but impose limits on number and size. Restrictions on the size of a dog are ill-founded, because some small breeds—terriers, for instance—are more likely to yap a lot or nip people's ankles in the elevator, while some large breeds—retrievers, for instance— are famous for having mellow temperaments. Many rules regarding dogs are thought up by people who know nothing about dogs, but that's life.

Choosing the kind of dog you want is your next consideration. Very few dogs are misfits in cities, but many are the wrong dogs for the homes they're in. Selecting an appropriate dog seems a matter of common sense, but if it is really so self-evident, why do we see so many poorly matched pets and owners?

I have seen a frustrated young Giant Schnauzer pulling at the leash held by an elderly lady who loves him dearly but had not anticipated the exercise needs of that spirited animal, or the difficulty she would have in controlling him. The problem with this dog is not that he lives in the city. He could thrive with an urban dweller who took him for long daily walks and trained him properly.

On the other hand, I have also seen muscular male joggers accompanied by panting little doggy skeletons trying miserably to keep up. Why didn't those human athletes get themselves dogs to match?

I once met a couple at a party who told me about a mistake they had made. They had thought it was a nifty idea to get a pair of glossy

Irish Setter puppies, not realizing how much time they'd need to devote to them. With husband and wife at work all day, the pups demolished the apartment. And as the dogs quickly grew into hyperactive adolescents, neither partner felt like walking the two maniacs for an hour at the end of the day, much less like taking them to obedience classes. It was not easy to find new homes for them, and in the end they had to be separated and given away.

Be realistic about your lifestyle and what you wish for in a dog, and don't have unfair expectations of the animal. Naturally, time is especially important during a dog's first weeks in your home. Arrange a free weekend so you can adopt a dog on Friday and devote the entire weekend to getting to know it and helping it settle in with you. Some dogs learn faster than others; some may need several weekends of undivided attention, with brush-up courses in between, to become truly good urban dogs.

Are you very fussy about your home and easily upset by mess? Though the great pleasure and comfort of having a dog far outweigh the nuisance of cleanups, in this book we are talking about a dog that lives with you in your home, where it ought to live. (Don't get me started on dogs that have to live outdoors chained up, with doghouses. There should be laws against that.) The presence of a dog is bound to have some impact in your house or apartment. My dog Sally had a long, silky coat and shed mightily year round. Susannah has a smooth, rather short coat—and sheds mightily year round. Your feelings about dog hair and paw prints are a consideration in your choice of dog.

Also, of course, you'll take into account your children, if any (see below), and the presence of other pets (see Chapter 9).

YOUR SPACE, THE DOG'S SIZE

How big is your house or apartment? If you think I'm going to suggest that, unless you own a big townhouse you should have nothing but a tiny dog, you're wrong. Much more depends on the type of dog and how much time you can devote to it.

As a rule of thumb, small or medium-sized dogs may be more practical than large ones for some city people who work outside the home. Certain small breeds do need quite a lot of exercise, but they generally don't need the distance exercise that the retrievers and other big-chested, long-legged, active types need. A little dog can let off steam running around indoors, and to it, a turn around the block is an excursion, while a large, spirited dog needs a lot more than that.

I had for one month a huge, exuberant young dog I called Lucy, whom somebody gave me after my dear fifteen-year-old Sally passed away. During that especially cold January, I walked Lucy four or five times a day, but that plainly wasn't enough for her. I often hired athletic teen-age boys—"Take her out and run her to the ground!" I begged them. They would come back forty minutes later, sweating and panting, while Lucy wasn't even breathing hard and seemed to say, "But I was just getting started!"

Lucy would have been fine as a city dog in a house with a yard, or with an active owner who could take her for several long walks, or to a dog run, where she could play hard, every day. Fortunately for both of us, a friend found the perfect home for Lucy—in a big house in the country, with a young couple and two children. The moral of this story is that you should always pick your own dog, keeping your age, energy level, and preferences firmly in mind.

If there's a dog run in your neighborhood, the exercise problem is virtually solved. Both you and your dog walker, if you have one, can take advantage of that. But, property values being what they are, only the most enlightened cities have enough dog runs.

If you do want a running partner, or enjoy and have time for long walks, you might want a big, hardy dog. Even a Great Dane could live happily enough with an owner who could provide plenty of long, time-consuming walks. In that case, if you fall in love with a big, lovable hulk of a dog and you're certain you'd like to live with it day in, day out, I say go ahead.

Dogs under 20 pounds are small; dogs 20 to about 60 pounds are considered medium-sized; large dogs are roughly between 65 and

120 pounds; and any dog that weighs in above 120 probably falls into the giant breed category. When you are deciding between big and little, remember that a small dog can be toted about the city in a carrier, even on public transportation. That's helpful when you want to take it to the veterinarian, to visit a friend, or on a plane trip. Anyone who has ever tried to hail a taxi with a medium-sized or large dog on a leash knows what a frustrating experience that can be.

Of course, if you have a car, then size doesn't matter. And in many cities there are pet taxis or car services that will chauffeur dogs of any size hither and yon, with or without their owners.

Another basic consideration is whether to choose a puppy or an adult dog. A dog is considered a puppy until it is nearly a year old, though very small breeds may reach their full growth at six months, while large breeds may take as long as fourteen months. How can you tell how big a little handful of a pup will grow up to be? With a purebred dog, that's fairly easy, because its eventual size will be within a predictable range. Also, females tend to be somewhat smaller than males. The full-grown size of mixed-breed pups is harder to estimate, unless the parents, at least the mother, are known. Often, the coat can give you a clue to a pup's parentage. A popular belief is that you can judge a puppy's eventual size by the proportions of its feet. But sometimes a mixed-breed pup with huge paws becomes only a medium-sized dog with big feet. Or vice versa—once in a while a pup with paws that aren't anything much to speak of grows up into a rather big dog with comparatively little feet.

A puppy will require much, much more of your time, for many months, than an adult dog will (see Chapter 2). In a household of very busy people, the dog that will cause the least trouble and require the least amount of time, comparatively, is an adult dog. Nevertheless, if your idea of the dog for you is a large puppy, then that's what you should have, even in the city. But do yourself a favor and at least get one that is as temperamentally suitable for city living as possible (see below), and be sure to obedience-train it.

THE COST FACTOR

Think hard to be sure you can afford a dog, now and in the foreseeable long-term future. I'm not talking about the initial outlay, but the cost of feeding and maintaining the animal for its entire life.

Big dogs, of course, cost more to feed than small ones. That adorable Yellow Lab puppy will grow up and need a large dinner every day for maybe twelve or thirteen years.

You'll need a license every year, and you may want to take the dog to obedience classes (a great idea). It will need a collar, leash, shampoo, and maybe a coat. Better add regular, or at least occasional, professional grooming fees to your estimate, especially with certain breeds. And there may be dog walking or boarding fees.

Be sure to figure on veterinary bills, whether your dog is big or small, purebred or mixed breed. Unless you adopt from a shelter that automatically spays or neuters its pets before adoption, you'll need to pay for that operation. Even a dog that enjoys good health for most of its life will need annual checkups and vaccinations. In its old age, the dog will most likely need frequent, expensive medical care.

And in case your pet has a serious accident or illness, would you mind laying out big bucks, even sacrificing, if necessary, to get it well? Every animal shelter with a clinic can show you dogs that were brought in sick or injured and then abandoned when the owners learned what the vet bills would be.

One shelter manager told me the story of a beautiful young Husky whose owners brought her in to the veterinary clinic with fractured forelegs; she had been hit by a car. When her owners were told what the charges would be for setting the poor animal's legs, they balked.

"We'll give her up and adopt a new, healthy dog," they offered.

"Not from this shelter, you won't!" said the outraged shelter manager. "This dog is hurt but not incurable. You don't bring in a broken dog and trade it in for a new one, like a vacuum cleaner or a radio."

The veterinarian set the Husky's legs, and the shelter publicized her case, complete with a picture in the newspaper. Sure enough, several prospective owners materialized, and the lucky dog went off with one as soon as her legs were out of the casts.

With proper care, your dog will be with you for many years. While this is good news, it is also an important consideration if you contemplate retiring and living on a lowered income in a few years.

SEX AND LIFE EXPECTANCY

Female dogs are said to be easier to train than males, and they are likely to be more docile, a desirable trait for city living. Some dog lovers consider females more affectionate and companionable, though in loyalty to the memory of my male dog, Benjy, and my childhood dog, Laddie, I have to question that. There's no evidence that one sex is more intelligent than the other.

Here's something you may not have thought of: A female dog can hold her urine longer that a male—some can wait as long as twelve hours if necessary—which might be an advantage in a household where no one is home during the day. And on walks, a female will usually empty her bladder all at once. A male dog may urinate in little spurts here and there, and it can seem to take him forever to relieve himself, especially on cold winter nights.

But if your dog is not already spayed or neutered when you get it, you will certainly want to have that done (see Chapter 6), and it is more expensive to spay a female than to neuter a male.

As to life expectancy, be aware that the common belief that each year of a dog's life equals seven human years is inaccurate. A year-old dog is a sexually mature teenager, not a seven-year-old child. A two-year-old dog of any breed is comparable to a human adult in his or her mid-twenties. After that age, you might estimate that each year of a dog's life equals roughly four human years—but you have to figure the breed's life expectancy into the equation, and life spans vary greatly.

In general, the toy breeds and other small dogs live longest: twelve years on average, and many are still perky at fifteen years or more. A medium-sized dog (say, thirty-five to sixty pounds) can easily live to ten, and longer with luck and good care. Both Dandy and Sally, who were medium-sized, lived to nearly sixteen. Although nine years is about average for large dogs, Lennie, the Golden Retriever next door, is hanging in pretty well at fourteen. A Great Dane or other of the giant breeds has an average life span of six or seven years, and it's a miracle if one lives to ten.

CHILDREN AND DOGS

If you're acquiring a dog that's to be a pal to the children, think ahead to the time when the kids will be out of the nest for good.

I'll never forget seeing a spaniel turned into an animal shelter by a man who, grinning sheepishly, explained that the dog was his daughter's, but she was off at college now, and he and his wife didn't want the trouble of keeping a dog. The frightened animal apparently guessed what was happening and had to be dragged bodily into the building, all the while frantically trying to ingratiate herself with the man and everybody else.

The spaniel may have been a devoted, sweet-tempered, well-behaved pet, but no matter—she had outlived her usefulness and was no long convenient to keep. So she was discarded like an outgrown toy. Her chances of being adopted from the shelter were nil. She was middle-aged and not particularly beautiful. The shelter was crowded with dogs that needed homes, dogs that were younger and more appealing than she. I learned later that she was killed within two days, days during which she suffered total fear and abandonment.

By contrast, for several years I saw in my neighborhood a gray-haired man walking a very old dog who, he told me, had been left behind by grown children. When this dog finally died, it was not replaced—but it had been allowed to live out its life comfortably in its own home.

Lily gets a thrill when she is allowed to walk Susannah
(Don't worry—there were seven adults virtually within arm's reach)

The age of a child who can appreciate a dog and learn to treat it gently varies according to the child, of course, but the consensus seems to be about three. Younger than that, a child is likely to yank and pull and poke a dog, and unless the dog is unusually long-suffering, this treatment can hurt the dog and cause it to defend itself by snapping.

If you already have a dog and a baby is born into the family, make sure the dog doesn't feel replaced. Most dogs will quite readily accept the baby as a new member of its pack, but some are jealous at first. Try to spend some time alone with the dog; take it for walks by itself, without the baby carriage. Greet the dog as you always did whenever you come home, and don't push the dog away when you're holding the baby.

That being said, never, ever leave the baby and dog alone together. A dog is a dog, and while it's extremely rare for a dog to suddenly act out of character, or in a way that seems irrational to us, it can happen. Remember that statistically, most dog bites are from owned, family dogs, and most victims of dog bites are children. You can prevent this by treating the dog well and teaching the children to do the same, and by being prudent.

Never get a dog with the idea that the dog will "teach the child responsibility." Although a dog can be a wonderful companion, playmate, confidant, and comfort to a child, it should not be expected to be a teacher. It will not, by itself, transform a child into a responsible person, no matter how much the parents wish it could. And it is unfair to make a dog dependent on a little kid for its food, walks, and other needs.

Don't try to motivate your child with the threat: "If you forget to walk Max one more time, we'll get rid of him." This makes the pet seem like a disposable object, a message you never want to give anybody. It also will make the child feel guilty, especially if you do carry out the threat and give the dog away, an act for which the child will probably never forgive you.

And while a dog is an especially good pet for a teenager (as a friend of mine put it, "My dog got me through my adolescence"), the well-known forgetfulness and self-preoccupation of even the best-intentioned teenagers usually make them poor candidates to be the sole caretakers of living creatures.

It comes down to this: Parents must be willing and able to assume the care of a dog themselves. You can insist that the child help, you can continually remind a child to see that he or she fulfills a task, but you are the role model. It's up to you to protect the rights of the dog. Isn't it a good idea to teach a child that others have rights?

Never give a dog to a child as a Christmas present—or rather, don't bring it into the household just at Christmas. There is too much noise, activity, and excitement. The animal will either feel frightened and want to hide, or become overstimulated and keyed up. In either case, it will probably get an upset stomach (at both ends), or grow exhausted and start to nip in self-defense.

A child old enough to understand can be given instead a leash, a collar, and maybe a picture of a dog with the promise that the pet is coming in, say, a week. Better yet, take the child to help pick out the dog after the holidays.

While pet shops do a brisk business selling puppies at Christmas, many good shelters refuse to allow their pets to be adopted during Christmas week. They ask instead that people come back after New Year's, when the holiday season has quieted. This greatly lowers the chances that the gift animal will be returned to the shelter by mid-January.

Many breeds, and many individual dogs, while fine with older children and adults, are not suitable for families with infants, toddlers, preschoolers, or even kindergartners. While this is not generally true of puppies (see Chapter 2), many adult dogs are unnerved by the unsteady gait, abrupt gestures, and screams and other noises of very young children, and will shy away or even bite in fear.

Also, a grown dog may already have had bad experiences with children and formed a dislike for them. Some breeds have better track records with kids than other breeds, and so, keeping in mind that every dog is unique, it might be wise to choose a breed or mix that is considered good with kids. (For some suggestions, see Temperament, below.) And, if you're adopting a dog from a shelter or private home, it is sometimes possible to find out in advance how an individual dog feels about children.

My dog Benjy was as pleasant a dog as you could possibly want around adults, but children made him nervous. He once, to my intense embarrassment and concern, snapped at the child of a visiting friend. But Dandy and Sally, who had not to my knowledge been raised around children, were sweet and patient even when being poked in the eye and petted the wrong way, back to front against the grain. Susannah, according to the amount of friendly licking she does, simply likes the way children taste.

But if parents are prepared to teach children how to treat a dog with kindness and respect, they can't give them a better gift. Those of us who enjoyed the devotion and companionship of our childhood dogs never forget them.

TEMPERAMENT

A prime concern of a city person choosing a dog should be the animal's temperament. The type of dog that will be easiest to live with in an urban environment is not easily startled and upset by sirens, traffic, and crowds, and is low in dominance. I'm not talking about a timid wimp, but an easygoing dog that won't be difficult to train, won't give you an argument every time you say "No" or "Heel." A high-dominance dog is usually hyper, headstrong, and difficult to control.

The reason dominance is an important quality is that dogs are by nature pack animals, and you, or someone in your family, will be its pack leader. A submissive dog won't be forever challenging the pack leader and trying to get its own way. I'll talk more about dominance in later chapters, but because it figures in your choice of a dog for city living, it is important to mention here.

Claire DeSilver

Robin, a champion English Cocker Spaniel

Dogs are very quick to recognize a pack leader. In fact, Dandy would become ridiculously submissive whenever a friend of mine who happened to be a dog trainer came to the house, even though he had never given her a command. She knew a pack leader when she saw one.

When I was a child, we took in a little stray dog who became my loyal playmate and companion. Laddie loved us all, but he obviously decided that my father was pack leader. My father was always kind to Laddie, but never spent much time alone with him or trained him. But Dad was a strong personality—my sister and I called him the Benevolent Despot. Laddie decided he was top dog and automatically obeyed him, no matter what.

It's easy to assume that the smaller the dog, the more suitable it is for city living. Not necessarily. Some of the toy breeds, such as Pomeranians, Pekingese, Yorkshire Terriers, Chihuahuas, and Toy Poodles, and mixtures of these, can be noisy yappers. They not only bark when a burglar tries to pick your lock, which is good, but they also bark at neighbors, guests, the super, deliverymen, and imaginary intruders, which is not good. If you really want a dog that will fit in your briefcase, choose carefully. If you get a real barker (and those little dogs' barks can be earsplitting), you or your neighbors—or your landlord—may lose patience before you can train your pet to bark only selectively.

Some breeds of dogs are reputed to be higher, or lower, in dominance than others. There will always be an exception among individual dogs, of course. But in general, here is a short list of breeds that are said to be amenable to training and tolerant of children (your own or those you meet on the street), which makes them good choices as city dogs. You might want to consider one of these, mixed or purebred:

Bearded Collie
Bichon Frisé
Boston Terrier
Boxer
Brittany
Cairn Terrier
Cavalier King Charles Spaniel
Cocker Spaniel
German Shepherd Dog
Golden Retriever
Labrador Retriever
Lhasa Apso
Miniature Poodle
Shih Tzu
Springer Spaniel
Standard Poodle
Welsh Corgi
West Highland White Terrier
Wirehaired Fox Terrier

You will see plenty of other types of dogs on the streets of every city in America whose owners think they're the best and should be included on this short list. My apologies to them.

There are trends in dogs, as in everything else, and one popular dog these days is the Rottweiler—big, handsome, alert, and strong-willed. This breed must be socialized very early as a puppy and gently but firmly trained, because it will try to dominate you and everyone else, every day of its life. Although I have met many gentle "Rotts," they can sometimes be difficult to deal with as city pets.

A city person choosing a dog should also be aware that certain breeds—some hounds and pointers, for example, and Irish Setters—are thought to be difficult to housebreak.

So why ask for trouble? Better to choose from among those breeds with a suitable track record for city life, and at least start off with an advantage. One person you might want to consult for advice is a dog trainer (carefully chosen, see Chapter 4) or perhaps an urban veterinarian, who has certainly had a chance to observe the temperament as well as the general health of many different types of dogs.

I asked Josephine Gassner, who has been walking and boarding dogs professionally in my Brooklyn neighborhood for over twelve years, if there was a breed she thought made an especially good city pet. "Shepherd mix," she said. "They're smart and trainable. The various retrievers are usually nice dogs, but they need a lot of exercise, they need a job. Spaniels may be overbred and high-strung."

"But," she added, "any dog is a good dog in the right home."

PUREBRED VS. MIXED BREED

If what you want in a dog is affection, beauty, intelligence, fun, trainability, and perhaps some protection, a creature that will be your companion and enrich your life a million times over, then it doesn't matter whether you purchase a fancy purebred from a breeder or bail a mongrel waif out of a shelter. Many a dog, given love, training, and proper care, can provide what you're looking for.

Dogs share certain qualities of dogginess, and therein lies their wonderful gift to human beings. All domestic canids, in their marvelous, infinite variety, are still dogs.

All the different breeds, from the 3-pound Pomeranian to the 174-pound Mastiff, from the practically hairless Chihuahua to the Komondor with its floor-length ropes of hair, were created by human beings. From that wolflike creature that took to hanging around us so many millennia ago, dogs have not followed an evolutionary path of their own but have been molded by people into whatever we needed or fancied.

It's impossible to get an accurate figure on the percentage of purebreds among owned dogs in the United States, but a reasonable estimate is perhaps as much as one-third. Some people have a strong preference for a certain breed of dog, and for them, nothing else will do. I know a man who simply loves English Bulldogs and has had one after another, putting up with their wheezing and snoring and drooling because he likes their funny faces and endearing personalities. If he couldn't have an English Bulldog, he might pass up having a dog at all.

There is something to be said on both sides of the purebred vs. mixed breed debate.

With a purebred dog, you'll have some clues to the temperament you can expect. In some mixed-breed dogs, the ancestry is quite apparent, and you can be guided by what is known about the personalities of the breeds they combine. Nevertheless, a dog's environment plays a big role in its temperament. And the bottom line is that dogs are individuals. A neighbor of mine had a Shetland Sheepdog who was timid and snappish, but his successor, also a male Sheltie from the same breeder, was poised and agreeable.

Purebreds and mixed breeds seem about equally liable to develop behavior problems. Many people believe that purebreds are more likely to be nervous and high-strung; however, if they have been carefully bred for temperament as well as looks, this shouldn't be true.

It's sometimes said that mixed-breed dogs are innately healthier than purebreds. It is true that with purebred dogs there's the risk of harmful inbreeding, especially among those from unscrupulous or amateur breeders. Inbreeding can cause health defects to become dominant.

Unfortunately, many purebred dogs have been bred for qualities that appeal to the dog fancy but aren't in the best interests of the animals. Some examples are the Pekingese, whose pop eyes are subject to chronic lacerations; the English Bulldog, whose short snout causes severe respiratory problems; and that rare and expensive curiosity, the Shar-Pei, whose deeply wrinkled skin results in chronic dermatological disorders. Inbreeding of some popular breeds, such as German Shepherd Dogs and Golden Retrievers, has caused them to be at risk for hip dysplasia.

One problem with purebred dogs is that when a breed becomes trendy there is a responding upsurge in the production of these dogs. Puppy mills get busy. Puppy mills, in case you aren't familiar with the term, are wholesale factory-like places where masses of dogs are "manufactured" as fast as the bitches can give birth. The offspring, who may already be in poor health because their mothers were, are then shipped to pet shops throughout the land to meet the demands of the dog-buying public.

Transportation takes a heavy toll on those young puppies, and many sicken and die en route, or arrive at the pet shops half dead. Then, the atmosphere in the average pet shop is conducive to the spread of disease, so even puppies that have survived shipment may become sickly (see Chapter 2).

Backyard breeders—enthusiastic amateurs who have one or a few pedigreed dogs but who lack professionalism—often jump on the bandwagon, too, and turn out pups to sell.

These profit-motivated breeding practices usually pass on from one generation to the next a chronic predisposition to the health problems that plague so many breeds, including hip dysplasia, eye defects, tumors, lung problems, deafness, and bloat. When dogs are bred to make a buck, little or no attention is paid to genetic excellence—or temperament.

The irresponsibility of puppy mills, pet shops, and the uninformed dog-buying public can have disastrous consequences for dogs. When kids who saw the "101 Dalmatians" movies demanded Dalmatian puppies, animal shelters were soon flooded with discarded Dalmatians whose owners had found out the hard way about the demands of raising pups of a high-strung, stubborn, and often sickly breed.

If you feel you must have a designer dog—an adorable Bichon Frisé or a magnificent purebred Labrador Retriever—try your local animal shelters first. They usually have some purebreds for adoption. Or go on the Internet and find a rescue group for the breed you are interested in. There are rescue groups nationwide for virtually all

Dandy, the South Irish Spaniel

breeds, who have purebred or even mixed-breed dogs for adoption. They list on their websites people who are fostering purebred or mixed-breed dogs whose owners had to give them up but didn't want to surrender them to shelters. You might find just the dog you are looking for, one who has been living in a home and not a cage.

The Internet is a great source of information about dogs, including dogs for adoption. There's a National Breed Club Rescue Network, for example, and an All-Breed Rescue Alliance.

For important information about professional breeders and pet shops, see Chapter 2.

As far as I am concerned, mixed-breed dogs have everything purebreds have except "status." This matters more to some people than to others. When Dandy was young, a friend once said to me that I should not refer to her as a mixed-breed, but give her a little class—make up a breed just for her.

"What would you suggest?" I asked, looking at my beautiful dog and wondering which of her forebears had contributed the dominant genes.

"Well, she probably has some spaniel in her, and she has red hair," he observed. "Why not call her a South Irish Spaniel?"

A few days later a man standing next to me in line at the bank was petting her. (Strangers were frequently attracted to Dandy because of her sweet expression.) "What kind of dog is this?" he asked. Now was my chance. "She's a South Irish Spaniel," I replied, deadpan.

"Oh!" said he. "Those are marvelous dogs!"

SHELTER DOGS AND STRAYS

Of the many, many city dogs I know personally, well over half of the most attractive—good dispositions, good behavior, good looks—were adopted from shelters or found.

Animal shelters offer a wide selection of dogs—young and not so young, big and little, homely and gorgeous, you name it. On a national average, over one-fourth are purebreds. Staff members can usually give you some information on the temperament and background of a dog that interests you.

A shelter dog that has just been surrendered from a private home may be a good choice—it depends on why it was given up. A dog whose owner died or for some other reason could no longer be cared for can be a better pet than a dog from a breeder or pet shop, who has never lived in a home.

True, a shelter dog may have been surrendered because of a behavior problem. Sometimes people won't admit that the dog they are abandoning has bad habits because they don't want to jeopardize the dog's chances of being adopted by somebody else. But that should not discourage you. Any dog that has lived in a cage, whether at a breeder's, pet shop, or shelter, will almost certainly have to have at least a brush-up course on housebreaking, and may bark when left alone until it get used to a new home. An understanding person, using good sense and how-to information, can usually correct a behavior problem (see Chapter 4). Also, a dog that behaved badly in one home may turn out to be perfectly well-mannered in the hands of the right owner in the proper environment.

One difficulty in judging a shelter dog is that a normally well behaved pet may be so upset at having been abandoned by its family, or may have had such terrifying experiences as a stray, or may be suffering so much from the confinement of a cage, that it is simply not itself. Some become depressed and fearful; some become hysterical; most hurl themselves at the doors of their cages and bark madly at all visitors, as if saying, "Me! Me! Take me! Get me out of here!" You want to give a dog the benefit of the doubt. Confinement in a cage at a shelter is highly stressful to most.

If a dog comes up to you and acts friendly but doesn't go berserk with excitement, that's a good sign. Try to spend some time alone with a dog that appeals to you, and, if the shelter permits, take it for a walk.

A major concern at some shelters is health. I have seen many shelters that are able to keep dogs decently in relative comfort, but some seem to me to resemble Auschwitz. Most fall somewhere in between. However, any clean, well-run shelter will probably have clean, healthy dogs.

Many shelters advertise themselves as no-kill, which attracts donations from kindhearted but unthinking people. Since no-kill shelters will accept only those animals that they consider adoptable, and that they have room for, this means the pets who are turned away, whatever the reason, go to a city-run shelter. Those shelters are usually in charge of Animal Control and, by contract with their local government, must accept any and all comers. A truly wonderful pet may be denied admission to a no-kill shelter because that shelter is full, so the pet will wind up in a city-run shelter, which is usually underfunded and therefore a less decent place. Since we seem to need animal shelters in our society, it is regrettable that as citizens we don't seem to care that so many shelters are awful.

Remember, too, that some dogs in the no-kill shelters may have had the bad luck not to be adopted and have been there, shut in cages, for months, even years. This is obviously not good for any animal, especially a dog.

Certainly, it's easier to adopt a clean, healthy dog from a good shelter, but the other one, the poor animal suffering in the hellhole shelter, really needs you. If you can bail it out, by all means do it. Know your capabilities and limits—I want adopting a dog to work for both of you.

Over ten million unwanted and homeless dogs end up in shelters nationwide each year. In spite of vigorous adoption campaigns waged by shelters, only about a third of them ever leave. Those facilities that by contract with their local governments must accept any animal brought to them are forced to become mercy killers for the community. Most simply haven't the resources to care for the animals that aren't quickly adopted, and so euthanasia is their only option.

Many people still believe that animal shelters find homes for all the pets that are discarded, and they don't like to think about the statistics that show otherwise. That is magic thinking and eases any guilt owners might feel about surrendering a pet—as well as any guilt about the conditions in many community shelters.

So, one very good reason for adopting a shelter dog or taking in a homeless one is the wonderful feeling you get from knowing that you are giving a home to a dog that needs it, maybe saving its life. A dog, when it realizes that you are taking it out of the shelter or off the street, will go crazy with joy, leaping about, trying to lick your face, wagging its tail till it nearly flies off. A powerful bond can form on the spot. A dog will never forget that you were its savior.

2. PUPPIES
The Joys and the Problems

The fact that puppies are so downright adorable is a mixed blessing for them. No animals are more cuddly, lovable, enchanting, and fun—yet few can cause so much trouble and exasperation. Puppies are often adopted or purchased by people who don't know what to expect in the behavior of a very young dog, or the care and patience it requires. As a result, puppies are punished when they shouldn't be, ruined in disposition and behavior, and abandoned by roadsides or turned in to animal shelters.

Puppies are probably the greatest single victims of impulse buying. People look in the window of a pet shop, or encounter somebody in front of the supermarket with a basketful for giveaway, and they're hooked. People walk down the line of cages in an animal shelter, and this appealing little creature comes wagging at them, licking fingers, begging to be picked up. Nobody, not even a kitten, gets its message across more successfully than a puppy.

Then the person who has succumbed to this hard sell gets the animal home and soon discovers the down side of living with a puppy. A puppy makes puddles and piles, throws up, yelps, whines, sheds, chews things up, and knocks things over. Human patience quickly wears thin and out the puppy goes—frequently to a shelter.

One perceived advantage of adopting or buying a puppy is founded in the belief that when you raise it yourself, you stand a good chance of ending up with just the pet you want. Presumably, if you get a dog accustomed very early to your habits and preferences, it will work out better than one that spent its puppyhood with someone else. Certainly with a puppy you have a golden opportunity to train it properly and establish yourself as pack leader in its eyes, right from the start. Yet I have, in my lifetime, acquired five adult dogs that became wonderful pets. The experiences of many of my dog-owning friends and acquaintances are similar. Early conditioning can't be crucial.

I don't mean to suggest that city dwellers should never take on a puppy. I do urge you, though, to do a lot of serious thinking.

SPACE AND TIME

Bear in mind that initially you'll have to spend an inordinate amount of time with your puppy, much more than with an adult dog, socializing it and training it to do well in a city environment. Since a dog doesn't reach adulthood until it is ten to twelve months old, maybe older, it may take as long as eight or ten months of effort on your part to train it well. Besides house-training it, you'll want to teach it not to mouth or chew on people or things, not to get into the garbage, not to wail when left alone, not to pull when walked on the leash, and not to jump up on people. This takes time!

Ideally, a puppy should only be brought into a household where someone is home most of the time. It needs a great deal of love and attention, for the best city dogs—or any dogs, for that matter—are those that feel wanted and secure in their knowledge of what's expected of them.

A pup may be lonely and howl if left alone for long hours, disturbing the neighbors. Working people who are away from home for nine or ten hours at a time can't give an infant dog the companionship it needs, so they must arrange for extra help for a while.

Margery Cornwell

So much for the notion that dogs and cats are instinctive enemies

A puppy needs frequent feedings. (For what, how much, and how often to feed it, see Chapter 5.) You can expect to be cleaning up after it for quite a while. A pup can't achieve good bladder and bowel control before it is four months old, and most veterinarians recommend that you not take it out on the street anyway until it has had its last shots (between sixteen and eighteen weeks). Once you begin house-training it, that means frequent excursions to the street or fenced yard to teach it to relieve itself there (see Chapter 4).

If you're sure you want a puppy but can't provide all this patient care during its first few months, you must make arrangements in advance with a reliable person to come in a couple of times a day.

Plan to devote your full attention to the puppy during your first few days together. This is not as much work as it sounds, because the pup will sleep a lot, giving you some time to yourself. Those first days are almost like caring for a human infant. When my children were babies, I used to flop down for a nap the minute they closed their little eyelids—I needed it!

JUDGING TEMPERAMENT

You'll want a dog that is between eight and twelve weeks of age—old enough to be taken from its mother without undue trauma, young enough to adjust well to people.

Puppies that have lived too long—say, over twelve weeks—almost exclusively with their mother and littermates have a harder time when brought into a human home. Also, a pup that has lived in a cage for its first twelve weeks may be shy and withdrawn in a strange environment. For this reason, good breeders, and the staffs of good animal shelters, try to put their puppies in foster care, to help socialize them.

If the mother dog is present when you go to choose a puppy, observe her to see if she is friendly. Normal protectiveness of her babies is one thing; severe anxiety or hostility is another. If the mother is unduly suspicious, she may have passed on this trait to her pups.

Spend some time alone with the puppy you like. Even a very young dog will exhibit definite personality traits.

One personality test you can give is to cradle the dog on its back in your arms like a baby. A trusting dog will just lie there, and if you put your face down close, it will try to lick you. Then slowly tilt the dog's body so the head is slightly downward. If the pup whines, struggles, or tries to jump out of your arms, or if it becomes so terrified that it goes rigid with fear, this animal will be harder to socialize.

A puppy that simply lies down and presents its stomach, however, is showing submissiveness and may be a lot easier to live with in the city than a swaggering extrovert would be. Submissiveness is not to be confused with timidity; it simply signifies low dominance. A submissive dog is just not into power. Bill Berloni, a former theatrical dog trainer, used to recommend the runt of the litter as a good city dog. "The runt will be easier to train," he said. "It has already accepted its low status and will not be competing to be boss in your household."

A pup that's excessively fearful or highly excitable isn't hopeless, but it will need more attention and probably longer training than a friendlier, calmer dog. A busy urban person might find it hard to devote the time it will take to help a puppy overcome extreme characteristics that might present problems in city living.

Female pups are often gentler and easier to train than males.

A puppy that has been abused may be withdrawn and shy, even snappish, with strangers, but can become trusting and affectionate in the hands of a kind and patient person. If it has been seriously traumatized, it may always be shy with people it doesn't know, but will be even more devoted to you and your family.

A family I know adopted a ten-week-old puppy that had been abused. The previous owner, a man, had punished her until she was covered with bruises and cuts from his beatings and could do little more than cower in a corner of her cage at the animal shelter. The family spent a long time rehabilitating her, and she became a happy, loving dog, but she has never forgotten her early mistreatment. She is now four years old, but if a man she doesn't know enters the house, terror strikes her heart, and she is off like a shot to hide, trembling. She will possibly carry this fear all of her life. This is an example of what physical punishment can do to a dog's spirit.

Jane Sapinsky

Bernese Mountain Dogs are mellow, and
in the right hands can be good city dogs

JUDGING HEALTH

A healthy puppy will have a firm, rounded body, clear eyes, and white teeth in pink, firm gums. Its ears will be clean, with no foul odor of infection or parasites. Its coat will be free of the patches that can indicate skin disorders or parasite infestations, and the skin under the fur will be white and healthy-looking. It will be alert and playful. If the pup has a little bump in the middle of its stomach or in its groin, that could be a hernia. It may go away by itself, or it may have to be surgically repaired by a veterinarian.

You will definitely want to make an appointment to take your dog to a veterinarian immediately for a checkup. Also, the pup will need a series of vaccinations. If the person from whom you obtain a young puppy tells you it has had all its shots, be suspicious, because the final immunizations are usually not given before eighteen weeks. Ask for its vaccination records, and if those are not available, your veterinarian will be able to advise you.

Hardest to resist sometimes is the sickly puppy, because it looks so vulnerable and helpless. Symptoms such as a potbelly (which usually means worms), a cough, a discharge from the eyes or nose, and evidence of diarrhea can be found in puppies in shelters, pet shops, and even in breeding kennels. If there's ever an animal that can awaken compassion and the nurturing instinct in all but the hardest of hearts, it's a pitiful pup.

It is very rewarding to take a poor little sick pup and, with love, care, and good veterinary support, restore it to health. But if you have other dogs, you must protect them from whatever the pup has. And it could be devastating if the pup was seriously ill and, after you invested a lot of time, emotion, energy, and money, it died anyway.

That being said, I know a number of healthy, beautiful dogs that were near death when rescued by sympathetic, capable people. So by all means take on the job—just be sure you're up to it.

PET SHOPS

The most rewarding and responsible thing you can do to obtain a puppy is head for an animal shelter and choose one that needs a home. A good shelter will have healthy puppies, usually (though not always) mixed-breeds, for you to choose from.

However, if you have your heart set on a particular breed and no shelter in your vicinity has one at the moment, then you may be trying to decide between a breeder and a pet shop.

As I explained in Chapter 1, pet shops are commercial establishments that acquire their animals from puppy and kitten mills, or from disreputable breeders, and sell them like merchandise. A puppy mill dog has never lived in a home or had human companionship. It will probably have inherited health defects because it will have been produced on a wholesale basis with no genetic screening.

If you buy a puppy at a pet shop, you're paying the retail price, which includes the puppy mill's price, plus the shipper's, the wholesaler's, and the pet shop's markup for what could very likely be an unhealthy or unstable dog. The other day I met a man on the street with an adorable puppy of some new fancy breed, which he had purchased in a pet store (probably for big bucks). He told me that on the first visit to his veterinarian, it was discovered that the puppy had both tapeworm and "kennel cough" (tracheobronchitis), an infectious disease usually caused by being crowded in a kennel with poor ventilation (like puppy mills and many pet shops).

An ordinary pet shop has a pronounced smell, unless it has glass-enclosed cages that hide it. Overcrowding is usual, with cages too small for the animals to lie down or move about comfortably. The cages probably have openwork metal floors, with trays underneath to make cleaning easy. Such floors mean less work for the employees but are uncomfortable for the animals, and if a dog or cat is kept for more than a couple of weeks in this type of cage, its legs and feet can be damaged.

I'm not the only person who will caution you against pet shops. Other dog books and many veterinarians will tell you the same thing. So consider yourself well warned.

BREEDERS

I know it's asking a lot of you, as a city dweller, to buy a purebred pup from a breeder instead of a pet shop. Pet shops are all over town; you have only to look in the Yellow Pages. Dog breeders don't live in cities—they're in the suburbs, small towns, or the country. To locate a good breeder, you'll have to do some research. It's a lot more trouble to buy a purebred puppy from a reputable breeder, but if you must have a designer dog, it will be worth it for you.

There are national breed clubs, consisting of breeders, owners, and aficionados of specific kinds of dogs, and these are a good way to locate a breeder of the dog you're interested in. You can find breed clubs on the Internet. Also, dog magazines and some Sunday newspapers list breeders.

But once you have the names of some breeders, how do you judge a good one?

A good breeder keeps dogs in the house as pets, so they are well socialized from the start of their lives. He or she usually breeds only one type of dog, not several, and gives a lot of personal attention to each animal. The best breeders are purely hobbyists, not commercially motivated. They will furnish you with references—people to whom they have sold dogs. They do not sell to pet shops.

He or she will encourage you to take the dog you select to a veterinarian for a health checkup within forty-eight hours and will offer to take the pup back and refund your money if it is found to be unhealthy.

A good breeder breeds for temperament as well as for points in the show ring, and for city people, temperament is of paramount importance.

If the dog's parents are registered with the American Kennel Club or other registry, the breeder should have registered the litter and therefore will be able to provide you—at the time of purchase, not later—with a partially filled out application form for registering your individual dog. The registration form is for you to complete and send, with the fee, to the registry. The fact that it is registered, in itself, says nothing about the quality of the dog you are buying. It only means that the pup is the offspring of registered parents.

You might, by the way, be able to buy a puppy at a discount if the breeder believes it is not of show quality. That doesn't mean you're getting a less desirable dog. It just means you wouldn't have a champion in the show ring. If what you want is a pet, what do you care about its potential as a show dog?

The subject of breeders raises the question of ear cropping and tail docking. Dog show standards for some breeds—Great Danes, Dobermans, and Boxers, for example—dictate that the animals must have parts of their ears or tail, or both, cut off, and the ears forced upright instead of hanging down normally.

Tail docking—cutting the tail off to a specific length—is usually performed on the puppies when they are only a few days old, so you probably won't have any say in the matter if you buy from a breeder. It is performed without anesthetic and hurts the puppy at least temporarily.

Ear cropping, however, is another matter. It is usually done when the dog is three or four months old. The operation must be performed with the dog under general anesthesia, by a qualified and experienced veterinarian if you can find one who is willing to do it. Part of each ear is cut off, and the ear cartilage is forced into the desired shape—the ear must be upright. Then the ears are taped and bound for many weeks. There is a risk of major complications such as infection and gangrene, and even without these there must be considerable pain for the dog while the ears heal.

These surgeries are purely cosmetic and offer no health advantages to the dogs. Because of the risks—from anesthesia, blood loss, infection—and the pain and distress they produce, they are outlawed in a number of countries, including Britain, Germany, Norway, Sweden, and Australia. They are controversial in the United States. The American Veterinary Medical Association takes a cautionary but ambiguous position: "Veterinarians should counsel dog owners about these matters [the risks] before agreeing to perform these surgeries." But many veterinarians stopped cropping dogs' ears long ago.

Ear cropping and tail docking may be illegal by the time you read this book.

I find it reprehensible to mutilate a dog's ears and tail for such a trivial reason as style. As for meeting show standards, dog shows are a pastime that some owners of purebred dogs enjoy, and though many dogs tolerate them (what choice do they have?), being crated and shipped around the country and caged or tied in crowds and noise for hours and days on end can't be what any dog would choose for itself.

There's another, gruesome kind of ear cropping performed routinely by some owners of pit bulls (American Staffordshire Terriers when purebred). Inspired by the upright-ear look of the show dogs, these folks simply cut off part of their dog's ears themselves with scissors. You can imagine what this feels like to the dogs. When you see a pit bull with those ears, especially one accompanied by a macho, usually young, rough-looking man, you can suspect two things: that the owner cut his dog's ears himself and that he uses the dog in the clandestine "sport" of dogfighting.

Dogfighting is not the occasional tomfoolery of a few backwoods rednecks, but a secret pastime involving huge sums of money. Dog fights, though illegal, go on in all parts of the United States, victimizing dogs that are bred and brutalized to become fighters.

Another reason owners of fighting dogs crop their dogs' ears is that in a fight, natural, pendulous ears can be a hazard to a dog. Its opponent might rip its ear, causing such pain that the dog retreats and loses the fight—and its owner's money. So ears that don't hang down are an advantage.

An example of this kind of vicious ear cropping is a case that came to the attention of the Michigan Humane Society some years ago. Acting on a tip, the humane authorities rescued a suffering dog whose ears had been cut down to bloody stumps. "I wanted him to look mean," explained the owner in court. The owner was fined and

Jonathan Pearl

Trowser and friend: A Boston Terrier pup

put on probation for two years, during which time he was forbidden to own a dog, any dog. His injured dog was confiscated and later adopted by a caring, nonviolent family.

CHILDREN AND PUPPIES

A puppy could be an excellent choice for a family with children. While an adult dog may or may not like little kids, a puppy has an open mind. When carefully supervised, a child and a puppy can be great playmates, and very strong bonds often form between children and dogs who are raised together.

I want to stress, however, that a mother who is the sole caretaker of a baby or a very young child should not have the responsibility of a puppy—she has her hands full enough as it is. This is especially true for a city mother because of the difficulty of house-training a puppy where the outdoors is not easily accessible. Walking a puppy the required six or seven times a day would certainly be a burden on her. Some of my urban friends have raised puppies by paper-training them, but it might be undesirable to have soiled newspapers lying around with a baby or toddler in the house, and sometimes it's harder to curb-train a dog that has already been paper-trained.

In Chapter 1, I suggested that your child should be at least three or four before you adopt a dog. Add several years onto that when you're considering a puppy. Children must be old enough to understand clearly that a puppy is not a toy. They must be carefully watched to make sure they don't hurt the puppy—they can literally, if unintentionally, maul a puppy to death. A pup, like a kitten, is very vulnerable, with soft, fragile bones.

A veterinarian I once knew described a scene in his clinic: "A mother came in with three little girls and a sick puppy," he said. "Each child was trying to carry the puppy, and they were pulling and snatching at it between them. They couldn't even keep their hands off it while I was examining it. I soon realized that the only thing wrong with this dog was that it was being handled to death. I kept it in my hospital overnight, just to give it a much-needed rest, and when I returned it, I had a long talk with the children and especially with the mother, explaining that the puppy needs a lot of rest and mustn't be handled all the time. I could see my advice had absolutely no impact. What I suspect will happen is that sooner or later the pup will bite in self-defense, and then the family will get rid of it, saying it has a bad disposition."

Playtime should be supervised, both because children may need to be taught not to engage in rough play with the puppy, and because an exuberant puppy can unintentionally knock down a small child.

A young child should not try to pick up or carry a puppy at all. Instead, have the child sit down on the floor or in a low chair and place the puppy in his or her lap. That way, the child can have the pleasure of cuddling the dog—with your supervision—but can't hurt it by dropping it.

Here is a list of important rules for anyone—including children—raising a puppy:

- Never pick up a puppy by the scruff of the neck.
- Never pick up a puppy by the legs, head, ears, or tail.
- Never drag a puppy by the legs, head, ears, or tail.
- Never tease or frustrate a puppy.
- Never disturb a puppy while it's sleeping or eating.
- Never strike, shake, or spank a puppy.

The fact that mother dogs sometimes carry their pups in their mouth by the skin of their necks doesn't mean we should pick them up that way. The proper way to pick up and carry a puppy is with one hand under the chest, with the other hand supporting the hindquarters.

Let a puppy sleep as much as it wants—it needs the rest.

A pup should be trained, but never physically punished. Hitting or spanking will only make it afraid. It can't get the connection between the spanking and the act you're punishing it for. That's like hitting a tiny baby for soiling its diaper. Physical punishment will not teach a dog anything but will make it fear and hate you.

Children especially must be firmly taught never to punish a dog. Very young children should not try to train or discipline a dog; that's your job as pack leader. A child and a puppy should be pal and playmate, fellow comforter and companion, not master and slave.

TOYS AND PLAY

The time when you will probably be spending the most time playing with your dog, and providing it with toys, is during its puppyhood. Also, puppies will make up their own games with whatever attracts them—your shoes, for instance—and must learn what items are off limits.

Some people give their dogs old socks or shoes to play with and chew on. This might be fine for some older dogs, but most, espe-

Jane Sapinsky

Boomer, a Yellow Labrador, grew up to weigh ninety pounds

cially puppies, will have trouble distinguishing between theirs and yours, since theirs were yours in the first place. Your average pup won't understand why it's okay to chew on a discarded loafer but not one of your new Ferragamos, or what distinguishes the worn-out sweatsock you gave it from the good pair you left on the bathroom floor. My advice is not to give your dog anything at all of yours to play with. Let it have its own toys.

The best dog toys are made of rawhide, hard nylon, fabric, or hard rubber—unpainted. Soft rubber toys are too easy to chew up, and when bits of the rubber are swallowed, they can play havoc with the dog's insides and even cause death. Painted toys can cause lead poisoning. And wooden toys are dangerous, too, because they can splinter.

Enjoying a puppy's capacity for play, and its comical antics, are among the reasons for having it in the first place. By all means, play with a puppy, and encourage children to do so—but with these caveats in mind:

- Don't play just before or after feeding.
- Don't play on a slippery surface, such as wood, vinyl, or tile. The puppy needs secure footing, or it can tear a muscle or dislocate a joint.
- Don't do anything to provoke aggression, even in play.
- Don't play tug-of-war with a puppy.
- Don't encourage or permit a puppy to bite anything but its own toys.
- Don't play with a puppy for more than a few minutes at a time, because it will become overstimulated and exhausted— or aggressive. Extended romping is especially harmful to a large-breed pup, whose bones are not yet strong enough to support its weight in hard play.

Of all these warnings, probably the hardest to heed is the one about playing tug-of-war, because the pup itself will initiate this game. Don't accept the challenge. It's amusing to see a young dog grapple with a rag or piece of rope, shaking its head and even hanging on so hard with its jaws that it can be lifted into the air. The trouble is that the pup never learns that its jaws can hurt.

A veterinary researcher at Purdue University, Dr. John Stump, once explained the reason: "When two puppies play together, the one that gets bitten will squeal or yelp. That's the signal meaning, 'That's enough,' so the biter learns something about the strength of its jaws," he said. "But when the dog bites a piece of rope that some-

Donna Knipp

Portrait of Max as a young dog

one is pulling, it gets no sense of how hard to bite before letting go, since it hasn't learned that shut-off signal."

It may be cute when a little puppy play-bites your hand, sleeve, or pant leg, or chews on your shoelaces, but this should be gently but firmly discouraged. Otherwise, before you know it, the dog grows up and, meaning no harm, sinks its teeth into someone's hand, or rips a sofa pillow. Then the confused dog finds itself in big trouble—for using its jaws in a way that you encouraged or permitted in the first place.

A dog should never get the idea that its teeth are to be used on clothing, household objects, or any part of the human body. You will just be setting it and everyone else up for a bad incident.

If a puppy bites you in the course of play, tell it "No!" quickly and sharply, and stop the play. In fact, it might be a good idea to let out a yelp, even if it hasn't hurt you, and then stop the play for a while. The dog should get the message that it has done something wrong.

Margery Cornwell

Cleo the cat may think she has finally found a use for dogs

It's great fun for a puppy to chase and retrieve a ball. Just don't let it scamper across a slippery floor, or it can wind up at the vet's with a dislocated hip or shoulder. Be sure the ball is small enough for the dog to grasp in its mouth but too big to swallow.

After a puppy has had all its shots, it can be taken outdoors. If you have access to a well-protected yard, dog run, or other confined area that permits dogs, that's a good place for vigorous play. Just make sure the fencing doesn't have spaces big enough for a little body to squeeze through. And don't make the mistake of letting the dog off the leash unless you are in an enclosed area. You'd be surprised at how fast a pup can run. Many a misguided owner has assumed he or she could catch a fleeing puppy and discovered that the only thing that stopped it was the wheel of a passing car.

PROTECTING A PUP

You want not only to protect your possessions from the pup, but to protect the pup from household items that can hurt or kill it. It's best to put away anything valuable for the duration of its puppyhood.

Keep all closet and cupboard doors tightly closed; cover the garbage securely; put books, plants, and other tasty valuables out of reach; and disconnect lamps and other electric appliances except when you are home and supervising the puppy. Better yet, when you're out, confine the pup in a large wire cage, the type called a kennel crate—unless you're going out for several hours. (More on kennel crates in Chapter 4.)

A veterinarian at the Animal Medical Center in New York City, one of the largest animal hospitals in the United States, once listed the following items as among those that have been removed by surgery from the stomachs of dogs: chicken bones, nylon stockings, Brillo pads, string, pillow stuffing, splinters of wood, and pieces of wicker.

One puppy owner took off her earrings and placed them on her night table while she took a nap. When she woke up, she couldn't find one of her earrings. After searching everywhere, she gave it up for lost. A few days later, her pup became ill. At the Animal Medical Center, x-rays revealed the earring lodged in the animal's stomach. It was an earring for pierced ears, so the point was stuck neatly in the stomach wall. After it was removed surgically, the puppy recovered, and the poorer but wiser owner got her earring back.

N.B. Don't forget to enlarge a puppy's collar as it grows. It sounds incredible, but some people forget to do this, allowing the collars gradually to strangle their poor dogs. I have heard several shelter workers speak of having to euthanize dogs that were found sick and deformed from just this oversight. The collar should be just loose enough for you to slip two fingers between it and the animal's neck.

If you have stairs, better install a gate at the top until the dog is grown and can go up and down safely. Uncarpeted stairs are especially dangerous to a pup.

As to where a puppy should sleep, you're not going to get an argument out of me if you feel it's okay in your or your child's bed. But it should also have its own cozy bed, placed away from drafts.

If the puppy misses its mother and siblings and cries the first few nights, you might try putting a softly playing radio near its bed, or wrapping a ticking clock in a towel and placing it in the bed; these have been known to lull and soothe a homesick little animal.

Housebreaking and obedience-training a puppy are much the same as for an older dog. You'll find advice on these subjects in Chapter 4, Training, and information on feeding dogs of any age in Chapter 5, Diet.

One advantage to having a city puppy: While you are socializing it to be friendly with people and other dogs on the street, you'll have a chance to meet a lot of new people, because most will want to stop and pet your puppy.

3. UNDERSTANDING

How Your Dog Thinks and Feels

There seem to be some people who believe dogs shouldn't live in the city—that dogs must be free to run all day in wide-open spaces. This romantic notion is out of date, since there are few wide-open places left where dogs can safely run free. In a nation criss-crossed with roads, unleashed dogs are killed and maimed by cars every minute of the day. In recognition of this fact, most country dog owners keep their dogs chained up more or less permanently, and frequently alone. Drive out to the countryside and count the dogs that are able to roam free—to the end of their tethers and that's it. What a life for a social animal.

A properly cared-for city dog can live a good life in the steward-ship of a loving and enlightened owner; in fact, that dog lives a much longer life than a country dog. The domestic dog seems perfectly programmed to adapt to living with its family in a city house or apartment.

City dogs and their owners are likely to spend a lot of time indoors together, perhaps even sleeping in the same room. And the very act of going for walks together strengthens their bond. Backyard and rural dogs may get to interact with their owners only at feeding time.

Lenny, Susannah, and Tao, the three stooges

Robin Holland

But a city dog must get used to a lot—for example, the constant presence of other dogs and people, traffic and noise. My dog Susannah pays little attention to the traffic on the streets of my neighborhood except for motorcycles, against which she defends me at the top of her voice. I haven't been attacked by a motorcycle since I've had her!

City dogs must be able to go up and down stairs, they must remain poised in elevators, and in many places they must learn to urinate and defecate on pavement, a surface that undoubtedly seems unnatural to them.

Even though the evolution of the domestic dog as a species or subspecies parallels that of human beings, and it has lived with us almost forever, it still shares certain primitive traits with its wild relatives. This chapter will give you some background on the nature of dogs that will help you get ready for the behavior training in Chapter 4.

THE PACK

Wild canids, primitive and contemporary, live in packs with well-defined hierarchies and carefully observed rules. That's why feral dogs form packs whenever possible and stick together. There is a pack leader, and often an alpha female as well (top female dog, mate of the leader). Each dog is aware of its rank in the pack, and looks to the leader for direction, protection, and maintaining order. Members of a pack observe rules, help care for the pups, display greeting behavior, and are sensitive to one another's emotional states. Being a pack member makes a dog feel comfortable; to it, nothing is worse than not belonging or being driven out.

Wild canids are also denning and territorial animals. The pack has a den in which the alpha female (usually the only one who gives birth) raises the pups. And the pack will defend what it considers its territory. The animals scent-mark their territory throughout by urinating in little spurts on vertical surfaces (trees, shrubs, boulders, etc.). A wild canid always knows when it is in its pack's territory because of the scent-marks within it. No matter how far it may wander, it can always use its nose to find its way home.

To the domestic dog, its human family is its pack, the family home is its den, and the family property is its territory. You, or someone in your family, are your dog's pack leader. Usually that leader is the person who feeds and walks it, though not necessarily. Sometimes in the dog's eyes, the leader is whoever fills the role of head of the household. If you live alone with your dog, you're unquestionably It, unless you abdicate the role to your dog.

Among wild canids, pack leaders are male, for the simple reason that males are larger and the alpha female is often pregnant or nursing and therefore not in a position to be in charge of the pack, settling arguments, keeping out intruders, and the like. This distinction about the gender of the leader is apparently lost on domestic dogs, however, for they will accept a woman as pack leader as readily as they will a man.

If a dog has been pack leader itself (perhaps in the litter) or aspires to be one, it may not automatically relinquish that position to you. You will have to assume it yourself and convince the dog that you are in charge, or you may wind up in second-rank position to your dog—at least, in its mind. It's as unbecoming and unwholesome for a dog owner to be a slave to his or her tyrant of a pet—for that's what the animal will become—as it is for a parent to relinquish leadership to a spoiled brat of a child. With a dog, it can even be risky, both for the dog's safety and everyone else's.

You must be able to brush and bathe your dog, give it medicine, take stuff out of its mouth when it has picked up something it shouldn't have, and obedience-train it. If your dog dominates you, you'll find it difficult, maybe impossible, to do any of these things.

You enter the relationship with a built-in advantage, since you provide the shelter and control the feeding, walking, games, and protection. So, if you play your cards right, it shouldn't be hard to assume leadership over even a born leader. The dog will become a fine companion as a result, and the bond between you will be strengthened.

It is primarily the pack instinct that accounts for the dog's legendary loyalty and also its protectiveness. Remember that nature programs a species for survival—either survival of the individual or, in the case of social animals, survival of the group. The primitive dog looked to the pack leader for guidance and approval because that meant its survival. It instinctively defended the pack and the pack's territory because that helped the group as a whole to survive. Each member of the pack was loyal and protective, whatever its rank within the group.

Certain species of social animals—some mammals and birds—are known to risk, to sacrifice if necessary, their individual lives for the protection of their particular groups. We know, for instance, of birds that hobble along the ground and feign injury to lead predators away from their nest, or risk detection themselves in order to give warning to their group. Certain primates when they are attacked will help protect the offspring of other members of their troop. Stories abound of dogs who have saved members of their families from harm, at great risk to their own lives. It's clear that the modern dog has simply substituted its human family for its own canine pack.

THE DEN, THE TERRITORY

Just as it regards one family member as pack leader, a dog considers its family's home as its den, its territory. Therein lies its value as a watchdog. A subordinate dog will be as protective as a dominant dog will.

The denning instinct may also be the reason it is possible to house-train dogs. A basic tenet of den dwellers is that you do not soil your den. (Come to think of it, perhaps that's the reason we can housebreak our children; human beings, unlike many other primates, have been denning animals ever since we began to live in caves, tents, huts, igloos, and the like.) Non-denning animals, such as horses and cows, are virtually impossible to house-train—it's not in their instinctual makeup.

In their own way, domestic dogs have retained their wild ancestors' practice of defining their territory with scent marks. When your dog wants to stop and sniff at every tree, lamppost, and hydrant, it is reading the newspaper, so to speak. It is finding out who went by recently, whether the other dog was familiar or unknown, male or female, perhaps in estrus. And when your dog urinates in your yard, or along your block, it is not only relieving itself but marking its own territory, sending a message to other dogs.

Cats are not pack animals and don't recognize the authority of a pack leader. That's why cats have the reputation for being independent, even aloof, and why people who demand absolute subservience in their pets can't stand cats.

A well-treated domestic cat will be loving and companionable, and you can of course train it to a certain extent—that is, you can modify its behavior so that it will observe reasonable house rules.

And anyone who has ever watched a cat drive an intruding cat out of its backyard can see the territorial instinct at work. Some cats have even been known to warn their owners when strangers were sneaking around the property.

But you can't teach a cat to lead the blind or to round up sheep, and the only way you can get one of its captive wild cousins to jump through a flaming hoop in a circus is to brutalize it. The dog, however, can learn to do what its pack leader asks because compliance is built into its makeup and because being obedient to an owner it loves makes it feel comfortable and happy.

Training is crucial to successful urban dog ownership but can be a frustrating experience for owner and dog if the owner repeatedly tries to teach in a way that works against, rather than with, the dog's nature. Using the dog's denning instinct in house-training is a lot more successful than punishing the animal for making mistakes. And understanding a dog's behavior not only smoothes your relationship with your own pet but is extremely helpful in handling its encounters with people and other dogs.

BODY LANGUAGE

It's certainly not hard to figure out what your dog is telling you when it meets you at the door after you've been out for a while—the joyful grin and madly wagging tail say it all. Most of us quickly learn our pet's basic repertoire of overt language. But some of the signals dogs give are subtle or confusing. Being able to read a dog's body language and to understand how the animal thinks and feels is especially necessary for urban dwellers. You not only want to be able to interpret your own pet correctly but, on the street, you want to be able to tell friend from foe.

Let's say your dog meets a strange dog off the leash. The other dog approaches with great interest, ears alert and tail wagging. Doesn't a wagging tail mean friendliness? Not necessarily.

This dog is giving out other signals that spell hostility. The wagging tail is stiff and held high. The eyes have a hard expression and stare into your dog's eyes. The dog's hackles (the fur along its shoulders and back) are raised. The animal's whole posture signifies aggression. Even without growling or showing its teeth, a dog behaving like this has a chip on its shoulder. You should remove your dog from the scene quietly and quickly.

On the other hand, a friendly—or merely curious—dog's tail will most likely be wagging, but in wide sweeps, hanging down. Its ears are down and its fur is smooth along the shoulders and back. The dog will not attempt to look you or your dog in the eye. It will go through the typical sniffing pattern with your dog—first nose to nose, then the genitals. Offer this dog the back of your fist to smell, and then you can probably pet it if you wish.

In another situation, let's say your dog, after the usual preliminary sniffs, suddenly bounces down on its chest and elbows with its ears flattened and its rear end in the air. Unless the other dog's owner recognizes your dog's body language, he or she may snatch the animal away protectively, misinterpreting your dog's behavior as aggression. Your dog was giving off perfectly clear signals—"Let's play"— yet was misunderstood. A dog that merely wants to play may also jump excitedly and bark, grin and wag its tail, run around in circles, and roll over.

It is not uncommon for dogs to pretend not to see people or other animals they dislike. They may also keep their distance while watching out of the corner of their eye.

Sometimes a dog meeting another dog, or a person, lies on its belly with its ears flattened and the fur along its back flat and smooth. It looks away and may roll over onto its back. Is it afraid— a coward, a wimp? In most cases not—it may well only be showing submission. It is probably saying, "I am recognizing that you are the boss (pack leader)." Or it could be telling the other dog, "I'm not into power—I don't want to fight." Puppies and low-dominance dogs often display this behavior. A dog that avoids confrontation in this manner usually makes a good city dog.

Fear is a more obvious signal. A frightened dog lowers its body, with its tail hanging low or tucked between its legs. Its head is down, its ears are laid back, and its hackles are usually raised. The dog may instinctively crouch close to the ground to protect its belly, and it may tremble and approach you and your dog in circles. Because a scared dog can quickly become a fear-biter, the best course is to stand still with your hands by your sides and refrain from looking the animal in the eye—that's a real challenge. Don't corner it or turn your back on it, but speak to it in a soothing voice. Unless it gets over its fear, relaxes, and shows friendliness or submission, it's best to move away quietly.

Correctly interpreting a hostile dog's body language may not only help you protect your dog but save you from getting bitten yourself. If a strange dog approaches you giving off signals of aggression when your dog is not with you, behave as you would with a frightened dog, especially by not looking it in the eye and not extending your hands. If the dog is barking, that's all the more reason to be cautious. It's very important not to turn away—that stimulates the chase response. Speak to the dog in a normal voice until it walks away or stops giving off the unfriendly signals. Then back away calmly yourself.

A dog's mouth can tell you a lot. Dogs do grin by pulling the corners of their mouth back and baring their teeth. Sometimes a blissfully relaxed dog will close its eyes and actually smile. But when a dog wrinkles its nose, raises its upper lip, and shows its incisors and canine teeth, that's a snarl (see Aggressiveness, below).

Every observant dog owner learns to recognize the body language of his or her pet when it's sick. Refusal to eat is of course a primary signal, yet there are many illnesses of which loss of appetite is not a symptom. A dog walking with its head somewhat down and its back arched, for example, could have an orthopedic problem, or perhaps stomach pain. Even such subtle signals should be investigated by a veterinarian.

Laddie, a great family dog

A dog's range of vocalizations is another meaningful form of language. Every dog owner can tell from the pitch of his or her pet's bark the mood or even the message that the animal is communicating. (An experienced dog lover may even interpret fairly accurately the message a perfectly strange dog two blocks away is putting out.) A bark can be welcoming or playful, or can signify loneliness, fear, or anger.

In the city, much of a dog's natural inclination to bark must be discouraged. It's asking a lot of a dog to learn to differentiate between the "whish" of the handyman mopping the hall of your apartment building and the quiet scrape of a burglar picking the lock on a neighbor's door. Teaching a dog to bark only selectively requires a difficult manipulation of the animal's instincts, but in town, it's often necessary, for everyone's sanity. (See Chapter 4, Training.)

Dog owners who are close to their pets will swear that their dogs often imitate their own moods, mirroring their excitement, joy, depression, anxiety. I believe this is true. Dogs certainly become greatly upset when their owners are in a rage about something, or quarreling, or weeping. Some very definitely react to hearty laughter—they'll grin and wag their tails and try to take part in the fun. Dogs pick up on our body language and usually read it more correctly that we do theirs.

They do sometimes misinterpret situations. But irrational fears in dogs can be understood if you look at a situation from their point of view. Holidays are a case in point. Halloween, for example, can be heaps of fun for children, and we may enjoy the little kids in costume trick-or-treating. Your dog, however, may think the world has gone mad. It will most likely get upset at the masks and funny clothes and the constantly ringing doorbell, and can even become aggressive because it is scared. If your pet is unnerved by Halloween festivities, keep it away from the front door, confine it in a comfortable place, and keep a firm grip on the leash when you have to take it out on the street.

And I have never known a dog who enjoys the Fourth of July. Some dogs sensibly hide under the bed or in a closet, but Sally would start to tremble and hyperventilate at the first firecracker, and if left alone would total the house in her terror. Susannah's teeth actually chatter as she tries to get in my lap.

As for Christmas, some dogs retreat to the back of a closet on December 24 and don't voluntarily emerge for more than a few minutes at a time until January 2. Whatever the holiday, help your pet remain as calm as possible.

AGGRESSIVENESS

The vast majority of pet dogs never bite and in fact may live their entire lives without ever so much as growling at a person. However, aggressive behavior is a major problem that prompts many owners to give up their dogs, often unnecessarily.

What causes a dog to be aggressive? There are several possible reasons. Brutal treatment is certainly one—aggression begets aggression. Stress can make a good-natured dog turn snappish. Fear of a real or imagined threat to itself or a member of its pack can of course cause a dog to attack. A traumatic experience it had as a young dog can cause an animal to become hostile if a similar situation occurs later.

Illness can be a reason; even a normally sweet-tempered dog might growl or snap if you attempt to handle it when it's in pain or if it feels so wretched that it wants to be left alone. An unspayed or unneutered dog is far more likely to bite than a spayed or neutered dog. On the street, a dog tied up may be more likely to bite because it feels cornered. And jealousy can bring on aggressive behavior, especially if the dog is insecure or overly protective in the first place.

Josephine Gassner, a professional dog walker and boarder, has noticed that high-energy breeds can become snappish toward other dogs if they don't get enough exercise. "It's called displacement aggression," she says. "The dog doesn't really mean to be aggressive—it is just trying to relieve pent-up energy." In high population areas—cities—dog bite can be a concern of everyone, dog owners in particular.

Of the four million instances of dog bite that are reported each year, virtually all of them are caused by owned, not stray, animals. And while deliverymen and meter readers suffer a share of attacks, most victims are the dog's owners, family members, or neighbors.

Sixty percent of dog bite victims are children, and nearly half of all children between ages four and eighteen suffer dog bite at some point. This fact raises the question of whether some children may unwittingly or purposely provoke these incidents. It's important to teach children not only to be gentle with their own dogs but to treat all dogs with proper respect. That means no teasing, even in fun.

On the other hand, some parents unfortunately instill fear of dogs: "Watch out, that dog will bite you!" they say, automatically pulling their child away from every dog they meet. In trying to prevent their child from ever being bitten, they also prevent the child from being able to appreciate and enjoy dogs or to be comfortable around them. It could even establish a phobia that could haunt the child all of his or her life.

Children should be taught a few basic, cautionary rules: They should learn, for instance, always to ask the owner before petting a strange dog and always to be gentle. They should be taught very early never to swoop down on a dog from behind, never to grab it around the neck, never to take food or a toy away from it, and never to put their hand through a fence to pet it. Children seem to be born with an interest in dogs, but I think a civilized quality such as empathy with animals has to be taught.

What if an aggressive dog attacks you? Above all, don't run—that will encourage the dog to chase you. Don't look the dog in the eye. Fend it off not with your hands but with whatever arm you don't use for writing or anything you have handy (if it's a small dog, you might try kicking it, hard). Yell "No!" with all the authority you can summon, but try not to get hysterical, because that will only excite the dog more.

If a hostile dog attacks your dog, the recommended solution is to turn a hose on it or pour a bucket of water over it, but how often do you have a hose or bucket of water with you on a city street? All you can do is try to hit the attacking dog with a stick, umbrella, or any similar object you can seize, but don't get your hands in the way—even your own dog might bite you by mistake in trying to defend itself. Whether the aggressive dog is attacking you or your dog, it's a terrifying scene. Nobody should have an aggressive dog in the city, or any dog off the leash.

You have probably heard it said that dogs often look like their owners, and you may even know amusing examples of it. A notion that may make more sense is that dogs will take after their owners in temperament—nice people will have friendly dogs, hostile people will have unfriendly dogs, and so on. Since dogs appear to have an uncanny ability to read our thoughts, or at least our body language, it's tempting to accept this supposition as fact.

However, in my own experience I know of many exceptions that make me wonder about this theory. For instance, one neighbor of mine has a quarrelsome little dog, but she is a very sweet person. And another neighbor of mine, very macho with the sensibility of Attila the Hun, has a gentle, friendly dog.

Human beings have a lot of ambivalence about submissiveness. We love dogs for their loyalty, for their obedience, for the unconditional friendship they give us. But we also scorn these very subservient qualities, and the word "dog" in our language (not to mention bitch, cur, and the like) is pejorative. In many parts of the world today, dogs are still treated with horrible cruelty—and in this country we are far from being the nation of dog lovers that we like to assume we are.

We train our dog to do our bidding and take pride in its accomplishments—but secretly, unconsciously, we may look down on an animal that is so obedient. The dog is in a no-win position, damned if it is totally devoted and damned if it isn't.

These contradictory feelings about dogs may be deeply embedded in our collective unconscious. When an individual dog owner regards aggression as a quality to be admired, his or her dog could very possibly respond accordingly. The owner might unconsciously encourage belligerent behavior in the pet.

A hostile dog has no place in a city, where it is in constant contact with people and other dogs. Such an animal is a danger to itself and others. The only situation in which a dog should be aggressive is one in which there is a very real, immediate threat to it or to a member of its human family. Otherwise, something is very wrong.

Unless the cause is biological, firm, patient training and loving treatment can sometimes change a dog with this type of personality (see Chapter 4).

PROTECTIVENESS AND JEALOUSY

A dog cannot be relied upon always to interpret correctly the behavior of strangers. A perfectly friendly person with a loud voice and hearty manners who comes up to you on the street or enters your home can be perceived by your dog as an enemy, at least until it reads your reaction to the person and realizes that everything's okay. You don't want a pet that bites first and figures out afterward. Not only can the animal hurt someone, perhaps seriously, but it might get you a lawsuit.

A dog who has lived with a single owner can feel very threatened when the owner marries or acquires a roommate and will try to "protect" its owner. If the dog knows that aggressive behavior won't be tolerated, it may resort to other means of expressing its anxiety—breaking house-training, chewing up things around the house, or barking when left alone. A wise owner will understand the dog's point of view and realize that sympathy and patience are in order. The behavior can be prevented or stopped, or the dog may discontinue it of its own accord as soon as it feels reassured.

Because dogs have such a close relationship with people, they have picked up certain primarily human emotions, of which jealousy is a notable one. Jealousy is touching to see in a dog because it reveals its dependency and love. But this emotion can also cause aggression, so if your dog has any possible reason to be jealous of someone, you will want to pay attention and help your dog overcome it.

The arrival of a new baby in your household is a case in point, particularly if the infant is a first. Initially, to your dog, this small creature is an intruder, especially because it makes strange noises and gets an enormous amount of your attention—attention that perhaps used to be lavished on the dog. The dog's feelings are the canine equivalent of sibling rivalry and can be dealt with in much the same manner, by giving the dog extra affection. When the dog tries to inspect the baby, let the dog approach, and don't push it away. Keep control of the encounter, but let the dog smell the baby. Give the pet every reason to feel it has not been replaced, while making sure it understands that the baby is a pack member.

As often as possible, take the dog with you when you go out with the baby, and try to include it when guests make a fuss over the new family member. When you bring the baby a new toy, bring the pet one also, or at least give it a treat. Whenever you return home after being out, don't rush to the baby immediately and ignore the dog. A working couple I know noticed their dog becoming somewhat cross over their new baby but found that if they gave the dog a big, warm greeting, even for just a few minutes, when they came home at the end of the day, the dog was content.

And never leave the dog alone in the room with the baby. Be aware that a dog may seem to accept the newcomer at first but then build up a resentment gradually.

I don't mean to make your dog seem sinister—in the over-whelming majority of instances, people introduce new babies into their households with no problems whatsoever from their dogs. I'm just suggesting keeping the dog's point of view in mind. Its nose may be out of joint for a while. A dog is a dog—a wonderful, intelligent but complex creature.

Know your dog, be aware of its feelings, and don't take chances. Some cities' shelter societies (such as the SPCA or Humane Society)

Peanut relaxes in his frog position

have animal behavior counselors. If your dog has a particular behavior problem, you might call one of these societies for advice.

Some dogs are simply one-person or one-family dogs. Such a dog loves its person or the members of its pack, and that's it. There's nothing wrong with this so long as the dog isn't actually hostile to other people. You want your dog to be pleasant to visitors, accept delivery people and workers in your home, be polite to everyone on the street. And you want someone besides you to be able to take care of your dog in case of an emergency.

My dogs have always loved me but a lot of other people as well. My friend Linda Thompson, a professional dog walker and cat sitter, is a case in point. Susannah adores her. When Linda comes to my house, Susannah is ecstatic; if we run into her on the street, Susannah is beside herself with joy and can't bear to part from her. Talk about jealousy—I'm glad, of course, to have such a trusted person available when I need her, and I'm especially glad Susannah is happy with her. But gee, does Susannah have to be that happy?

4. TRAINING

The Well-Behaved City Dog

I believe the future of dogs in cities depends a great deal on how well they and their owners behave. Dogs are already a threatened species, and the trend in housing rules and city ordinances could soon place them on the endangered list. The best hope for those of us who wish to keep these marvelous animals with us in our urban homes is to see to it that they are good canine citizens. Your urban dog must be far better behaved than its suburban or country counterpart. This sounds unfair, but actually, having your dog under control not only enhances your own peace of mind and respects your neighbors' rights; it also helps assure your dog's comfort and safety. A dog that barks and whines when left alone is not only a pain in the neck to all within earshot but is itself miserable, suffering from separation anxiety. A dog that picks fights with others on the street is not a comfortable dog and can get into serious trouble, hurt, or even killed.

It seems to me that the training priorities for the owner of a city dog are house-training and socializing. House-training covers not just learning to control body functions but being quiet when left alone and not damaging household property. Socializing includes helping a dog to become gentle and friendly, teaching it proper street behavior, and training it to obey basic obedience commands (come, sit, down, stay, heel, and no).

Because a dog intuitively expects and even welcomes directions from its pack leader, it isn't cruel to train it to do what you want, as long as the training is done humanely, with love and understanding and rewards, working with rather than against the animal's instincts. You want to communicate, clearly and firmly, in language the dog can understand.

TOUCHING

It is no accident that an animal that's kept as a companion and object of affection is called a "pet." This word reveals the importance of the touching, fondling, caressing, and nurturing that are summoned forth in the relationship between ourselves and our companion animals. And petting is a two-way street, because it not only involves the pleasure of stroking on our part, but encourages affectionate responses in the animal.

A well-socialized cat when petted will arch its back, purr, and rub against you; a horse that is treated like a pet will bow its head and nuzzle. And a dog will express its pleasure in many ways—tail wagging, "smiling," dancing about or rolling on its back, perhaps even leaning against you with a dreamy expression on its face. When its beloved owner's hand drops affectionately on its head, a dog will almost certainly acknowledge the gesture with some happy response.

In fact, one of the greatest pleasures of having a dog is touching it—hugging it, playfully scratching its ears, running a hand soothingly down its warm head and shoulders. But these acts go beyond the enjoyment they bring to us. They are a way of strengthening the bond between pet and owner, of making the dog feel loved, and of socializing the animal to human beings.

If you are entering dog ownership with a puppy, now is a good time to start it out on the right paw, so to speak. It is probably unnecessary to advise that you pet your puppy a lot, because how can you resist? Encourage other people to do the same. Every hug and cuddle goes into the pup's little bank of experience and helps inculcate in it the belief that human beings are just swell and can be trusted. That's the right attitude for a dog to have, especially in the city. Your job is to provide a life for it in which nothing serious happens to destroy this belief in the goodness of humankind.

Get your puppy accustomed to being manipulated as if being given a thorough physical examination. Look in its ears and under its tail; open its mouth and put your fingers in. Examine your puppy's toes. Start brushing and combing and grooming the pup very early. Do all this frequently while it is growing up, and keep doing it even after it's grown.

Stroke your puppy even when it is eating, and take its food bowl away for a moment, then give it back. You don't want a dog that will bite your hand off if you touch it or its bowl while it's eating—a common reaction of a dog that hasn't been properly socialized. I remember when a new kitten ran over and, before I could intervene, stuck its head in Dandy's bowl while she was eating—a potentially dangerous act, since many dogs would have growled, snapped, or bitten. But Dandy's reaction was simply to eat faster.

It's good to cradle a puppy on its back as you would a baby. Get it used to being carried about, by you and by other people. But please don't forget the advice I gave you in Chapter 2 about the right ways to hold and play with a puppy, because they are important in the socializing process.

I don't mean to suggest that you handle a young dog nonstop, never giving it a moment to rest or just be quiet by itself. Children especially should learn to respect an animal's right to be left alone when it's tired or has had enough. For this early touching to socialize your puppy and defuse any possible aggressive tendencies, it must be pleasurable to the dog—otherwise it will have the opposite effect. If the puppy is pestered and mauled, rather than handled in a gentle and understanding way, the opportunity for it to develop an angelic disposition will be lost.

An adult dog can be socialized in much the same way as a puppy, except that you might have to go slowly if it has been abused, neglected, or mishandled in any way. Be especially careful, for example, about touching its food bowl when it is eating. If the dog has ever gone hungry, it might have developed an anxious attitude toward food and can react instantly to what it perceives as a threat to filling its belly. But with constant reassurance and good treatment, the dog will eventually learn to trust you and other people.

Most dogs hate to have their feet touched or handled, and it's a good idea for city people especially to get their pets used to this. Not only will you probably need to clip your dog's toenails occasionally, but you'll want to wipe its feet when it comes in with wet or muddy paws, and it's no fun to have to cope with a struggling animal in order to do it.

HOUSEBREAKING

Three important pieces of advice, before we get down to the nitty-gritty of housebreaking: Don't even attempt to housebreak a puppy until it is around four months old, because that's as hopeless as trying to toilet-train an infant. The dog simply hasn't developed reliable bladder and bowel control.

Second, forget about scolding or otherwise punishing a dog that has already made a mess. You absolutely must catch it in the act. Some people say their dog always acts guilty when they point to the puddle or pile and scold, so therefore the animal knows what they're talking about. Not so. The dog is reacting to the tone of voice—it knows by its owner's behavior that it has done something wrong, but it has no idea what. All it knows is that you're mad because it has relieved itself; it has no idea that you're objecting to where it did it. Just wipe up the mess without comment.

When you catch your dog in the act, say "No!" and carry it or lead it immediately out to the appropriate spot. Even if it's the middle of the night. Always praise the dog enthusiastically when it goes where you want it to go.

And third, along the same lines, if anyone tells you to punish a dog by rubbing its nose in the mess, ignore that advice. This tactic is not only cruel but totally ineffective.

Be especially patient with a dog that has lived in a cage or been confined, as in a shelter, pet shop, or even a breeder's. Being caged or confined in a small space suppresses a dog's instinct not to soil its den, because the animal has no choice. You have to start almost from scratch with it. However, if a shelter dog has been a housebroken pet fairly recently and hasn't forgotten, or if the shelter has enough staff or volunteers to walk the dogs outside regularly, it won't take long to get it back into good habits.

If you have just moved from the country or suburbs to the city with your dog, it may refuse at first to relieve itself in the street because it is nervous and afraid of the traffic and crowds. The same applies to a pet you are adopting that formerly lived in a home or a shelter where it was housebroken to relieve itself outdoors on grass or on a dirt road, not on pavement. The street simply doesn't feel right under its paws. And it is very stressful for such a dog to have to urinate or defecate at the curb, with traffic zooming by. Give the dog a break.

One city friend of mine adopted a charming dog from a rural shelter but was very annoyed at discovering that, although the shelter had told her the dog was housebroken, it clearly didn't have a clue that it was supposed to use the street. Then she realized that the dog probably was housebroken, but accustomed to relieving itself on grass. It took a couple of weeks of patient work before her pet caught on that it must overcome its previous habit and learn always to go outdoors at the curb.

Begin housebreaking a dog when it's old enough by taking it to the street at regular times—upon waking in the morning, after each meal, after play, when it gets up from a nap, and the last thing at night. A young pup may need to go more often, but an adult dog can soon be trained to three or four well-spaced trips outside. Keep a regular schedule, and also take the dog to the same place on the street each time. Whenever it performs at the curb, pet and praise it extravagantly. (And don't forget to clean up any fecal matter.)

When you're with your dog in the house, keep it with you and watch for signals that it might have to go out. (Use a baby gate if necessary to prevent it from going to a room where you can't watch it.) The animal will start sniffing in corners or on the rugs, often turning in circles and acting agitated. That's your cue to spring to your feet and whisk your pet outdoors—and this will reinforce the learning process.

When you're not home, the best plan is to confine the dog to a place where it can't hurt the floor—the bathroom or kitchen—or in one of those folding, heavy wire cages called kennel crates, lined with newspapers. The confinement space should be big enough for the animal to lie stretched out and should contain newspapers, its water bowl, and some toys. Unless you make the mistake of pushing the dog in, or use it as a place of punishment, the dog will instinctively adopt the crate or confinement area as its den. And because dogs are loath to soil their den, the animal will try to hold its elimination needs until it is taken out.

Don't crate the dog for more than a few hours at a time. As it begins to relieve itself on schedule and only outdoors, then you can gradually let it have the run of the house when you're out.

Some trainers recommend establishing a time limit within which an adult dog must learn to relieve itself at the curb. If the animal hasn't done its business within, say, half of a city block, bring it back in and make it wait until next time. The dog's discomfort may inspire it to react more quickly when taken out. Otherwise, you may find yourself pacing up and down at the curb some winter night waiting and waiting for your pet to perform. When it gets the idea and urinates or defecates at the curb within a reasonable time, reward it with praise and a treat until it gets the habit.

Some city dwellers prefer to paper-train their dogs. Follow the same general procedure as if you were taking it to the curb, but instead, take it regularly to a place where you have spread newspapers thickly. When it has relieved itself at the right place, reward and pet it.

There will be accidents. These can be exasperating, but try not to get mad at your pet. One way to clean up a puddle on a carpet or upholstery, by the way, is to blot it first with paper toweling, if possible putting several thicknesses of paper towel under the spot as well. Then wash the spot with a commercial product made for the purpose. Or try a solution of one part vinegar to two parts water. Let the vinegar solution sit on the spot for a little while, then blot with more paper towels.

A dog may break house-training when it is anxious about some change in the household, such as a death in the family, the arrival of a baby, a new person living in the house, a move, or the acquisition of a new pet. Dogs are creatures of routine and habit and can feel very threatened even when they merely sense a change coming—which they may perceive as impending doom. But a previously housebroken dog doesn't start soiling in the house out of spite; rather, it is upset. The way to deal with that is to figure out what's bothering the animal and take steps to reassure it.

PROBLEM BARKING

One of the most important things you will ever teach your dog is not to bark, howl, or whine when you're out. Not all dogs vocalize when left alone, but if you hear yours making a ruckus as you approach your door, or if a neighbor has complained, you must deal with this problem immediately and successfully—for your animal's sake, for your neighbors', and for your own if you wish to keep your pet.

Human beings are innately social creatures, and most of us suffer greatly if separated for very long from our fellows. Dogs, almost without exception, are also social beings. Laboratory dogs that are kept in isolation for experimental reasons suffer even more than human prisoners that are sentenced to solitary confinement, for the dogs have no understanding and no hope. And a pet, especially a puppy, deprived of companionship for many hours experiences the same feelings of abandonment that a human baby would feel; both express separation anxiety.

According to Dr. Peter Borchelt, an animal behavior consultant, the first reactions of both babies and dogs to being left alone are crying, elimination, and destructive behavior. Many dog owners misunderstand these actions on the part of their pets—they interpret the dog's "naughtiness" as an effort to punish them for leaving.

"Dogs don't have the complicated thought processes that would be required for them to punish their owners for doing something they didn't like, such as leaving them alone," says Borchelt. "When the dog vocalizes, it is simply expressing anxiety. Young animals in the wild, when separated from their mothers, will call and call, an instinctual reaction that helps their mothers locate them. Possibly the dog's reaction is similar—it may be signaling its location to its absent owner. When the dog eliminates, it is leaving its scent. And when it totals the house, it is trying to escape, trying to get out so it can reattach to its owner."

Most puppies, when separated first from their mothers and littermates, then from their owners when the owners go out and leave them alone, will instinctively begin to cry. Borchelt also points out that a dog that has been passed around among successive owners, attaching itself to someone only to be permanently separated from him or her, is more likely to suffer from separation anxiety than a dog that has lived for a while with the same owner and feels secure.

But the important thing to remember is that a dog that cries or shows other signs of anxiety when left alone is not a bad dog, is not misbehaving or trying to bug you, but is reacting to normal insecurity. You need to let it know that its anxiety behavior displeases you, that you will return, and that it must wait for you quietly.

One thing that helps is to not make a big deal of going out or coming back. Don't make a big fuss over the dog before you leave; this just makes the animal feel worse about not going with you. And when you return, greet the dog casually and affectionately, but don't get down on the floor and throw your arms around it and act like you feel guilty.

To train a dog not to bark, you must catch it in the act. Pretend to leave your house. Most dogs will begin to wail or bark within fifteen minutes, so you won't have to hang around for hours. Don't wait just outside your door, by the way—your dog will certainly know you're there. You must go down the hall or down the block, staying within earshot. When the dog starts up, rush back in and reprimand the surprised animal with a loud, stern "No!" Shake your finger and go out again.

In the beginning, you may have to go in and out at ten-second intervals, but you'll find that you can gradually extend the time. Keep up this training for fifteen-minute periods, several times a day. Don't give up.

If you are friendly with your neighbors, you might enlist their cooperation. Ask them to let you know whether your pet has complained or been quiet when you were out. That way, they will know you are concerned and actively working on the problem, and their feedback can help you to ascertain how quickly your dog is learning.

Some dogs are helped by the sound of a radio playing quietly. Others are comforted by the presence of another pet. But the main thing is that your dog gets the message about how you expect it to behave when you're not home.

You don't want to teach your dog never to bark—that would be like expecting a child not to speak or a bird not to sing. Also, if you reprimand your pet every time it makes a sound, it might keep quiet when there's a prowler outside, or when there's a fire. True stories abound of instances in which the barking of a pet has saved lives by attracting help when needed. Also, it is natural for a dog to bark for joy when playing or greeting its owner, and that should be allowed. What you want is for your pet to bark selectively, so it only has to remember the few instances when barking is forbidden.

If your dog barks every time a neighbor passes the door of your apartment, you might open the door and let the dog see who it is, reassuring it at the same time. If the dog learns to recognize the sounds that are regular and normal, not suspicious, it will know not to sound the alarm. Susannah has a short, sharp yip that tells me, "Somebody I don't know is in the hall."

But if a dog always barks nonstop at some feared object that it encounters with some regularity—a vacuum cleaner, for instance—then it's necessary to desensitize the animal so it won't drive you and the neighbors crazy every time you clean the house. Start by having someone else use the cleaner at some distance from the dog, and only for a few minutes. Reassure the dog continually when the motor is on. Reward it as soon as it can tolerate the cleaner without barking. Then gradually step up the time the cleaner is on and slowly decrease its distance from the dog. Be patient—remember that the animal is only trying to warn you about a fearsome object.

OTHER BEHAVIOR PROBLEMS

Other annoying behaviors that a dog might exhibit include jumping up on you and others, and—if you have forbidden it—lying on your furniture when you're not around. And while most dogs are afraid of explosive noises, such as thunder and fireworks, some dogs are so panicked that they become destructive. Here are some ways you can help your dog change these behaviors.

Jumping on People

One of the first things your dog will do, especially if it's a puppy, is jump up on you and on everyone who gives it attention. The animal is only trying to get close and establish eye contact, but it's best to discourage this behavior. You don't want it jumping up when it has muddy feet, for instance, but you can't expect the animal to understand what's wrong with muddy feet. A big dog jumping up on an elderly or frail person, or a child, even in the friendliest way imaginable, can hurt. So you'll want to teach your pet to keep all four feet on the ground when interacting with you or other people, period.

There are several recommended ways to teach a dog not to jump up: You can step lightly on its hind toes, you can bump it in the chest with your knee, or you can grasp its front paws and push it backward so it is off balance. Any of these should be accompanied by the command, "No!" Then, after the dog gets down, walk away and ignore it for a few minutes.

After a moment, when you're sure your pet has got the message and has stayed down, pat and praise it. Remember, be consistent. Don't confuse the dog by letting it jump up just this once, and then pushing it down and saying "No!" the next time. And don't give up.

Jumping on Furniture

Jumping on the furniture when left alone—any dog with sense will try it at least once. There's an old joke about a dog that had a habit of sneaking up on the sofa or a chair for a nap when its owners were out. Though the dog was always at the door to greet them when they came home, the owners would go around the room feeling the seats of all the furniture, searching for telltale warmth. Whenever they discovered the dog had been naughty, they'd punish it. So one day, as the story goes, they came home and found the dog blowing on the sofa cushion to cool it off.

If you don't wish your pet to lie on the furniture, you must catch it in the act, when it is jumping up or has settled in. Scolding the dog after it has already gotten down won't do it. To catch the animal, you have to outsmart it by going out and waiting in the hall till you think it's had time to settle on the sofa or wherever, then returning unexpectedly. Burst into the house and, if the dog has indeed sacked out on the cushions, yell "No!" The dog will probably jump down and run, but if it stays where it is, push it down to the floor and say "No!" Do this several times a day.

Also make sure to go out and come back in before the dog has had a chance to get up on the furniture, and then reward it. Keep extending the time you wait before coming back in.

When you have to go out for other than training reasons, though, don't reward the dog unless there's some way you can be sure it hasn't been sitting on the furniture and jumped down the minute it heard your key in the lock. It may have blown on the cushion to cool it off!

Remember, most dogs are lonely when left alone. One thing that might help is to provide a place where your dog can look out a window, especially a window that faces the sidewalk or street, or even a tree with a lot of birds and squirrels. You can't blame a dog for getting up on a chair or sofa so it can see out a window, so provide a chair or ottoman or other comfortable piece of furniture for the purpose.

A puppy is going to want to sleep in your bed with you, and this is a matter of choice on your part. Lots of dog owners let their pets sleep with them, and I certainly don't see anything wrong with that. But if you prefer that your pet sleep in its own bed, at least keep the bed in the room where you sleep. Remember that your dog loves you, and its idea of where it should always be is at your side—especially in the dark of night.

To help a little puppy get used to sleeping alone in its own bed, try putting a warm hot water bottle (wrapped in a towel) and a clock with a tick loud enough to hear (also wrapped in a towel) in the bed with it, to approximate the warm bodies and heartbeats of the mother and siblings it misses.

Chewing

Just like babies who go through a stage of putting everything in their mouth, puppies tend to chew on anything they find that looks tasty—socks and shoes, handbags and books, electric light cords, you name it. They do this especially when they're teething, of course.

The way to deal with this is to confine the pup when you're not around to keep an eye on it. Shut it in the bathroom or kitchen, or invest in a kennel crate and settle the pup there whenever you go out.

Adult dogs also sometimes chew up household objects or their owners' possessions when they're left alone. According to Borchelt, this is another expression of separation anxiety. This redirected behavior is similar to the way some of us bite our fingernails or drum our fingers when we're nervous.

A dog that's ordinarily a paragon of perfect house behavior can resort to destructive chewing when left alone at times of dramatic change in household routine. Seeing packing cartons around before moving, or suitcases before a trip, for example, can trigger it. A kennel crate is also useful at such times if the dog is already used to the crate. A normally well-behaved dog will stop misbehaving of its own accord as soon as the household settles down again and familiar routine is restored. Remember the dog's denning instinct; putting it in a small room or kennel crate for short periods of time is not cruel but protects both the dog and your possessions. Put its bed, a towel, anything cozy and comfortable for it to lie on in the room or at one end of the crate, spread newspapers as far from the bed as possible, in case of accidents, and give it some safe toys to chew on. Chew toys are an important part of a dog's accoutrements anyway—hard nylon bones, hard rubber toys, objects that can't splinter or break up if chewed (for example, not plastic, wood, or soft rubber).

If you confine a dog in the kitchen or bathroom, be sure to put poisons, garbage, and the like—anything the animal might get into—out of its way. And never confine a dog anywhere for longer than four or five hours—or, if overnight, seven or eight hours tops.

Some dogs, especially puppies, have a tendency to mouth you— take your hand or arm in their mouth and gnaw on you, not enough to hurt, usually, but just enough to be annoying. When a dog does that, don't snatch your hand away, or push the dog away. Instead, say "No!" loud and firm, remove the dog's mouth, hold it closed for a moment, and then ignore the animal. You might even get up and walk away, get involved in something else for a while, to make your point.

I think it is a bad idea to give a dog something of its owner's to chew, like an old shoe or sock, because the dog can't tell a worn-out sneaker from a brand-new Gucci loafer. When I put that in a magazine article, a reader wrote and told me that her dog used one of her old shoes as a chew toy and never bothered her good shoes—and she sent me a cute snapshot of her dog biting its very own, old shoe. Obviously, I was wrong as far as her dog is concerned, but I pass this advice on to you anyway.

Fear of Thunder and Fireworks

Thunder and fireworks—virtually all dogs are afraid of them. They have no idea what's going on, and they probably think it's the end of the world. Some dogs simply go under a bed or to the back of a closet and wait it out. But some dogs are so afraid they react pathologically. Sally would pace, roll her eyes, tremble, and hyperventilate till her tongue was hanging down almost to the floor. She would chew up whatever she could reach. She could not be distracted with toys or play. I once shut her in the bathroom where I thought she might feel safe, and she ate part of the door until her gums bled. Susannah is even worse—and her teeth literally chatter.

One of the widely recommended solutions for thunderstorm fear is to get a cassette or CD of storm sounds and try to condition the dog to the noise by playing that. In my opinion, no dog is going to be fooled. Sometimes when I've been watching a TV program there's a scene with a huge loud storm, or a program that shows the fireworks displays on the Fourth of July, with all the accompanying din. No reaction from my dog. It could be a program of chamber music for all she cares. A dog's fear is apparently triggered not simply by the noise but by the whole atmosphere during a storm. Sally could sense a storm coming long before it hit—I think the change in the barometric pressure warned her. Even in her old age, when she was virtually deaf, she still went into a frenzy of fear even before a storm. Susannah is also an accurate predictor.

You might ask your veterinarian about tranquilizers, and give your dog one if you have enough warning that a storm is coming. But most tranquilizers take thirty to sixty minutes to take effect, and by then the dog is likely to be already terrified.

I try to be with Susannah during a storm; if I'm out, I may ask a neighbor or family member to stop in. At least she is prevented from damaging herself or the furniture in her hysteria. All the dog trainers say not to soothe or cuddle a terrified dog, or let it in your bed if you normally don't, because that reinforces their fear—the dog figures there must be something bad going on. Just keep your pet safe and try to convince it that nothing dangerous is happening.

DEALING WITH AGGRESSIVENESS

Mouthing is not an aggressive act, but growling and showing teeth definitely are. A growl, snarl, or warning bark is the prelude to a bite. City dog owners cannot afford to have aggressive dogs. Even if your dog is gentle with you and your family and only hostile to others, this just won't do in the city, where the animal is constantly exposed to other people and other dogs.

I can't imagine that it would be pleasant to have a dog you had to watch constantly, worrying about what it might do. If your dog hurt someone, you would be held responsible for the suffering the dog had caused. Not only would you be open to a lawsuit, but your dog might be destroyed by the authorities of your city.

Be aware that aggressive dogs can also turn on their owners. It is known that not only do the vast majority of dog bites occur from owned dogs, not strays, but a sizable proportion of them occur when dogs attack their owners. Certainly something is very wrong when this tragedy occurs—the dog may have had irreparable harm done to it in the past, or its owner might abuse it. Or it might be sick. But if you take on a dog with an unstable disposition, even if it seems perfectly loyal to you, you can't trust it.

Also, dogs can make mistakes, just as we do. We once had a bad experience with Dandy and a guard dog. My son was walking Dandy peacefully on her leash on the sidewalk past a garage. Suddenly a huge German Shepherd came roaring out of the garage and attacked Dandy. He bowled her over and bit her in the chest—a bad puncture wound that narrowly missed her lung—before the garage owner and my son could pull the dog off her. This dog made two mistakes: He perceived the public sidewalk as a part of the territory he was supposed to guard, and he attacked before he discovered Dandy was a female. (Normally, male dogs do not attack female dogs, and vice versa.)

The Shepherd's owner apologized all over the place and paid Dandy's veterinary bill. But this is an example of why guard dogs, and attack dogs, are a bad idea. I think it is wrong to turn dogs into weapons; it perverts their nature and distorts the loving and loyal relationship they normally have with human beings. The episode also indicates how a presumably well-trained dog can get confused at times. And if a befuddled dog happens to be aggressive, it can be dangerous.

Physical punishment increases, not decreases, aggression. As I pointed out earlier, the vast majority of reputable dog trainers consider hitting a dog counterproductive, and this goes especially for aggressive dogs. The owner's attitude plays a prime role: If the owner becomes angry and impatient, in any type of training, it will upset the animal and make the problems worse.

Don't worry that if you have a submissive dog it won't try to protect your home in a threatening situation—in all likelihood it will. Its readiness to do this stems from the pack and den instincts I discussed earlier. Your dog will defend home and loved ones not out of aggression but because it is programmed by its heritage to do so.

It may be that some dogs are more likely to remember and act on those instincts than others. While I think my former dog Benjy might have gone for the jugular of a mugger, I doubt very much that Susannah would. People have told me, Oh yes, she would be a different dog if an ugly situation arose and you were in danger. However, her job is just to be a pet and a companion, not to guard me or mine.

The first thing to do at the first sign of an aggressive tendency in a dog is to have the animal spayed or castrated. That will help to calm the dog and make it much more trainable.

Next, obedience training. Many urban SPCAs or humane societies, as well as private trainers, offer dog training classes. If your dog is especially difficult, it's best to hire a professional trainer to work privately with you and your pet. Otherwise, the animal's bad habits will just get worse, and then you will have a serious problem.

If you do hire a private trainer to help you, be very selective. There are a lot of nuts out there in the dog training business. There seems to be an especially high proportion of authoritarian men who use this profession as a means of getting rid of their own hostility and frustrations by brutalizing dogs into submission. One type you should particularly look out for are those who use electric shock collars on the dogs during training. Even if your idea of the dog for you is a high-strung Doberman or a Shepherd with a big chip on its shoulder, the worst thing you can do is subject it to this kind of torture. You want a kind, firm, knowledgeable professional who really likes dogs and has trained the pets of people you know personally whose judgment you trust.

It goes almost without saying that you should also give the dog a great deal of affection and patient but firm leadership. In addition, help it to get used to other people in nonthreatening situations (on the street is a good place to start, as opposed to the dog's own home). Careful, regular, and casual contact with friends who like dogs will go a long way toward reassuring and socializing an aggressive dog. I can't stress it too much—city dogs must be well socialized.

SIMPLE OBEDIENCE TRAINING

Fundamental in having a city dog that's a joy to you, to itself, and to everybody else is teaching it to obey a repertoire of simple commands. This won't be hard to do if you have reasonable expectations of your pet and approach the training in a positive way. Ask not, How can I *stop* my dog from doing a specific thing? Ask, rather: How can I *get* my dog to *do* the opposite? For example, instead of thinking, How can I stop my dog from pulling on the leash when I walk him/her, concentrate on teaching your dog to walk properly at your side.

Paul Glassner/ San Francisco SPCA

Dogs attending the San Francisco SPCA's annual Wingding participate in "the world's longest down-stay"

Simple obedience training consists of teaching a dog to come when called, to sit and stay, to lie down, to heel (walk at your side), and to respond correctly to the word "No." Stick to one-word commands and be consistent—come, sit, stay, down, heel, and no. Don't say, "Cut it out," or "Stop that, sweetheart, I don't like it when you do that," when what you mean is "No!"

Don't feel apologetic about training your dog, as if you were being mean to it or taking away its rights. Remember that the animal will feel better when it knows that you're in charge, that you know what you're doing, and that it will get love and approval from you when it does what you want it to. Be clear and firm in giving commands, and reward the dog lavishly for good behavior.

I once knew a woman who adopted an Irish Setter named Katy, who had been turned in to the SPCA because she was "bad with kids." Katy was a cowering, shy, slinking dog who did not know her name, was not housebroken, and was afraid of everyone and every-thing. The first thing the owner did was take Katy to obedience classes. "I can honestly say that obedience training made Katy blos-som," she reported. "It gave her a sense of purpose and accomplish-ment, developed her self-confidence. She has served as my teaching dog in SPCA humane education programs and is wonderful with children. And in fact, she has won first place in obedience classes at many dog shows, including the American Kennel Club's most advanced title."

Bill Berloni, formerly of theatrical performing dog fame, points out that there's a difference between teaching and correcting. "People are too quick to reprimand a dog," he says. "If your dog persists in doing something, in spite of your efforts to the contrary, ask yourself if you simply haven't gotten the message across—maybe the dog just needs more teaching, or a different method of teaching, instead of correcting. If the dog already knows what you want it to do, and has been doing it for some time, but for some reason suddenly does something else instead, then and only then can you assume it needs correcting."

There are two schools of thought about using food as a reward when training a dog. The only trouble with the food reward is that sometimes you'll be giving lessons out on the street, so you'll have to carry dog treats with you. Also, the dog will learn to expect a treat and will be disappointed if that reward is not forthcoming every time it does what you want. For that reason, I'd suggest giving praise and a pat or hug along with a little treat such as a bit of cheese or dog tidbit in the beginning when your dog masters a simple obedience lesson. Then phase out the food reward gradually while stepping up the praise and petting. Eventually your dog will be just as ecstatic about "Good boy!" or "Good girl!" as it initially was over a food treat.

Use "No!" sparingly, but in a way that communicates firm dis-approval, making sure the animal knows exactly what it is you object to. Adjust the severity of your tone to the dog's temperament—some dogs will cringe pathetically at a reprimand, while others won't pay any attention at all unless you raise your voice. Your tone of voice should definitely be different for the word "no" than for the other commands. If you lose your temper and yell "Come!" in an angry voice, what dog is going to want to respond? Give the obedience commands in a friendly voice, and express annoyance only with "No!"

Frequently precede or follow a command word with the dog's name. The late Job Michael Evans, an excellent dog trainer, recommended eye contact for three or four seconds whenever you give your dog a command. He felt this helps let the animal know that you are pack leader.

Some trainers recommend corporal punishment—a rap on the nose or swat on the behind—when a dog misbehaves. You may have heard the folded newspaper theory—that you should smack a dog with a rolled-up newspaper when it has been "bad." I wouldn't use any hitting at all, and the best dog trainers I know are also vehemently against it. If you are patient and persistent, you should be able to teach your dog by making clear what you want and then rewarding it with displays of your love and approval.

Before you start obedience lessons, two important pieces of advice: Don't try to obedience-train a puppy before it is between two and three months old, or you will just confuse it and frustrate yourself—and wait till it's five to six months old before you take it to an obedience class with other dogs. And don't try to train a dog for longer than ten to fifteen minutes at a time, or it will become tired or bored and will grow to hate rather than enjoy the lessons. Two sessions a day should be about right.

Also, be sure that every member of the family agrees on how the dog should be trained. If the animal gets conflicting messages on its do's and don'ts, it will be confused and training will break down completely.

"Come" is probably the easiest command to teach, especially when followed by the dog's name, because it indicates to the animal that you are calling it to you to give it affection. But you must insist that it respond every time, even when it has an interest elsewhere. If the dog doesn't come when you call it, go and lead it by the collar to where you were standing. Some dog trainers recommend using the leash, even indoors, to draw the dog to you when you say "Come!"

The importance of teaching your dog to come when called shouldn't be underestimated by city dog owners. Even though your dog will always be leashed on the street (I hope), there may be places such as fenced dog runs where it will be running loose, and you may want to get it away from troublesome dogs or people. Or you may accidentally let go of the leash for some reason. I know a beautiful Golden Retriever that was startled by a sound on the street just at a moment when his owner, her arms full of packages, had unknowingly dropped his leash for a few seconds. The dog bolted, ignored her call, dashed into the street, and was hit by a truck. So you want to be sure your pet's response to the "Come!" command is as reliable as possible.

Also, there will be plenty of occasions indoors when you want to call your dog to you and have it respond. You want to groom it, take it out, have it meet company. Or say you want to give it a bath, and you have a nice tubful of warm water all ready—you don't want to have to search for your pet and drag it out of hiding. One rule on which all dog trainers agree: Never, never call your dog to you and then punish or scold it. This will only make the dog hate and fear you and will more likely ensure that it will ignore you or run in the opposite direction when you call it. You can hardly blame it for that. Get the dog to associate "come" with pleasure and rewards.

"Sit," "Down," and "Stay" should be taught together, since there's no point in teaching your pet to sit or lie down if it gets up and walks away two seconds later. You teach a dog to sit by giving the verbal command and by pushing its rear end so that it sits down. If it stands up immediately, say "Sit!" again and push it into the sitting position. Keep this up until the dog remains seated long enough for you to say "Good dog" and stroke it. You may want to use the leash for this exercise, so that you can pull your dog's head up while you push its rear end down.

Use the leash for teaching "Down" also. Have your pet sit, and face it with your foot on the leash. Raise your hand, palm toward the animal, and when you say "Down," make a downward sweep with your hand and get the dog into a lying position. With a little dog, you can pull it down by the collar; a big dog may require a push at the shoulders or a gentle pull forward of the front feet. However you do it, get the dog into a lying position and praise it. Give it a food reward until it learns to obey the command automatically, then gradually phase out the food but keep up the praise. Keep practicing, making sure the animal associates "Down" and the hand signal with the prone position.

There probably won't be many occasions outdoors when you'll be telling your dog "Down," but indoors, a well-mannered dog might be told to lie down if, for instance, you are serving guests and your pet is getting underfoot, or if you are visiting with it in someone else's house.

"Stay" is a little harder, because when you walk away the dog will naturally get up to follow you or stroll away. Put the palm of your hand in front of the dog's nose while the animal is seated or lying down, and say "Stay." Then, bending over and keeping your hand in the same position, slowly walk around it. If it gets up, say "No" loudly, make it sit again, and repeat the exercise. When the dog remains seated, reward it. Once it has mastered staying still while you walk around it, try backing away, holding your hand palm-forward toward the dog. If the dog gets up, say "No!" and make the dog sit or lie down again. Repeat the exercise for ten-to fifteen-minute sessions, several times a day, until it gets the idea.

Job Michael Evans suggested that city dog owners might teach their dogs always to sit, even without command, at the door when they return from a walk, so they can get out their keys and unlock the door easily without having the dogs milling around waiting to be let in. This makes sense, doesn't it?

Paul Glassner/ San Francisco SPCA

Dr. Susy Atwell, a retired surgeon and SPCA volunteer, has trained dogs for forty years. She is teaching Nutmeg, a San Francisco SPCA Hearing Dog in training, to be a valuable aide to a deaf person.

LEASH TRAINING

Get your dog a good quality collar with a secure fastener, and be sure to allow a space of two of your fingers between the dog's neck and the collar. Remember to check the collar every few days on a growing puppy to make sure it hasn't gotten too tight as the pup gets bigger. Some people like those spring-retractable collars for a puppy, because they won't have to get a bigger one later on. Get a puppy used to wearing a collar gradually, in the house. But take it off when you're not around. A pup who's not used to a collar will shake its head and try to chew it off, and might get its lower jaw stuck in the collar.

For a strong and somewhat unruly dog, a nose halter will be a godsend, much better than a chain-link choke collar. Some people may think your dog is wearing a muzzle to prevent it from biting, but actually, a dog wearing a nose halter can open its mouth easily to eat, drink, pant, yawn, or even bark if necessary. Lucy, the strong, lively dog I had so briefly, pulled me into snowdrifts and puddles, even with a choke collar. When I put a nose halter on her, I had no trouble controlling her, and she was perfectly happy wearing it. I don't suggest a nose halter instead of training your dog to walk nicely on a leash, but as an addition to leash training.

Few experiences are more aggravating than trying to walk a dog that is all over the place, straining and lunging forward on the leash, or dragging behind. You'd be surprised how strong even a little dog can be when it is not properly leash-trained. But what a pleasure it is to walk down the street with your dog trotting properly at your side. Walking your dog should be a matter of give and take. Let it sniff the trees, lampposts, and hydrants for a little while—"reading the newspaper" is one of a dog's great pleasures. And your dog does have the right to find just the perfect spot at the curb to relieve itself. Sometimes this takes a little circling, pacing back and forth, till the dog decides "this is the place." But once it has relieved itself, you have the right to insist that it come along with you if you are in a hurry or have errands to do.

As for teaching your dog to walk on a leash, if you haven't already enrolled yourself and your dog in an obedience class, this might be a good time to do it. Leash training comes more easily for some dogs in a class. Many humane societies and SPCAs offer classes, as do some freelance trainers. However, if your dog seems easily trainable, you could teach it yourself.

The consensus among many dog trainers is that you walk with your dog on your left, controlling the leash closely with your left hand and holding the end of the leash with your right. If the dog pulls ahead, give a quick, short tug on the leash with your left hand and say, "Heel, boy" (or girl, or say the dog's name). Don't yank the animal off its feet, but give a quick tug firm enough to be felt.

Your instinct might be to keep the leash so tight that the dog can't pull ahead of you. This may prevent it from ranging ahead, but it doesn't teach it to walk beside you. The dog must walk there on its own, not because it has no choice. Keep working on the "Heel!" command until the dog finally walks beside you, then give it a lot of praise and petting, even a treat. Ten minutes of lessons at a time, several times a day, are enough, otherwise both you and your dog will get tired and give up.

The same technique applies to a dog that's lagging behind. A puppy especially may do this when you first take it out on the leash. Don't drag the animal along, but coax it in a friendly voice, giving short tugs at the leash (again with your left hand) until it decides to come along. Then praise it and give it a treat. The dog should soon get the idea that what you want is for it to walk along at your side.

Job Michael Evans suggested that a puppy be carried for its first few excursions on the street. Hug the dog close to you at about chest level and let it take in the strange sights, noises, and smells from the protection of your arms. This makes a puppy feel secure, and it will be less likely to be afraid when you eventually put it down and start to teach it to walk on the leash.

Some dogs catch on very quickly and in a few days are walking at your side very nicely. Other dogs—many strong-willed little terriers, for instance—require an inordinate amount of training and patience. Hang in there.

I've seen dogs that have been trained not to look to the right or the left and to ignore other dogs on the street. I suppose this is necessary for people who have dogs that tend to be quarrelsome with other dogs and who haven't socialized them. But with a friendly city dog, I personally think it's fine to let it have plenty of social intercourse with other friendly dogs. Dogs in the same neighborhood get to know one another and form friendships. Susannah has several pals of her own species—Tao, Lenny, Zeke, Barney, and Molly—though she's a little wary of Dugout the pit bull, who is hysterically friendly, powerful, and rowdy. However, don't push dogs on each other. Josephine Gassner has noticed that one mistake many dog owners make is assuming their pet will automatically like other dogs. "Dogs have their likes and dislikes among their own species, just as we do," says Josephine. Even if your friend has a dog and you think it would be ever so nice if your dog and your friend's dog were buddies, the dogs are entitled to their preferences. They must not be unpleasant—that's against the rules—but they should be permitted to ignore each other if they want.

Incidentally, it's good to be cautious around children walking dogs, unless you know them. You can't always trust a child to have control of his or her pet on the street.

Here's a tip for good street manners with a dog: Naturally, you can't take your pet into a grocery store, restaurant, deli, or the like, because that would violate local health laws. But if you enter a non-food type of store, always ask the proprietor, or the first person you see who works there, if it's okay to bring your dog in. It's only appropriate to respect the preferences of the store owner or manager. And you'd be surprised how welcome you may be if you ask first. Not only that, but you'll help improve the image of city dog owners generally.

In the process of modifying your dog's behavior so that it becomes a perfect house pet and city citizen, the key words to remember are patience and perseverance. Training a dog can be boring, discouraging, and exasperating. Some owners give up and either learn to live with their pet's bad habits or give up the dog altogether, which is unnecessary. A dog can be such a pleasure and give such rewards in terms of love, companionship, loyalty, and fun, that it is well worth your while to invest the time and energy required to help it become well behaved.

5. DIET

Keeping Your Dog Well Nourished

F ood is more than just fuel for our bodies. It comforts us, nourishes our souls, and gives sensory pleasure. The preparation and dispensing of food is an expression of love and hospitality. Food carries much emotional weight and enters into the relationship between owner and dog in ways that go beyond merely providing sustenance.

Few dog owners just fill the feeding bowl and set it before the animal in a perfunctory way. Feeding is a social event for us and our pets, an important element in the bond between us. It's usually accompanied by an interplay of communication. Many of us, as we prepare each meal, talk what psychologists have termed "motherese"—nonsense chatter in soothing tones. Meanwhile, the dog plays its part in the little ceremony, gazing at us bright-eyed and eager, dancing about, tail awag. Chow time is frankly a pleasure for both dog and owner!

It must be relatively easy to sustain a dog, considering the bizarre dog diets I've heard of. I once knew a hound that subsisted for years on raw carrots, cottage cheese, and rawhide chips. But I've also known a Toy Poodle that was fed the same macrobiotic diet its owner ate; not surprisingly, the poor animal was soon malnourished

The hamburger Bailey is chomping on is only a toy

and became ill. Fortunately, the owner took it to a veterinarian who persuaded her to feed her dog properly.

Years ago, pet dogs lived mainly on leftovers—meat and vegetables—from their owner's tables. Today, many people give their dogs table scraps as a treat or supplement to the dogs' regular food. And some dog owners cook for their dogs, and the dogs seem to do just fine. Most dogs, however, are fed commercial dog food, and are better off for it. Despite the protestations of health food aficionados, most commercial dog foods that you can buy in supermarkets and pet supply stores are well-balanced and give our pets the nutrients they need.

Though dogs are considered carnivores, that doesn't mean they should eat nothing but meat. Even wild canids don't eat meat exclusively. Like their primitive ancestors, contemporary wild canids—wild dogs, wolves, foxes, and other cousins of our pet dogs—consume the vegetable matter in the stomachs of the herbivores they kill.

They also eat berries, fruits, vegetables, eggs, insects. By nature, a dog is something of an omnivore, like us.

I no longer eat meat myself for philosophical reasons, but my dogs and cats have always eaten commercial dog and cat food. Cats, by the way, are obligate carnivores, and need more meat protein and fat in their diet than dogs do. Animal nutritionists strongly advise against feeding cat food to a dog, and vice versa. Each type of commercial food is formulated specifically for each species.

I strongly believe that each pet should have its very own feeding bowl. Food is so important to animals that having to share can set up an unnecessary anxiety. Also, animals vary in the rates at which they eat. If two or more dogs eat from the same bowl, the speedy eater will get more than its share, and the slower may end up hungry. Also, the fast eater will often push aside its neighbor and finish off its food.

If you have several pets, you may want to feed the cats on the counter, and supervise everybody to be sure justice is served.

COMMERCIAL DOG FOOD

But how to choose a commercial dog food for your pet? Supermarket shelves offer an overwhelming abundance of types in cans, boxes, packages, and bags, all purporting not only to contain total nutrition, the best stuff we could possibly feed to our pets, but to delight their palates as well.

To help you pick the best for your dog, here is a brief overview.

Dog food comes in several general forms: dry, canned (that is, wet), and semi-moist. Dry dog food is kibble, or little dry nuggets in different shapes, packaged in boxes or bags. Canned dog food looks like stew, or like cooked cereal. Semi-moist dog food is formed and colored to look like hamburger, chunks of raw meat, or meat patties, and is sold in individual sealed packets in boxes.

All contain both animal and vegetable protein, fat, fiber, and the vitamins and minerals dogs need, plus moisture. They differ in composition and methods of processing.

A major difference is the amount of water each type contains. Dry dog foods generally contain 10 to 12 percent moisture; canned, 70 to 78 percent; and semi-moist, 30 to 35 percent. The water is necessary in processing the food and makes it edible and palatable.

Dry dog foods are cereal-based, containing mostly grain protein, with meat meal and bone meal. They may also be good for the teeth. Because they contain comparatively little water, a dog gets more nutrients per cupful of dry food than from the same amount of canned or moist food, and therefore dry is the least expensive to buy. Be sure to check the expiration date printed on the package. By itself, dry food has an exceedingly low spoilage rate, but if you add water or gravy to it, be aware that it will spoil in just a few hours if unrefrigerated.

Most of the canned foods and the semi-moist foods contain mainly grain protein with meat by-products. Some owners mix a little canned dog food in with dry, which seems to make it more palatable to some dogs. Semi-moist dog foods also contain salt and preservatives and a small amount of sweetener. The convenience and visual appeal of these foods make them attractive to dog owners, but they have no special advantages for dogs.

A dog doesn't care whether its food looks like hamburger or crackers or stew, yet somehow we feel we're giving our pets better stuff if it looks rather like something we wouldn't mind eating ourselves. What really matters is whether a food has the right proportion of ingredients for an individual dog and whether the dog likes it, not how appetizing it looks by our standards.

There are commercial dog foods for dogs with medical problems—bladder stones, kidney or heart disorders, or sensitive digestive systems—that require special diets. These foods, available through veterinarians, have helped extend the lives of many pets. Special commercial foods for puppies, overweight dogs, older dogs, and dogs doing high-stress work are designed to meet the needs of these groups. Some are sold in supermarkets, some through veterinarians.

Remember that each dog is an individual, and what one dog thrives on may not be easily digested by another. Dry dog foods, for example, give some dogs gas, and semi-moist foods give others diarrhea. Also, an abrupt change in diet can upset a dog's stomach and cause vomiting or diarrhea.

Then there are the finicky eaters, who have decided preferences and will turn up their noses at food that most dogs lick their chops over. I think it's best not to let a dog be too fussy. The little tyrant gets the idea that if it holds out for something it particularly loves, you'll cave in and serve that. I've heard people say their dogs absolutely refuse to eat anything but one particular food. If it happens to be the nutritious food the dog should eat anyway, fine, but sometimes what a dog gets hooked on is the canine equivalent of junk food, or a single food like liver, which can cause a toxic buildup of vitamin A.

If your dog is already a fussy eater, refusing anything but its one or two favorite foods, I suggest phasing other foods gradually into its diet—mixing small amounts in each meal, with the food the animal prefers, and increasing the amounts of the new food gradually. Be strong. It's very hard to hold out against the reproachful looks and hurt attitude you'll get from your pet, but remember, no dog becomes suicidal over food. It will eat eventually.

Dogs enjoy dog biscuits and other commercial dog snacks and treats, and owners enjoy giving them. Though they aren't intended to be a dog's sole diet, many are nutritious. They're certainly better for dogs than the sweets we eat. But I bet it would be hard to find a dog owner who doesn't give his or her pet a bite of cookie, a piece of cake, or a little ice cream now and then. This sharing is part of the pleasure of the bond between pet and owner. Unless what you're eating is chocolate—never give a dog chocolate, it can kill—giving your pet a taste won't hurt it if done in moderation. Just remember that sugar is no better for dogs than it is for us. (By the way, if someone tells you that sugar gives dogs worms, that is silly. Worms are living parasites that a dog can acquire from various means of contact with the organisms or their eggs, but not from sugar.)

Health food stores sometimes sell commercial "natural" pet foods. If the ingredients and guaranteed analysis are within the range that's right for your dog, there's no reason not to buy them if you like.

But there's every reason not to give your dog real bones. Bones are widely believed to be normal fare for a dog, and this notion keeps many veterinarians busy. Dogs that aren't lucky enough to get quick veterinary care may suffer and die. Steak, chop, pork, rabbit, chicken, and other fowl bones should never be fed to a dog under any circumstances. They splinter and can cause mouth and throat injuries and bowel impaction or perforations. Some dog experts give their blessing to knuckle bones. My feeling is, why ask for trouble? If there's any risk to your pet, better to give it something else to chew on—a commercial dog food bone or a hard nylon toy bone—that can't hurt it.

When you have bones in the garbage, by the way, get rid of them immediately, because even a well-trained, well-behaved dog won't be able to resist the temptation to pull them out and eat them.

Also, it's best not to feed your dog raw meat, because it can contain bacteria that is harmful to dogs.

READING THE LABELS

By law, all pet foods except treats and snacks must substantiate their nutritional adequacy on their labels. Standards for pet foods are set by the official regulatory body, the Association of American Feed Control Officials (AAFCO). A product that states it offers "complete and balanced nutrition" means that it has been formulated to meet AAFCO's nutrient standards, or else that it has passed AAFCO's animal feeding tests. In general, feeding tests are considered the better way to assure nutritional adequacy.

So, while it's not the whole story, the first thing to look for on the label of a package or can of dog food are the statements "complete and balanced nutrition for all life stages" and "animal feeding tests" on the label.

Next you'll see the guaranteed analysis, followed by the list of ingredients, or vice versa. The guaranteed analysis tells you about a food's four major ingredients: the minimum amount of protein and fat it contains, the maximum amount of fiber and moisture.

Protein—that is, amino acids—is essential in varying amounts to all animals. It can be supplied by animal or plant products. Animal protein can come from meat (skeletal muscle and tissue), meat by-products (including lungs, spleen, kidneys, brain, liver, and blood), and meat and bone meal (the dry rendered products from animal tissue). Plant protein comes from grains, such as corn, rice, and wheat; soybeans; and meal such as corn gluten and soy flour.

Adult city dogs who live as pets in comfortable circumstances need only moderate amounts of protein—18 to 20 percent in dry food, 8 to 10 percent in canned, and 16 to 18 percent in semi-moist. The guaranteed analysis doesn't distinguish between animal and plant protein; for that, you have to look at the list of ingredients. The label will name those in decreasing order according to weight—that is, the main ingredient first, and so on down the list. *N.B.* Be sure that a protein source is listed among the first two or three ingredients in your dog's food.

If the name of a canned dog food product includes the word "dinner" or "platter" or some such after the meat, poultry, or fish named (for example, "beef dinner"), the product must contain at least 25 percent of the named ingredient. That is, "beef dinner" must contain 25 percent beef. If the meat, poultry, or fish named is not modified, the product must contain 95 percent of the named ingredient or ingredients (for example, a canned dog food labeled "beef and chicken" must be 95 percent beef and chicken).

Fat is important in helping a dog maintain a good coat. If there's too little in the diet, the dog's coat can become rough and dry, its skin scaly. Sometimes a dog with dry skin will scratch so insistently, you'll think it has fleas. On the other hand, too much fat in the food can cause digestive problems and weight gain. A young or highly active dog can handle a larger proportion of fat than a more sedentary animal. Most dry dog foods contain 8 to 10 percent fat; canned, 2 to 6 percent; and semi-moist, 6 or 7 percent. These amounts should be plenty for healthy adult city dogs.

Fiber is not actually a nutrient and is not digested—it is simply bulk and helps intestinal motility. Dry dog food is generally 4 to 4.5 percent fiber; canned, 1 or 1.5 percent; semi-moist, 3 percent. High fiber content (above 5 percent) in a food will cause an increased amount of stool.

It's best not to supplement your dog's diet with extra vitamins, minerals, or whatever unless your veterinarian specifically advises it. Very tiny dogs might need extra nutrients because their stomachs won't hold enough at a meal to give them the daily quota they need, so if yours is a pint-sized dog, ask your veterinarian about this. But in general, dog foods are quite carefully balanced, and gratuitously adding certain nutrients could push their concentration up above optimum levels. It's not true that if a particular vitamin is good for a dog, more of it is automatically better.

Designer or so-called super-premium dog foods will not necessarily make a dog healthier or help it live longer. And a food high in protein will not give an active dog more calories to burn—the way to do that would be by adding fat to the food.

HOW MUCH IS ENOUGH?

A well-treated adult city dog in comfortable surroundings lives an undemanding, generally nonstressful lifestyle, unlike that of, say, a working ranch dog, a guide dog for the blind, or a dog that has to live outdoors year-round. Therefore, its food energy needs are relatively low.

A dog's calorie requirements differ according to its stage of life, and to some extent vary according to the individual. Growing dogs need more calories, older dogs fewer. And we all know people who can pack away prodigious amounts of food and remain slim, while others of similar age, height, and build have to count calories—dogs are a little like that.

Unfortunately, pet food products don't include calories on the labels. And in order to ensure that dogs fed a commercial diet will get all the nutrients they need, the manufacturers tend to recommend amounts at the high end of the scale. City dogs generally need less. For example, the company that makes the dry food that Susannah eats recommends 2 ¼ cups a day for a dog of her weight, but she eats about a cup and is well padded and healthy.

So, unless your city dog gets an unusual amount of exercise and is young, you will probably feed it less than what's suggested on the packages and cans of the food in its diet. When caring dog owners err in how much they feed their pets, it's usually on the side of too much.

With some dogs, you can tell whether or not they're the right weight just by looking at them. But with long-haired or wire-haired dogs, it may not be easy. Try this with your own dog: Stand behind the dog and place your hands over its ribs with your thumbs meeting at about the middle of its back. Spread your fingers on the ribs and press down a little on the vertebrae with your thumbs. Now slide your hands gently forward and backward. You should be able to feel a thin layer of fat over the ribs. However, if you feel the rib bone ends too easily, the dog is thin. If the ribs feel smooth and wavy and you can scarcely feel the rib bone ends, the dog is fat. (See Feeding an Obese Dog, below.)

Don't count on your dog to control its own food intake to maintain a desirable weight. And if you get in the habit of overfeeding it, that will be hard to stop. Once the pet gets used to receiving a certain amount of food, it will feel deprived if it gets less. It will complain and look at you reproachfully, and it's a hard-hearted owner who can hold out under this kind of pressure. So it's best not to let your dog become overweight in the first place.

Dr. Ben E. Sheffy, of the James A. Baker Institute for Animal Health at Cornell University, once told me something I've never forgotten. "The two key words to remember in feeding an animal," he said, "are moderation and regularity."

Free-choice feeding, by the way—keeping a full bowl of food always out—is probably not a good idea for city dogs. Most will quickly gobble up all that's in their bowls and look around for more. Some eat a little more leisurely. But if the bowl is always refilled, the dog will surely gain weight. Also, you want to get your pet into the habit of eating at more or less the same time so you can predict when it will have to relieve itself.

If a dog doesn't eat all of its meal at a feeding, and it's canned or moistened dry food, it may spoil or at least become hard, crusty, and unappetizing. (Also, food left out can attract bugs.) So pick up the bowl as soon as your dog walks away. If there's food left, put it in the refrigerator and add it to the next meal. Wash the bowl after each feeding.

One good meal a day can be appropriate for most adult dogs. Some city dog owners prefer to give their dog its meal in the morning. Since it takes twelve hours for food to pass through its system, the animal will have its major bowel movement during the evening walk. However, some people prefer to feed their dog when they have their own evening meal. Your pet is less likely to beg to share your dinner if it has its own right under its nose.

However, Dr. JoAnn Greenberg, veterinarian to my dogs and cats, recommends that all dogs get their daily amount of food in two portions. She believes that twenty-four hours is too long between meals, and hunger can cause a dog to beg from the table when its owner is eating.

The dog's size or age may also be a factor. Toy breeds may not be able to consume enough at one meal to get all the daily nutrients they need and therefore may require two or even three meals a day—ask your veterinarian. Also, old dogs may do better if their total food amount is divided into two small meals a day, to avoid overload on the digestive system. (See Feeding an Old Dog, below.)

Dr. Greenberg suggests that dividing the daily intake into two or three small meals instead of one large meal may also be preferable for very big or giant breeds, which can be susceptible to bloat, a life-threatening though fortunately not too common gastric disorder that requires emergency medical attention.

Cats normally eat twice a day, and if you have a cat as well as a dog, how can you feed one and not the other? That not only hurts the dog's feelings, but might set up feelings of competition and jealousy in the dog. It's only fair to feed everybody at once. Susannah gets her daily amount of food in two portions—morning and evening—with my cats.

Be sure water in a clean bowl is always available to your pets (see Water, below).

FEEDING A PUPPY

In choosing a good commercial food for your puppy, you have two choices: You can buy one labeled "Complete and balanced nutrition for all life stages"—that is, a food that is sufficiently high in protein and fat and other nutrients for puppies, adults, or geriatric dogs. Be sure it carries the AAFCO label, preferably a label stating the food has passed animal trials. Then you can serve that throughout the dog's life and not have to change unless there is some particular reason to, such as obesity or a medical condition that requires a food your veterinarian recommends.

The other choice is to buy one of the foods especially formulated for growing dogs. It can be canned, dry, or semi-moist. Canned puppy food is the most palatable to many puppies, and while it is the most expensive per ounce, it is the most nutritionally dense, so smaller amounts are needed. It may be preferred for small breeds that can't eat large quantities at a time.

Semi-moist puppy food is somewhat less expensive and less nutritious per ounce than canned, and has higher moisture content than dry. Some dogs are allergic to some of the ingredients in semi-moist food, so if you decide to feed it to your pup, proceed with caution.

Dry puppy food is the least expensive, but because it is lower in nutrients per ounce than canned, feed your dog as much as the label suggests. It's often preferred for large-breed dogs that need to eat a lot of food to fulfill their energy requirements. Some puppies like a combination of dry food mixed with canned, and this is a good choice, but if the pup doesn't eat it all at one meal, be sure not to leave it out to spoil. Let refrigerated food come to room temperature, or heat it slightly, before serving it again. Again, be sure any food you choose states on the label that it has met AAFCO standards.

When the pup is about six months old, or about half grown, you can start changing from puppy food to adult food. Puppy food may be too rich and cause the dog to vomit. Make the change gradually, mixing in the new food in small but increasing amounts. (In fact, any time you change your dog's food, you want to do it gradually.)

Keep an eye on your puppy's figure as it grows. A roly-poly puppy is cute, but for its future health, it's not good for it to be headed for real obesity. This goes especially for a medium-sized or large breed, or a medium or large mixed breed. Letting a pup become too fat sets it up for serious skeletal disorders later on—hip dysplasia, swollen joints, and other orthopedic problems. This is because the bones of a growing dog can't remodel fast enough to support excess weight. Not that your puppy should look skinny and malnourished—just a well-padded slim.

Up to thirteen or fourteen weeks of age, a puppy can eat dry food freely whenever it wants to. If its food is canned or semi-moist, it needs four evenly spaced meals a day.

After that you can phase the meals down to three a day until the dog is about six months old. Giant-breed pups may need three meals a day beyond six months because they mature later than smaller dogs. Great Danes, for example, don't reach full growth until perhaps eighteen months to two years of age.

From six months to about eight months, pups need to eat twice a day—morning and night. But when they're full grown, they can do all right on one good meal a day (but see How Much Is Enough?, above).

A puppy of about six months may go somewhat off its food because it is teething and its gums are sore. You might soften its food and give it something to gnaw on, such as a hard nylon bone. But if your pup refuses two meals in succession, and you are certain it isn't teething, you should consult your veterinarian.

Remember, no romping with a pup just before or after a meal.

Treats—who can resist treats for one's pet, especially a puppy? Commercial dog snacks are best, though little morsels of food from your table are okay occasionally as long as they're not spicy or chocolate, and of course no bones, ever.

Milk is best avoided—it can give a puppy, or even an adult dog, diarrhea.

And one more thing: Some dogs have a real food anxiety and growl when they're eating. If your pup gets in the habit of growling over its food, this is unacceptable behavior. Feed it from your hand, keep your hand in the bowl, pat it gently on the back a few times while it's eating. If it doesn't growl, say "Good boy (or girl)!" but if it growls, say "No!" and take the food away for a few seconds. In fact, from time to time take the bowl away anyhow for a few seconds and then return it, so the pup gets used to that. Get your pup accustomed to eating when other people are around.

Home cooking for your dog is not necessary, but if you want to do it, be sure to get information on nutrients and balance from your veterinarian.

FEEDING AN OLD DOG

Old dogs digest and utilize nutrients as well as young dogs do. Unless a dog has been diagnosed as having chronic renal failure or some other serious medical problem, in which case it needs a special diet, it can be fed a good commercial food that's formulated for adult dogs. Just be sure the food you choose has met the AAFCO standards, and look for one with "complete and balanced nutrition for all life stages" on the label.

According to an extensive study made by Consumer Reports a few years ago, it is not necessary to put your old dog on a diet of commercial food labeled "senior." Just as there are no regulations governing the use of the term "natural," there are no standards from AAFCO or even the FDA that manufacturers must meet in order to use the word "senior" on their product. This doesn't mean the food is not good—it just doesn't mean it's necessarily better for geriatric dogs than other good dog foods.

However, your old dog might need fewer calories in its diet than it did when it was younger and more active. To lower the calories in its diet, you might choose a food lower in fat.

If you include dry food in the dog's diet, you might moisten it to make it easier to chew. Rice is considered the most digestible of the grains that are used in commercial dog foods.

Dogs with kidney failure, heart disease, and other major disorders of aging will need specially formulated commercial foods. These are not available at the supermarket, but must be obtained from a veterinarian.

Any change in diet should be phased in gradually, to avoid upsetting the animal's digestion and habits. And if you have been feeding your dog once a day, this might be the time to change to two small meals, nine to ten hours apart. This helps digestion and utilization of nutrients.

You'll be taking your dog to your veterinarian more often anyway (see Chapter 13, The Geriatric Dog), so your pet's weight can be monitored. Many old dogs are somewhat bony, but you want to be aware of significant weight loss. On the other hand, obesity is especially hard on an old dog.

You'll find yourself filling the water bowl more often for your old dog. Not to worry if it drinks somewhat more, but if it's at the water bowl every little while and can't seem to get enough, a prompt visit to your veterinarian is recommended. Excessive thirst can be a sign of kidney problems, liver disease, diabetes, or other disorders.

An old dog with stiff joints might have difficulty bending down to eat on the floor, in which case you'll want to get it one of those tables or raised frames specially designed for dog food bowls.

FEEDING AN OBESE DOG

Obesity is a real health hazard for a dog, and one to which city dogs are especially prone. One obvious cause, of course, is lack of exercise. For the dog of an extremely busy owner, mealtime may also be the time when the dog gets the most attention, and so food takes on an exaggerated importance for the animal. The dog craves more and more food, and the owner responds because that's his or her way of showing the pet affection. Food may also mean more than it should to a dog that isn't walked enough and allowed to interact with other dogs and people, or that has to spend many long hours at home alone.

The best way to deal with obesity of course is not to let your pet become fat in the first place. Losing fat once it's on is as hard for a dog as it is for most of us. However, if you can stand the begging and the reproachful looks, the simplest way to help a dog lose weight is just to feed it less and cut out snacks. I know this is easier said than done, especially if your pet is accustomed to getting a bite of almost everything you eat and is rewarded with treats for good behavior, but it is in the animal's best interest.

You might try feeding your pet very small meals more often. This will keep it from getting ravenous between meals and convince it that it's getting more food than it really is. Just be sure the dog's total daily intake is less. Adding lettuce to its food is another way of filling the animal up without increasing calories.

There are commercial "light" or "lean" dog foods for obesity that contain plenty of nutrition but also a lot of fiber. However, they may not be lower in fat. Check the guaranteed analysis. City dog owners should also be aware that these foods may create more stool, so be prepared.

Increased exercise will of course help a dog to lose weight. But don't suddenly subject a fat dog to vigorous exercise. Work up to it very gradually.

There's another good way to help an overweight dog slim down: acquire another dog, an active, younger dog. In all probability, they'll become friends and play together. But even if the older dog only grudgingly accepts the other, the stepped-up walks and change of pace around the house will keep it more active. For suggestions on the smoothest way to introduce a new pet, see Chapter 9.

WATER

While it's not a good idea for city dogs to have food left out for them to eat at will, they should be able to drink water whenever they want. Fresh water in a clean bowl should be available at all times. (By the way, allowing a dog to lap water out of the toilet is not only tacky-looking but also unhealthy for the dog.)

Some city people might be tempted to withhold water from a dog to prevent elimination accidents, especially when they're trying to house-train it. But that's cruel and deleterious to the animal's health.

Excessive drinking can be a danger signal. It might be that the dog is merely thirsty from exercise or an overly warm house, but it could also be a sign of disease, especially in an older dog. Normal daily intake of water is approximately one pint for each ten pounds of the dog's weight.

6. HEALTH

Keeping Your City Dog Fit

I strongly suspect that well-kept urban dogs are healthier than suburban or country dogs. Dogs that live as our close companions are probably more carefully looked after, and any illnesses they do get are more quickly noticed and treated. In general, veterinary care is easily available and immunizations are routine among urban pets.

Nevertheless, because your pet is likely to be in contact with many other dogs, it is important that you keep its vaccinations up to date and that you recognize early signs of sickness so you can provide prompt medical care when your dog needs it. Also, not all illnesses are preventable by immunization, and no matter how well you care for it, your dog will almost certainly get sick at some time or other, especially as it gets old.

As a city dweller, you will probably have your choice of several veterinarians and be influenced by the advice of your friends, just as we all are in selecting our own doctors. Listen to dog-owning friends whose judgment you trust.

In picking a veterinarian, you'll want to balance the wisdom and experience of an older professional against the sophisticated training of a more recent vet school graduate. Naturally, you'll want him or her to have a clean and tidy clinic, with no overwhelming smell of

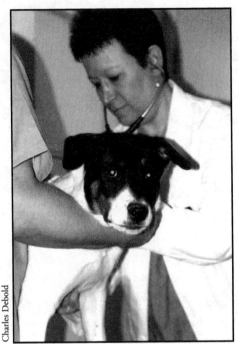

Charles Debold

Buddy gets a check-up from
Dr. JoAnn Greenberg

either animals or disinfectant. Notice how he or she handles your pet. Can you sense a genuine liking for animals?

If your pet must be hospitalized, ask to see behind the scenes first. Will it be kept in a clean and comfortable cage?

I tend to like a vet who explains everything thoroughly, who spells out technical matters and gives me credit for normal ability to understand them. I also appreciate an easy, unpretentious manner. I wouldn't put up with being treated in a pompous or brusque way, and in a city with plenty of veterinarians, nobody has to.

If you don't have a car, one factor you might want to take into consideration is a veterinarian's distance from your home. If your dog is too big to fit into a carrier, you'll have a problem getting a taxi to pick you up, unless you have the great good luck to hail a cab driver who likes dogs. Your city might have an animal ambulance service: Check the Yellow Pages. But otherwise, bear in mind that in very hot, bitter cold, or rainy weather, a sick, injured, or elderly dog will have a hard time walking many blocks to the doctor.

Today there are many veterinary specialties—ophthalmology, cardiology, oncology, and neurology, to name just a few—which require several years of extra training, board examinations, and certification. If your dog should develop a problem that you want to consult a specialist about, your primary veterinarian can probably recommend one, or your city or state veterinary medical association can refer you to one. Also, specialists are generally available at veterinary colleges or at large animal hospitals, such as the Animal Medical Center in New York City or Angell Memorial in Boston.

VACCINATIONS

Immunization against five of the common canine diseases—distemper, hepatitis, leptospirosis, parainfluenza, and parvovirus (see below)—can be given in a single vaccine. A puppy should receive its DHLPP inoculations in a series: usually, the first at six to eight weeks of age, the second at nine to eleven weeks, and the final one between sixteen and eighteen weeks. (Some vets recommend a fourth shot in certain cases.) Don't expose the urban puppy to other dogs on the street until after the last vaccination.

Every dog should be given a booster of DHLPP vaccine annually.

There is a vaccine for distemper, hepatitis, parainfluenza, and parvo that does not include leptospirosis. In the past, vaccinating against leptospirosis was often viewed as unnecessary for well-kept city dogs. However, several new strains of the disease are affecting some dogs, and it's best to ask your veterinarian what is appropriate for your particular dog.

Rabies is another matter. In some states, all dogs are legally required to be vaccinated against rabies; in other states, it's optional. You might think, rightly, that the chances of an urban pet coming into contact with rabies are slim. Rabies is rarely transmitted from dog to dog; generally, an animal has to be bitten by a rabid wild animal—usually a skunk, bat, raccoon, or fox—in order to become infected. The image of rabid stray dogs roaming neighborhoods threatening pets and people is unfounded, according to the U.S. Center for Disease Control. Though nearly all the rabid dogs examined in one study were unvaccinated, nearly all of them were owned.

Even though your pet is unlikely to meet a rabid skunk while walking down a city street on a leash with you, I think regular rabies shots are a good idea. For one thing, you might want to take your dog with you to the country for a picnic or vacation. And, in the event that something should happen to make your dog bite someone, you will most certainly want to be able to prove that it has been vaccinated against rabies, especially if there should be a lawsuit against you.

A puppy should have its rabies shot at about four to six months of age. Inoculation lasts from one to three years, depending on local regulations.

ILLNESS SYMPTOMS

You don't need me to tell you that obvious problems such as severe coughing; inflammation of or discharge from the eyes, ears, nose, or throat; discharge or bleeding from the vagina, penis, or anus; a lump under the skin; or evidence of continuing pain or tenderness in your dog require veterinary attention. In fact, any deviation from normal behavior and appearance should be regarded as significant and worthy of your attention, especially in a very young or old dog.

Some symptoms are subtle or confusing, however. A dog that hunches up its back and walks strangely may be suffering from back trouble, abdominal pain, or a problem in the anal region.

Here are symptoms that could indicate your dog is sick:

Loss of appetite is an early warning signal. Healthy dogs generally devour their meals with gusto. One theory about this is that in the wild a dog must grab its share of the kill in a hurry, before other pack members or other predators muscle in, and that modern dogs retain this instinctual sense of urgency. It's the only explanation I've heard that accounts for a dog's atrocious table manners.

Therefore, loss of appetite is probably one of the first things a dog owner notices when the animal becomes ill. Though it's not always an indicator of illness—it can be brought on simply by hot weather, change of diet, or some change in household routine—it is a symptom not to be ignored if it continues. Not to worry if your pet walks away leaving its food untouched once, but you should be concerned if it refuses a second meal, especially if it's an old dog or a puppy. If you have a pup of one of the very small breeds, missing even one meal could be harmful, for the puppy might become hypoglycemic (low in blood sugar).

Evaluating loss of appetite in a puppy is tricky. It can be a sign of serious illness—but on the other hand, a pup four to six months of age may simply go off its food or slow down because it's teething. If you have consulted your veterinarian and teething is truly the problem, soften the puppy's food so it can eat comfortably. Also, give it a harmless hard toy such as a hard nylon bone, hard rubber ring, rawhide bone, or even a raw carrot to gnaw on.

If a dog is really ill, loss of appetite is rarely the only symptom it will display. Keep your eyes open for others as well.

Weight loss is something you may not notice all at once. Usually, someone else who knows your dog will mention it, especially if the person doesn't see the dog every day. Then you'll take a hard look at your pet and see that it does seem thinner than usual. Unless your dog is too big for you to lift, weigh it on the bathroom scale. (Do this the way some veterinarians do: Weigh yourself, then weigh yourself with your dog in your arms; the difference is the dog's weight.)

You'll want to consult your veterinarian if your dog loses weight without an obvious reason such as increased exercise or a change of diet. Remember, even three or four pounds can mean something, depending on the size of your dog. A loss of four pounds in a twenty-pound dog is one-fifth of its total body weight. Obviously, in order to gauge weight loss, you'll need to know your dog's normal weight, so be sure to keep track of that.

Vomiting and diarrhea, however, are two symptoms that city dog owners can't miss. They too can mean everything or nothing. Dogs tend to vomit from time to time quite normally. Sometimes a dog will vomit a frothy, light-yellow liquid. This is probably just gastric fluid, caused by an empty stomach. If a dog vomits food right after eating, it may have eaten too much too fast, or eaten something undigestible. The vomitus will look elongated and ropelike, indicating that the food came from the esophagus.

If the animal seems well otherwise, a single bout of vomiting or diarrhea doesn't mean you must rush it to the vet. But do watch it closely for additional symptoms, and to see whether the vomiting or diarrhea continues. (For home treatment for occasional vomiting and diarrhea, see GI Problems, below.)

But frequent and violent retching or vomiting, frequent and forceful diarrhea, or evidence of blood in either or both means trouble. What sort? The dog could have any of several illnesses (especially if unvaccinated), it could be eating spoiled food (garbage, for example), it could be poisoned, or it could be suffering from extreme stress. Vomiting and diarrhea are characteristic of a whole range of disorders, mild or serious. With experience, you'll be able to recognize the difference in your own dog. Don't panic every time your dog throws up or has a single case of the runs. But if either persists for more than a day, you should take the animal to your vet, even if you don't notice other symptoms.

Fever is hard to detect; a dog is covered with hair, so you can't feel its cheek or chest to see if it's unusually warm. Don't go by the nose; it's not true that a dry, warm nose indicates sickness. You might be able to tell a little bit by feeling the inside of a dog's ear, but the only accurate way to find out if a dog is running a fever is by taking its temperature (see Basic Home Care, below).

A dog's normal temperature is between 100 and 102 degrees. Above that means fever. Below that could also be a sign that something is wrong. A temperature under 99 degrees is one of the symptoms of shock, which is very serious indeed. Fever is usually accompanied by increased water consumption, decreased appetite, lethargy, and depression, but these symptoms can also occur without fever. A dog that's dragging around and depressed for more than a couple of days should see a veterinarian, whether it's running a fever or not.

If your dog has any one of the following symptoms persistently, or displays a combination of several, it should be seen by a veterinarian.

- Persistent cough
- Inflammation (for example, of the skin, ears, eyes)
- Discharge (from any body opening)
- External bleeding
- Lump under the skin
- Continuing pain or tenderness
- Loss of appetite (partial or complete)
- Weight loss
- Persistent vomiting
- Persistent diarrhea
- Fever
- Lethargy, depression

BASIC HOME CARE

Here are tips on the ways and means of determining the state of your pet's health and rendering simple home care.

To take a dog's temperature, shake down a rectal thermometer and grease it well with petroleum jelly or KY jelly (or, if you don't have either of those, use face cream). Your dog is not going to stand still and let you insert the thermometer into its rectum, so you'll have to have somebody else restrain it, or else make it lie down on its side and hold it down the best you can, all the while talking quietly and soothingly. Lift the dog's tail and gently push the thermometer in one or two inches, about half the length of the thermometer, rotating it as you insert it. Don't let go of the dog or the thermometer. Leave the thermometer in at least one minute.

Remember, 100 to 102 degrees is normal. A temperature much above or below that is a matter of concern.

To get a urine sample, use a disposable aluminum pie tin or other good-sized disposable container to capture the urine in. Wait until the dog starts urinating, then slide the container into position. Then transfer the urine into a smaller disposable container with a tight lid. You can keep it in the refrigerator for a few hours, or overnight if necessary, before delivering it to the veterinarian.

To get a fecal sample, slip a plastic bag over your hand, pick up the feces, dispose of all but the sample, turn the bag inside out, and fasten it securely. If you have to keep the sample in the refrigerator for any length of time before delivering it to the vet, put the plastic bag into a disposable plastic container with a tight lid.

To give a dog a pill, first try to disguise the pill in food. If the medication is in a capsule and isn't too bitter, you can open the capsule and mix the contents in your pet's dinner. Try just a sample first, to see if the dog will eat it. You don't want to waste medicine if the animal is going to refuse its medicated food.

A pill can be wrapped in a piece of meat or cheese. I always give Susannah a plain piece first, to lure her into thinking she's just getting a treat, and then I put the pill in a second piece. Then I give a third piece as a reward.

However, if you have no alternative but to get the pill or capsule into your dog without food, put the animal in a corner, if possible, so it can't back away. Work from the side, facing the same way the dog is. Speak gently and reassuringly. Use one hand to grasp the dog's upper jaw and press the lips against the teeth behind the fangs. The pressure will cause the animal to open its mouth, and now you want to act quickly because it will probably be struggling. Don't throw the pill down the dog's throat, but place it on the tongue and then hold the mouth shut. Hang on and stroke the dog's throat until you're sure the pill is safely on its way. When the dog licks its lips, it has swallowed. Follow with praise and petting.

To give liquid medicine, use a plastic syringe or eye dropper. Raise the dog's head a little, pull the cheek out to form a pouch with the side of the mouth, and squirt the medicine in. Don't just squirt it straight down the throat. If you have to administer more than a few drops, give a little at a time; otherwise, the dog will spit it all out—all over itself, you, and the room. When the dog has swallowed it all, follow with praise and petting.

To test for dehydration, pull the dog's skin up a little at the back of the neck. When you let go, the skin should immediately settle back into place. If the skin remains standing up when you let go, the animal is dehydrated. By the way, it's a good idea to try this first on your pet when it is healthy, so you'll be able to recognize the difference should it ever become dehydrated.

MAJOR PREVENTABLE CANINE DISORDERS

Your dog can be protected against these seven diseases by vaccines or medication.

Distemper: This deadly viral disease attacks the dog's respiratory, gastrointestinal, and nervous systems. It is characterized by almost every symptom you can think of: weakness, lethargy, dehydration, lack of appetite, fever of 103 to 105 degrees, cough, discharge from the eyes and nose, vomiting, and diarrhea. It is highly contagious, spread in the air or through direct contact with an infected animal; it can even be brought in on people's clothing. There is no cure for distemper.

Hepatitis: Infectious canine hepatitis is a viral disease that particularly affects a dog's liver. Symptoms include lethargy, abdominal tenderness, fever of 103 to 105 degrees, cloudiness of the cornea of the eyes, possible discharge from the eyes and nose, and an orange cast to the inside of the mouth (jaundice). It is spread via the urine, stool, or saliva of an infected animal. (It is not the same virus as the human hepatitis virus, so is not contagious to people.) There is no cure for infectious canine hepatitis.

Leptospirosis: This bacterial disease attacks the kidneys. A dog with leptospirosis is weak and lethargic, with appetite loss and stiff muscles. It vomits, has diarrhea and fever, and may have discharge from the eyes and nose and red patches on the tongue and gums. The leptospirosis organism is spread through contact with the urine of an infected animal (rats may have it). This disease can be treated, but the treatment may be prolonged and is not always successful. Leptospirosis is contagious to people and can be spread by contact with the dog's urine, so dogs with this disease must be kept in isolation.

Kennel Cough: This term covers a number of viral and bacterial respiratory diseases, including parainfluenza and tracheobronchitis. A dog with kennel cough can have one or several of these diseases. While not particularly serious, it is highly contagious (the organisms are carried in the air). If one dog in a pet shop has it, you can be pretty sure the rest do, too.

Kennel cough is characterized by a hacking cough that is worse at night. This cough is dry, as distinguished from the productive cough of pneumonia. The dog may even gag and develop a watery discharge from the eyes and nose. With rest, warmth, cough suppressants, and antibiotics to prevent pneumonia, a dog can recover from kennel cough. But while it's sick, it should be isolated from all other dogs, even those that have received DHLPP vaccine, because the vaccine does not give complete protection from all the possible varieties of kennel cough.

Parvovirus: A particularly virulent disease, parvo is especially lethal to puppies. Symptoms include lethargy, depression, fever, extreme dehydration, especially severe vomiting, and watery diarrhea that is highly malodorous and occasionally bloody. Pups with parvo can die suddenly, and those that survive may have heart damage. It is spread in stool but can also be brought in by people who have walked where diseased dogs have been. There is no cure for parvovirus.

Rabies: There are two types of this killer. In the dumb type, the animal is stuporous, drools, and can't swallow. Its jaw drops open and paralysis follows. A dog with the furious type is crazed, attacks anything that moves. In the last stage, the dog is paralyzed. Rabies is spread through the saliva of an infected animal. A rabid dog dies after great suffering.

Heartworm: This is an insidious and very dangerous parasite that is transmitted from dog to dog by mosquitoes and is found in virtually all parts of the United States and Canada.

Heartworms, which can be twelve to fourteen inches long, live in a dog's heart and surrounding blood vessels. When an adult female heartworm produces larvae, these circulate in the dog's bloodstream. A mosquito sucks the infected dog's blood, and the larvae incubate in the mosquito for a couple of months. Then the mosquito bites another dog and transmits the larvae. It takes a few more months for the larvae to reach the second dog's heart and another couple of months before the larvae become adult worms and produce their own larvae.

Heartworms will eventually cause heart disease, with symptoms such as a cough, breathing difficulties, weakness, and fatigue. You can prolong the dog's life somewhat by treating it for heart disease, but sooner or later the heartworms will cause fatal congestive heart failure.

Heartworm can be prevented by a monthly pill taken year round, or by vaccination every six months. However, before starting your dog on the prevention, your veterinarian will order a blood test to be sure no heartworms are present, because if the dog has already become infected, the medication may be harmful to the dog. Also, if there is some slip-up in giving the medication on schedule, you must have your dog's blood tested again before you resume the medication.

While country and suburban dogs may be more at risk for heartworm, you should practice year-round prevention for your dog anyway, because, as you probably know, there can be mosquitoes at least occasionally even in the city.

PARASITES

Intestinal Parasites (Worms)

Puppies quite commonly have worms; if the mother has them, the pups contract them through her milk. Even healthy adult urban dogs can get them just from greeting other dogs or sniffing in the gutter. City parks are common sites of reinfestation. Before describing the different types of worms that dogs are subject to, a few words on worms in general:

Intestinal parasites will cause weight loss, dull coat, and possibly diarrhea. Some types of worms can cause a dog to have an itchy rectum, and the animal will drag or scoot its bottom along the ground, sidewalk, or floor, trying to ease the itch. But bear in mind that the dog could instead be trying to ease the discomfort of blocked anal glands (see Professional Groomers in Chapter 8).

If you suspect your dog has worms, be sure to have a stool sample checked by your veterinarian, because the medication prescribed to get rid of them must be specific for the type of worm. Never dose your pet with one of those over-the-counter, all-purpose worm medicines. Worms must be destroyed by carefully regulated doses of poison, and the goal is to kill the worms, not the dog.

Mild cases of intestinal parasites do not make a dog seriously sick in the initial stage and are easily gotten rid of with proper medical treatment. But if allowed to persist and multiply, worms can kill a dog, especially a puppy.

Home remedies such as garlic will not prevent or kill worms. (As a matter of fact, some toxicologists believe that garlic given in excess may cause a type of anemia.)

It's not a bad idea to have your urban dog's stool checked fairly regularly for worms, even if there are no obvious symptoms. You might not know your dog has them until the infection is bad enough to damage its health.

Roundworms (ascarids) are common in puppies. They're called roundworms because their bodies are round like spaghetti, not flat like tape. In fact, when you see roundworms in a dog's stool or vomit, they look like spaghetti. They can give a dog a bloated stomach and a poor coat, and cause diarrhea and weight loss.

Tapeworms are long, flat worms that can actually grow to several feet in length in a dog's intestines. But what you see in the animal's stool or perhaps around its anus is tiny segments, like grains of rice. Tapeworm may be asymptomatic, but if a dog has a big one it can cause mild diarrhea, weight loss, a dull coat, and an itchy rectum.

It's important to know that fleas are the host of the most common type of tapeworm, and if your dog has fleas, it will almost certainly also have tapeworm, and you must get rid of both.

Hookworms and whipworms, which have similar symptoms, may be far more serious than tapeworm. In addition to making a dog thin with a dull coat, they can cause bloody diarrhea and anemia. An anemic dog's gums are very pale.

Coccidia is usually found among pups raised in unsanitary conditions. A puppy with coccidia will not thrive but will have a cough, low fever, chronic diarrhea, and an emaciated appearance.

Giardia, a protozoan parasite, is difficult to diagnose and should be suspected when other types of worms have been ruled out. Urban dogs rarely have giardia, but a dog bought from a pet shop or brought in from the country could suffer from it.

External Parasites

A discussion of fleas and ticks belongs in this chapter on health, because they can become a health problem: a severe infestation can weaken a dog and make a small dog or puppy anemic and vulnerable to other disorders.

Fleas can not only cause weakness and anemia but can make a dog scratch and bite itself to the point of badly irritated skin and open wounds.

City dogs can get fleas from early summer until the first frost—in fact, in warm climates, year round. Fleas can hop from one dog to another, they can hide in bushes and grass, and they or their larvae can lurk in carpets and upholstery where an infested dog has been. One likely place to find them on a dog is on its back at the base of the tail. Fleas are also commonly visible around the head and neck, and in the "armpits" and inner thighs. You can see the tiny parasites scuttling through the hair, or, if you don't see the actual creatures, a telltale sign is black specks like pepper—those are flea droppings.

Some dogs are allergic to flea bites, and it can take only one flea to send the animal into paroxysms of furious scratching, without the baffled owner being able to detect the single parasite in the pet's fur.

Fleas require immediate action on your part before they infest you, your family, and your house. There are many products available for fleas, but today the treatment of choice is Frontline®, a liquid that your veterinarian will apply topically to the dog's back, between the shoulder blades. One application should do the trick. Another product, Revolution®, applied topically, prevents flea and tick infestations for a month.

When using other methods of getting rid of fleas, the first thing to remember is to use them one at a time, never in combination. There are prescription pills (one is called Program®) that you give the dog once a month to help prevent and control fleas. There are dips—these are pretty strong, and it's best to have your veterinarian or a professional groomer deal with a dip for your dog (and never dip a puppy). There are sprays and powders. Follow the directions on any of these faithfully.

And of course there is the flea collar, which I have found to be of limited value—and since the above, more effective products have become available, my feeling is, why use a flea collar? However, if you decide to try the collar on your dog, here are a few words of caution:

Let a collar air out for twenty-four hours before putting it on your dog.

Never put a flea collar on a puppy.

Never use a flea collar in combination with other remedies such as a spray, powder, or dip.

Don't put the collar on too tightly—you should be able to slip your finger easily between the collar and the dog's neck. But don't put the collar on too loosely either, because the dog might try to chew on it, get its lower jaw caught under it, and become poisoned by the substance in the collar. Always cut off any excess (and throw it away where your pet won't find it and think that it's something to chew on).

Examine your dog's neck regularly for any sign of redness or irritation and remove the collar at once if this occurs. Some dogs are unusually sensitive to the chemicals in flea collars. Don't replace the collar when the redness clears up—the irritation will just recur.

Remove the collar whenever your bathe the dog, and don't replace it until the animal is completely dry.

If you decide to use a flea powder, here are some tips:

It's no good just to sprinkle the powder on the dog's fur—you have to push the fur against the grain and powder the skin. Then, standing the dog on a newspaper, brush and comb it thoroughly. The fleas should drop off on the newspaper (be sure to roll up the newspaper tightly and burn it afterward).

Repeat this procedure periodically, according to the directions on the can. Regular combing and brushing your dog will help, too, but if you suspect your pet has a flea or two, do it over newspaper, burn the paper, and dip the comb and brush in alcohol.

Some people swear that giving a dog some powdered, debittered brewer's yeast in its food every day will keep fleas off the animal. I don't know if this helps or not, but brewer's yeast is nutritious and can't hurt.

Another home remedy, garlic, is unproven as a flea deterrent.

However, there's no point in getting fleas off your dog if they or their eggs are already in its bed and in your rugs and upholstery. You have to wash the dog's bedding and vacuum clean your house from top to bottom. (Burn the vacuum cleaner bag when you're finished.) Maybe vacuum clean every day during flea season where you live. For a really serious infestation, it might be wise to call in an exterminator.

Ticks can sometimes be found on city as well as country dogs. They can attach themselves to any dog that's walked in a park, a wooded yard, or even just on the grass. These bloodsucking parasites bury their heads in a dog's skin.

To get rid of one, dab it first with a cotton swab dipped in linseed oil, nail polish remover, or alcohol (whiskey will do). Then use tweezers to pull the tick off. Destroy it immediately by flushing it down the toilet. If you get only the tick's body but not the head, the dog's skin will be mildly irritated for a while, but in all likelihood there's no real harm done.

Ticks are hard to spot on long-haired dogs. Also, they don't usually drive dogs crazy with itching the way fleas do. The best way to deal with them is to give your dog a once-over examination after each walk in grass or shrubbery, looking particularly between the toes and inside the ears.

Especially difficult to see is the tiny brown deer tick that causes Lyme disease (named after Lyme, Connecticut, where the disease was first identified). Symptoms include lameness, swollen joints, lethargy, and fever, and the disease is usually diagnosed through an elevated blood count. Lyme disease is treatable with antibiotics, and there is now a vaccine that offers a dog protection against it. If you often take your dog to the country for walks on the grass or in fields and woods, ask your veterinarian about the advisability of getting the vaccine.

Charles Debold

Scruffy lost a leg in an accident seven years ago, but thanks to expert veterinary surgery, good home care, and his own great spirit, he runs and walks today as if nothing had happened

OTHER HEALTH PROBLEMS

While I can't describe every possible disorder that could afflict your dog during its lifetime, here are some fairly common ones whose symptoms you should know:

Ear Infections

These are especially common in flop-eared dogs such as retrievers, spaniels, and hounds. The reason these dogs are more susceptible to them is that a dog's ears need air circulation in order to stay healthy. Also, food allergies have been known to cause ear problems.

The symptoms of ear infection include tenderness, redness, a brown discharge or wax, and an unpleasant odor. The first sign you may notice is that the dog is carrying its head to one side, shaking its head, or pawing at its ear.

Ear infections require veterinary attention and medication. However, you can help prevent them by cleaning your dog's ears once a week with cotton balls dipped in ear cleaner (from your veterinarian, not over the counter). Never use Q-tips or other swabs, by the way—you could damage the ears.

Strays and other dogs that have had to live in unsanitary conditions, especially puppies, may have *ear mites*—microscopic organisms that cause itching, redness, and extreme discomfort. They are contagious to other animals. Ear mites can be eliminated by persistent use of prescription eardrops that contain an insecticide.

However, adult dogs with itchy ears almost never have mites, but may have a bacterial or yeast infection. Your veterinarian will be able to tell you what is causing your dog's discomfort and prescribe appropriate medication. It's not a good idea to use over-the-counter treatments on your dog's ears without a professional diagnosis.

Urinary Disorders

Cystitis, a bacterial infection of the bladder, is the most common urinary disorder in dogs. The dog strains to urinate, and there may be blood in the urine. A urinalysis and a culture and sensitivity test will confirm the diagnosis and determine the organism that is causing the infection. Then an appropriate antibiotic will usually clear it up.

Bladder stones, caused by chronic infection or metabolic problems, can be serious and painful. Dogs of all ages can be afflicted—females more than males, and small dogs somewhat more than large. Some types of bladder stones can be dissolved by prescription diet, but if the urethra becomes blocked, the dog will be unable to urinate and may die without immediate medical attention (usually surgery). Once a dog has had bladder stones, they can recur, so the animal should remain on a prescription diet and medication to help prevent the stones from forming. Prescription foods specially formulated for dogs that have a tendency to form bladder stones are available through veterinarians.

Tooth Problems

Dogs normally have forty-two teeth—twenty in the upper jaw and twenty-two in the lower. They're lucky in one respect: they rarely get cavities. But they can get abscesses, periodontal disease, gingivitis, and other tooth and gum problems just as we can.

A dog with a toothache will obviously have difficulty eating and may also shake its head and paw at its mouth. Its breath will usually be malodorous, and there may be facial swelling and irritated gums. Loose teeth will bleed. A dog with any of these symptoms should have veterinary attention.

The most common disorder of a dog's teeth is the buildup of tartar, which is a brownish stain just below the gumline. Excessive tartar can cause gum infection. It's usually more of a problem with older dogs, although some dogs seem to form tartar on their teeth more than others.

A good diet that includes crunchy food and hard toys of nylon or rawhide to chew on will help prevent tartar formation. And some dog owners wipe their dogs' teeth and gums daily with a cloth or a toothbrush dipped in baking soda. Better yet, dog toothpaste can help keep tartar from forming. (Don't use yours—human toothpaste shouldn't be swallowed.) It's good to accustom a dog to this from puppyhood; otherwise, only a very passive dog will tolerate it. If the tartar gets really bad, the veterinarian should scrape it off under anesthesia with an instrument.

Puppies cut their permanent teeth between the ages of three and six months, often with some discomfort. They need hard objects to chew on—nylon, rawhide, or leather toys. Be sure to check a puppy's mouth daily to be sure no new teeth are emerging in spots still occupied by baby teeth. When this happens, it's best to have the baby teeth pulled so the permanent teeth can come in straight.

Skin Disorders

When a dog has a dull, dry coat and suffers from persistent itching, the cause may be fleas, insufficient fat in the diet, or—the most likely culprit in city dogs—the dry heat or air conditioning of an apartment or house. However, itching can also be a symptom of an allergy, so you'll want to check with your veterinarian before the poor animal gets an infected spot from biting and scratching itself. All skin problems should be diagnosed by your vet and treated according to his or her advice.

Stray dogs or dogs that have been kept in unsanitary homes, kennels, pet shops, and shelters and exposed to a lot of other animals may have caught *ringworm* or *sarcoptic mange*, both of which manifest themselves on the skin.

Ringworm, which is not a worm but a fungus, is characterized by small, scaly circles from which the hair has fallen out, usually on the head, neck, and legs. The lesions enlarge and spread over the body, causing mild itching. Ringworm is contagious to humans and other animals. Prompt treatment with medicated baths is essential.

Sarcoptic mange is a parasitic mite that burrows under the skin, especially on the dog's head, ears, chest, abdomen, and back by the tail. Symptoms are hair loss and/or little red blisters that produce an intense itch and have a musty smell. The disease is contagious to dogs and people, and once your veterinarian diagnoses it, immediate treatment with a bath or injection is in order.

Demodectic or follicular mange ("red mange") is characterized by bald patches, typically beginning on the head and legs, that become raw and red. The patches may spread and cause the dog to lick and scratch itself constantly. Demodectic mange is not contagious to people or to healthy dogs and cats. It can be controlled and treated, but once it becomes generalized, getting rid of it is a full-time job. You must bathe your dog regularly and keep an eye out for any secondary infection, because a bad case can depress the immune system. An external factor such as stress can cause a relapse.

A puppy with demodectic mange may perhaps outgrow it, but because this disorder can be transferred from the mother, it's prudent not to adopt a puppy from a mother who has it. In fact, any dog who has had demodectic mange should certainly be spayed or neutered, because there is a genetic predisposition to it.

Orthopedic Problems

One of the most common orthopedic problems in dogs is hip dysplasia, a painful arthritic condition often seen in big dogs such as Golden Retrievers, Labradors, and German Shepherds. (However, it can develop in any breed, even the smaller ones.) There may be a hereditary factor, or the animal may have been overweight while growing. Hip dysplasia can show up in dogs as young as four or five months of age, but it usually comes on between nine months and two years. It affects the hind legs, causing the dog to limp or have an odd gait and to have difficulty getting up and lying down. Another fairly common disorder is elbow dysplasia, characterized by front leg lameness and often seen in young German Shepherds.

Patellar luxation is a problem of the kneecap of small breeds such as Toy Poodles and Yorkshire Terriers; it may cause the dog to run on three legs.

Arthritis is not uncommon, especially in older dogs. (See Chapter 13, The Geriatric Dog.)

Dachshunds, Cocker Spaniels, Beagles, Basset Hounds, Pekingese, Miniature Poodles, Dobermans, and Great Danes seem to be particularly susceptible to disc disease, which puts pressure on the spinal cord and causes back or neck pain. A dog with disc disease has difficulty walking, even temporary paralysis.

All of these orthopedic problems can be treated with medication or surgery, or sometimes with acupuncture or herbal remedies (see Alternative Therapies, below).

Heart Disease

A young dog can have heart disease from a congenital defect or from residual damage caused by a disease such as parvo. Old dogs may develop an insufficiency in the heart valves or degeneration of the heart muscle. Symptoms are a persistent cough, easy fatigue, and sometimes an enlarged belly. In some cases, congenital disorders of the heart can be repaired surgically. The life of an old dog with heart disease can be prolonged with rest, medication, and special diet.

Diabetes Mellitus

Much like diabetes in people, this disorder is first suspected when a dog eats more but loses weight, drinks excessive amounts of water, and urinates more frequently. If unrecognized and untreated, diabetes mellitus also causes depression and eventually vomiting and diarrhea. The animal must receive insulin by injection, which the owner can learn to give routinely, and its diet must be regulated.

Stress

Clinical stress is usually the result of severe anxiety, triggered by such events as moving; the arrival in the household of a new baby, spouse, or pet; the death of another pet or of a beloved person; being left alone too much and for too long periods; boarding; or showing. In some cases, aging, trauma, or illness can cause stress.

Prolonged stress can bring on symptoms much like those of other disorders: loss of appetite, vomiting, diarrhea, listlessness, depression, and behavior changes such as irritability, barking, or breaking house-training.

Whatever the cause, sustained stress can exhaust a dog. Its fight-or-flight response is kept in a continual state of alert, and this emotional wear and tear can adversely affect the immune system.

The first order is to rule out any physical causes of the dog's symptoms. Then, the best treatment for stress is to change the situation that produces it, if possible, or at least to help the animal adjust to it. A high-protein diet, acupuncture, massage, or herbal remedies may help (see Alternative Therapies, below).

The temporary use of tranquilizers can help a dog through a severely stressful period, but you should never give it your own tranquilizers. These drugs should be only of a type and dosage prescribed by a veterinarian for your dog in specific circumstances.

GI Problems

Occasional diarrhea, constipation, and vomiting can be quite temporary, isolated disorders in an otherwise healthy pet. As long as other symptoms are not present, they will respond to simple home treatment.

Diarrhea, as noted earlier, can be brought on by a whole host of physical and psychological causes, just as it is with us. If your dog's diarrhea has blood in it, or persists for longer than a day, your vet should examine the animal, even if nothing else seems to be wrong.

For a single bout of diarrhea with no other symptoms, give the dog Kaopectate or Pectolin every four hours—one teaspoon for a toy breed, one and one-half teaspoons for a small, two teaspoons for a medium-sized, one tablespoon for a large, and two tablespoons for a giant breed. Withhold food for twenty-four hours, then give bland foods, such as cooked chicken, cooked egg, cottage cheese, and rice. Make sure the dog has plenty of fresh water available, and keep it warm and quiet. After a few days, you can reintroduce the dog's regular diet—very slowly so that its system can adjust.

Constipation is relatively rare in dogs, so if your pet is constipated, be sure nothing has happened that could cause an intestinal obstruction. If your dog has been into the garbage and eating bones, for example, or if you have reason to believe it might have swallowed some hard object, be on the alert for straining and obvious discomfort when it tries to defecate. An intestinal obstruction can be serious and requires veterinary attention.

However, a dog can become constipated from a diet lacking in fiber, from insufficient exercise, or from not drinking enough water. Old dogs sometimes become constipated if they're arthritic and don't move around enough.

A laxative such as mineral oil (one or two teaspoons, depending on the size of the dog, sprinkled in its food), a little milk, or a teaspoon of milk of magnesia should give relief. But if the constipation persists or recurs frequently, your veterinarian should prescribe an individualized treatment.

As for *vomiting*, the first thing you need to do is determine the cause. Spoiled food? Heatstroke? Worms? Anxiety? Poison? Or is the dog merely throwing up light yellow gastric fluid because its stomach is empty, or getting rid of food that didn't agree with it?

If there is blood in the vomitus, or if the dog seems ill, then of course you should take it to your veterinarian. A second or third bout of vomiting should also be brought to your vet's attention. But if the dog seems otherwise normal, you can treat it yourself and watch it carefully.

Home treatment is simply to withhold food and water for about twenty-four hours, offering the dog ice cubes to lick because the vomiting may make it thirsty. (The reason for withholding water is that drinking may start up the vomiting again.) If the dog hasn't vomited during the twenty-four-hour fast, feed it a bland diet—cooked chicken, rice, cottage cheese, and the like—for a few days. Change back to its regular diet gradually.

SPAYING OR NEUTERING

Years ago, before I knew better, I avoided having Dandy spayed. I had no intention of breeding her, and she was never off the leash, so she couldn't get pregnant accidentally. So why put her through surgery? I asked myself. Well, I learned why the hard way. She had a couple of false pregnancies and then developed pyometra (an extremely serious uterine infection), and I almost lost her. The surgical and anesthetic risks involved in removing an infected uterus are far greater than those of a simple spay. There's no comparison in expense, either.

Also, because she had not been spayed earlier, Dandy developed mammary tumors in middle age that had to be surgically removed. I wouldn't want your dog to go through these life-threatening problems, and I hope to spare you the worry, guilt, and expense.

At first thought, it seems extreme to interfere surgically with an animal's natural urges to mate, but there are good reasons—medical, behavioral, and social—for doing it.

Domestication has changed the sexual habits of dogs. Wild canids have quite limited sexual activity—they reach sexual maturity later than domestic dogs, females are in estrus only once a year, and mating within the pack is restricted and often monogamous.

By contrast, today's small and medium-sized pet dogs are sexually mature before they are a year old, males are always able and eager to mate with any receptive female, and females, except very large breeds, usually have two heat periods every twelve to eighteen months.

If two modern dogs were to mate twice a year for six years, producing an average number of pups, who in turn had an average number of offspring, at the end of six years, 67,000 dogs would have been born! This is one reason why roughly two million unwanted dogs must be euthanized every year in animal shelters—there aren't enough homes to go around.

This unhappy situation is commonly referred to as the "pet overpopulation problem," which somehow seems to imply that it's the pets' fault. Until some progress is made in adjusting the number of dogs that are born to the number of people who want to give them homes, until there is some sensible regulation that balances supply and demand, it is irresponsible for pet owners to neglect neutering their animals.

There is ample evidence that neutering (castration) of males and spaying of females not only makes dogs better pets, especially in the city, but protects their comfort and health. It also adds to the comfort of urban dog owners, and any city dweller who even considers breeding his or her pet should be dissuaded. Here's why:

The Female Dog

An unspayed female dog goes into heat—that is, estrus—every six, eight, or nine months, depending on her breed and individual body rhythm. This is a stressful time for her, lasting three to four weeks. She is nervous and often breaks house-training, her disposition suffers, her vulva swells uncomfortably, and for nine or ten days of the heat period she has a discharge, which may be slight or copious and bloody. When she is walked on the street, she is often snappish with people and with other dogs, especially with males, who will pester her unmercifully.

When she is in estrus, the cervix (passage leading to the womb) is open. If an infectious organism gets in, it can flourish when the cervix closes at the end of estrus. She is also susceptible to pyometra, an endocrine disorder that can lead to a serious bacterial infection of the uterus.

If she is not bred, she will most likely eventually suffer false pregnancies, extremely stressful hormonal disturbances during which the dog is convinced she is pregnant. She makes a nest and is reluctant to leave the house. Her appetite increases, she puts on weight, and her breasts swell and produce milk.

On the other hand, mating is not always simple for her or for her partner and should not be attempted by well-meaning amateur owners, only by professionals. Strange as it seems, the dogs often need help. Otherwise, they can injure themselves or each other. Also, the female, in spite of being in heat, may hate the male dog on sight, panic, and attack him viciously. You can't always simply let nature take its course.

Whelping is difficult for many dogs. Many require cesareans, and some die. When that happens, the puppies must be hand-fed around the clock and may die anyway. If you have an especially superior purebred dog and are motivated by thoughts of making money selling the pups, you might instead wind up with staggering veterinary bills, no puppies, and possibly no mother dog.

If your idea was to breed your female pet dog to give her the pleasure of motherhood, be assured that she couldn't care less whether she ever becomes a mother or not. Dogs don't look at motherhood the way we do. Mating is simply an urge, and even if the mating and pregnancy have gone well, motherhood is an obligation that a female dog may fulfill only grudgingly. Many females that have been great household pets resent their puppies and won't even nurse or clean them.

You have probably heard parents say they plan to breed their female dog so that the children can learn biology or experience the "miracle of birth." This myopic and irresponsible point of view causes the animal welfare and animal control workers to despair, for they are the ones who must euthanize the millions of pets that don't get adopted into homes.

Uninformed and uncaring dog owners dump literally millions of puppies on shelters every year, telling themselves that the shelters will find homes for them. Some puppies do get adopted, but many of those are later returned or abandoned. Those that are not chosen for adoption, or have even the slightest health defects, may be put to death because the shelters must make room for the continual influx of unwanted dogs. Some private shelters can afford to have a "no-kill" policy, promising to keep every dog until it is adopted. That forces those public pounds and shelters that must accept any and all pets brought to them into the position of acting as the mercy killers for their communities, thanks to people who allow their pets to breed.

Even if you found homes for the pups your female dog produced, that could mean that the same number of other puppies already waiting to be adopted would go to their deaths because those homes were not available to them. Animal shelter workers often wish the misguided parents who bred their dogs for the children's sake would bring the kids into the shelter at euthanasia time so they could see the "miracle of death" that their actions brought about.

Now for the good news. Here are the medical advantages of spaying a female dog:

- She will be spared heat periods.
- She will be spared false pregnancies.
- She will be protected against uterine infections.
- She will be protected against ovarian and uterine tumors.

And, especially if she is spayed before her first heat, her chances of developing breast tumors (both benign and cancerous) are virtually nil.

The benefits to both dog and owner are obvious. The only disadvantage is that if she is a purebred of show quality, you can't enter her in dog shows, except in obedience classes.

The *spay operation* is an ovariohysterectomy: removal of the uterus and ovaries. It can be done as early as eight to sixteen weeks, though some veterinarians may prefer to do it at five or six months, preferably before the first heat. But the operation should not be performed while the dog is in heat, because the uterus is engorged with blood at that time.

There used to be a theory that a female dog should have a litter before being spayed, but that has been shown to offer no health advantages to the dog.

For the surgery itself, the dog is completely anesthetized, her abdomen is shaved, and the procedure takes about thirty minutes. She can go home that night or the next day. When you bring her home, she should be kept warm and as quiet as possible for a few days. In the highly unlikely event that she becomes lethargic, loses her appetite, and seems feverish, you should notify the veterinarian immediately. But in all likelihood, she will recover quickly, and except for having the stitches removed after a week or ten days, that's it. There will be almost no visible scar.

Your dog will not get fat and lazy unless you overfeed and underexercise her. Spaying in itself does not cause obesity or undesirable personality change.

Various other methods of birth control for female dogs, such as pills, liquid medications, or injections, are available. They act by suppressing estrus. Some have risky side effects or can be used for only two successive heat periods, after which you must let a third estrus pass without the contraceptive. Some are not recommended for lifetime use. A dog food containing one of the contraceptive drugs has been developed and may be on the market soon, to be fed daily to female dogs. It is presumably effective and safe when properly used and might offer advantages to the professional breeder. But none of the contraceptive drugs offers the health benefits that spaying gives. For the city dog that lives as a pet, spaying is the best choice.

The Male Dog

The word "castration" has unpleasant connotations, and perhaps the special status of dogs in many American minds and households makes some owners reluctant to do it. Most dog owners can handle the idea of spaying a female pet because it prevents unwanted puppies, but many have serious hang-ups about castrating a male. This seems to be particularly true of male dog owners.

Another reason it's less popular to neuter a male dog than a female is that if offspring result from a mating, they become the problem of the owners of the mother dog rather than the owners of the father, if indeed the father dog is even known. In areas where dogs are allowed to roam, owners of males often feel no compulsion to castrate their pets.

It is highly advisable to castrate a male dog, however, no matter where he lives. He will be far easier to control on the street, easier to train, and more obedient. Though many intact male dogs are affectionate, most become more demonstrative after neutering. And just as spaying offers health protection to female dogs, neutering offers health advantages to a male dog:

- He will be protected against tumors of the reproductive tract.
- He will be protected against infections and tumors of the prostate.
- He will be calmer, less aggressive toward other dogs, and far less likely to get into fights.

The only disadvantage—in a human's mind, not in a dog's—is that if he is a purebred, he won't be eligible to enter dog shows except in obedience classes.

The *castration operation* is much simpler than a spay because it doesn't involve cutting into the abdomen. It can be done at any age but should be done before the dog is a year old. The operation, performed while the dog is under general anesthesia, involves the surgical removal of the testicles from the scrotal sac through one or two small incisions. The dog can usually go home the same day or the next and may seem a little sore but otherwise none the worse for wear. The stitches may be the kind that dissolve and won't have to be removed.

If he has been an aggressive or hyperactive dog, don't expect a sudden improvement in his behavior, because it takes six to eight weeks for the hormone level to decline.

Contrary to general belief, castration will not make the dog fat. However, he may tend to put on weight if you feed him the same as formerly, so you may want to reduce the size of his meals or increase his exercise.

Spaying or neutering will not necessarily stop a dog from sexual behavior. Spayed female dogs sometimes try to mount other dogs—males or females, neutered or not—and engage in clearly sexual activity, especially during play. Castrated males also may try to mount other dogs that they are particularly friendly with. Both males and females sometimes clasp people's legs and carry on the same way, often to their owners' embarrassment. This is not deviant behavior, but a normal response to the animals' occasionally sexy feelings.

ALTERNATIVE THERAPIES

The burgeoning popularity of alternative therapies for human health has extended to the veterinary and other fields devoted to the care of our pets.

There are now so many veterinarians trained to administer acupuncture, and it is so commonly practiced, that it has become virtually mainstream. Some veterinary hospitals have acupuncturists on their staffs, and there is even an International Veterinary Acupuncture Society (970/266-0666; Internet: www.ivas.org; E-mail: office@ivas.org). Vets have found it especially effective for canine arthritic disorders, and even for some respiratory diseases.

A dog does not have to be sedated in order to undergo acupuncture—in fact, according to my veterinarian, most dogs seem to find it relaxing. Or, if a dog is especially anxious, an herbal soother such as valerian or kava can be administered first. But Dr. Greenberg cautions that acupuncture should never be used as an alternative to surgery or a traditional treatment when one of those is clearly the best remedy.

A similar treatment is massage therapy. Supporters claim that it can speed recovery after surgery, help a dog with arthritis, and even help curb behavior problems. It should certainly help socialize puppies and hyperactive or timid dogs.

You can learn to administer massage therapy to your dog yourself, without a veterinary appointment every time, which you do need for acupuncture. There are books and videos to teach you how to administer massage, and you can obtain information from the American Holistic Veterinary Medical Association (410/569-0795; Internet: www.altvetmed.com; E-mail: ahvma@compuserve.com).

But before you try massage or any herbal remedies, be sure to tell your veterinarian, especially if you are planning to discontinue whatever medication he or she may have prescribed for your dog. Your vet may be able to guide you in your choice of alternative therapies. Don't go ahead on your own and mix whatever you want to try with whatever medicine your dog may be on.

The American Veterinary Medical Association may also direct you to further information on alternative therapies (847/925-8070; Internet: www.avma.org/care4pets; E-mail: avmainfo@avma.org).

Alternative therapies may be just fine in place of—or in addition to—traditional medicine, but you need to adopt them with solid medical information from reliable sources.

PET HEALTH INSURANCE

If your dog needs a pacemaker, one can be had and will greatly extend its life, but it will cost you a bundle. If you are lucky enough to have several pets but are unlucky enough to have a run of serious illness among them, their combined veterinary bills can necessitate a bank loan. The increased sophistication of modern veterinary medicine, along with inflation generally, means that pet owners now spend many billions of dollars a year on medical care for their dogs and cats. Pet health insurance may be worth considering.

Supporters of pet health insurance believe it will make veterinary care available to more dogs and cats who need it, but detractors claim it will just drive up veterinary bills.

Arguments that pertain to city dog owners can be made on both sides. One factor in favor of having insurance is that because of their high overhead, city veterinarians usually charge higher fees than suburban or rural vets do. Many owners simply cannot afford the costly medical care that could prevent a pet's untimely death. And it might be practical if you have several pets, in which case you might pay at a reduced rate for their coverage.

Health insurance will pay some of the veterinary expenses, after deductibles, for many illnesses or injuries, even for routine care. If you live in a state where pet health insurance is available, you'll want to weigh all the factors before deciding whether or not it makes sense for you.

7. SAFETY AND FIRST AID

Protecting Your Dog, Giving Emergency Care

Statistics indicate that accidents hurt or kill more young children than all diseases combined. I'd be willing to bet the same is true for dogs. Although not all pet accidents are preventable, a good many are, especially if you are alert to their possibility and know how to take precautions against them.

After all I've said about how dogs live with us in perfect comfort in cities and how suited they are for urban life, I want to emphasize the fact that they must be under the stewardship of responsible people. Their instincts for survival and self-protection do not help them much when they're on their own in an urban environment; this is the one instance in which their genes have not caught up with their situation. A homeless dog in the city is doomed, for it will not last long against automobiles, hunger, disease, exposure, and human cruelty. And a day spent in any busy urban veterinary hospital suggests that even dogs with homes don't do all that well if their owners are careless about supervising them.

The point to remember is that the burden of your pet's safety is totally yours. In this chapter I'll point out common hazards. I'll also explain the techniques you might need in case of an emergency in which you must render first aid to keep your pet alive until you can

Patricia Curtis

Lucy, who tends to take off in all directions, is safe in a dog run

get professional help. First aid is for a critical, life-threatening emergency until you can get the animal to a veterinarian. It is not intended to replace professional medical care.

DANGERS TO AVOID

You can't guarantee your dog complete protection, of course, any more than you can guard your child or yourself against every conceivable accident. But if you are aware of common hazards of city living with a dog, you can avoid exposing it to danger needlessly.

The Unleashed Dog

"We had a dog, but he got run over," people say. This piece of information is imparted matter-of-factly, without the slightest trace of guilt or blame, and received without surprise, as if the owner had played no part in this event that kills hundreds of thousands, perhaps millions of unsupervised dogs each year.

In truth, except in the most remote countryside, where there are no busy highways for miles and miles, the time has long gone when dogs can safely be allowed to roam unsupervised. In the suburbs, rural areas, and small towns, vehicles take a heavy toll on dogs. I myself saw a beautiful Golden Retriever hit by a car, his back broken, on a country road in the exurbs fifty miles from New York. I saw a ranch dog killed on a highway in front of his home, in the foothills of Colorado. As for the city, dog owners frequently ignore leash laws, especially in residential neighborhoods, and dogs suffer and die daily because their owners don't protect them.

Yet, of all the risks people take with their dogs, none seems to be so fraught with emotion as the matter of the leash. While letting their dogs run loose seems to be a characteristic typical of irresponsible dog owners, it's also true that some people who otherwise take good care of their dogs turn brainless when it comes to the leash.

In my opinion, dog owners who walk their dogs unleashed fall into three categories, with a lot of overlapping. There are the misguided owners who believe that they're giving their pets pleasure by letting them run at their own pace and that leashing reduces the dog's fun. There are owners who believe that they have their dogs completely under control and that their pets are so well-trained and so street-smart that they would only have to give a command and the animals would obey absolutely. I think there's a lot of machismo among this type. And then there are the folks who view themselves as free spirits with free-spirited dogs and think their image would he sullied if they did anything so conventional as leashing their pets. Such an owner usually walks along paying no attention to the pet at all. In my observation, this is the also the owner least likely to clean up after the dog.

While almost every city in the United States now has laws requiring dogs to be leashed on the street, hardly any are regularly enforced, the authorities presumably having more important problems on their hands. All three of the above types of dog owners can get very ugly if you go up to them and ask them please to leash their dogs. So I'm not suggesting that you indiscriminately try to persuade other people to leash their dogs; I'm only going to point out good reasons why you should leash your own:

A dog cannot judge the speed and distance of an approaching vehicle and won't jump out of the way until the vehicle is right upon it. A dog at the curb cannot tell when a parked car is suddenly going to start forward or back up.

A dog seeing a friend or enemy on the other side of the street is very likely to dart across. (Unneutered pets are especially impulsive.) People who believe their dogs are too street-smart to run into traffic should see the injured and dying dogs brought into any city veterinary hospital after being hit by cars. I once saw a dog in the waiting room of a veterinary hospital with its leg heavily bandaged. "Broken leg—hit by a car," said the owner, a burly man. I expressed my sympathy and asked how on earth it had happened—hit by a car while walking with him, on a leash? The man became irate. "Wasn't on a leash—dogs don't have to be on a leash!" he bellowed, totally unaware of the irony of his opinion.

A dog frightened by a sudden loud noise such as a backfire, blast, crash, or whatever will instinctively take off, and you can scream obedience commands till you're blue in the face before it will hear you or pay attention.

A dog off the leash is at the mercy of any hostile dog that is also off the leash. (See First Aid for Bite, below.) At the very least, an off-leash dog is a nuisance to other dogs who are leashed.

A dog can lose sight and smell of its owner on a busy sidewalk all too easily and chase off in the wrong direction trying to catch up. If you ever saw the panic of an unleashed dog running up and down looking for its owner, you would not want to put your pet through that. Leaving aside its emotional state, such a dog will certainly dash into traffic in its single-minded search for its owner.

A dog off the leash and out of sight of its owner can be stolen. (More about the danger of dognapping below.)

A dog running loose stands an increased chance of picking up a disease, because it will sniff and lick or eat dirty stuff in the gutter. It could also be poisoned this way.

In contrast, a dog on a leash feels safe and can relax and enjoy its walk without having to worry about getting lost or losing its owner.

There is no question that dogs do love to romp and play freely, and if you can provide an opportunity for this in a protected place, great. Some cities have fenced dog runs available. If you take a small dog to a dog run, by the way, be sure to check the fence to make certain your pet can't slip through.

The Unattended Dog

Next to letting their dogs run off the leash, probably the biggest risk that city dog owners take is leaving them tied up outside on the sidewalk while they go into a store or restaurant.

In the first place, many dogs become severely anxious. Some bark nonstop, and if you look at the situation from their point of view, can you blame them? When my daughter lived in Soho, a neighborhood of New York City, she was forever distressed by the dogs she saw and heard tied up for hours outside the trendy bars, especially in the dead of winter. Sometimes she could get action by telephoning the managers of the bars, who would identify the owners and make them take the dogs home. On occasion, she could get the police to come—they would respond if she put the request in the form of a nuisance complaint because of the barking rather than a cruelty complaint, though once in a while she got the impression that the cops were sympathetic to the dogs.

But the main reason it is dangerous to leave your pet is that it can be stolen.

Who would steal an unattended dog? Someone who took a fancy to it, or a crazy person just for mischief. If it is a purebred dog, it might be stolen by someone who plans to sell it. And any dog can be stolen by dealers who will sell it to a research laboratory.

Stealing is one method by which Class B dealers obtain dogs. These are people who sell dogs to laboratories, perhaps at prices below what the laboratories would have to pay for animals obtained from regular companies that breed animals specifically for research. Class B dealers are licensed by the U.S. Department of Agriculture.

Of the millions of animals that are killed every year in the testing of household products and cosmetics, in teaching, in military experiments, in medical research, and in experiments conceived for the purposes of obtaining grants or graduate university degrees, some 140,000 are dogs and cats. Dogs may be battered, burned, shot, starved, exposed to radiation, forced to inhale or drink noxious substances, and used in medical and surgical experiments that are nothing less than torture.

They are also subjected to cruel psychological experiments. A favorite once used at Harvard's School of Public Health involved something called the "Pavlovian sling." Dogs were restrained in a sling and given a series of painful electric shocks. After a rest period, they were returned to the sling. "The sling environment evoked the behavioral and cardiac responses indicative of stress," reported the experimenters in the *American Journal of Cardiology*. Lo and behold, "the dogs were restless, exhibited somatic tremor, had sphincter relaxation, salivated excessively, and had a rapid heart rate." Some scientific breakthrough, right?

Even though experimentation using living animals has decreased in recent years, thanks largely to public pressure and the development of alternative testing methods, it is still the norm in many laboratories. Think about all this the next time you plan to leave your dog tied up alone somewhere, where it could easily be a temptation to a Class B dealer.

Stealing dogs is not the only way these dealers obtain animals to sell to research laboratories. If a lost or stolen pet winds up in an animal shelter that serves as the local pound and receives public funds, it might still be turned over to a laboratory. In some states, shelters that have the contract with the locality to pick up strays or accept all animals brought to them are required by law to supply Class B dealers. This is known as pound seizure.

The argument given out in favor of pound seizure is that because so many unclaimed dogs and cats are going to be euthanized anyway, it doesn't make any difference whether they die that way or in a laboratory experiment. However, many people feel that servicing laboratories perverts the purpose of a shelter. They believe that a shelter is intended to be a haven for strays, a place where lost pets can be reclaimed by their owners and where others can be offered for adoption. Also, if a shelter animal must be euthanized, they argue, in all but the worst shelters it is killed by painless injection. In a laboratory, it may be subjected to prolonged, repeated, and agonizing experiments before it dies or is killed. The humane community is vigorously opposed to pound seizure. Me, too.

I recommend attaching to your dog's collar a tag with your name, address, and phone number on it, in addition to an up-to-date license tag. Naturally, a person stealing your dog will simply throw away the whole collar, but in the event that the animal, instead of being stolen, just gets away from you and is found wandering, this tag will simplify things for a finder and increase your chances of getting your dog back. Also, if a dog thief found your dog and decided to hold it for ransom, the tag would help him or her get in touch with you.

One practice intended to reduce the possibility of losing a dog through theft or any other means is that of tattooing the animal, usually on the inner thigh, with a number that is kept on file at a registry. Veterinarians, shelter workers, and research laboratory personnel, as well as the general public, are supposed to notify the registry whenever a stray tattooed dog comes to their attention, so the owner can be traced.

This is basically a good idea that has not yet been very successful. For one thing, the public generally doesn't think to look for a tattoo and might not know what it meant if they found one. For another thing, there are a number of different registries, and if you found a tattooed dog, it might take a lot of research to locate the right one. Until there is some sort of national data bank, the registry idea may not be universally helpful to dog owners.

A more high-tech method involves a microchip implanted under a pet's skin, where it can be read with a scanner. So far, the problem with this otherwise fine idea is that just as there is no national data bank of tattoo registries, there is no compatibility between the different companies making the chips and scanners. And not all veterinarians and animal shelters have scanners to match all the different chips. There should be a universal scanner that can read chips from every manufacturer. Through a national network of cooperating registries and microchip companies, a lot of lost pets might be returned to their owners.

The Dog Left in a Parked Car

One crisp October day, I was at a football game when an announcement came over the loudspeaker, urgently requesting the owner of a car with a certain license number to go immediately and rescue the dog that had been left in the car.

I hope the owner reached the dog in time and learned a lesson. The person must have innocently assumed that since the temperature was only in the 60s, the dog would be comfortable and safe. What he or she obviously didn't realize was that in the sun, even with the windows left open a crack, the temperature inside the car could reach over 100 degrees. A greenhouse effect is created, and it can kill.

In a car parked in the sun on a 75-degree day, with the windows partially open, the temperature inside can reach 120 degrees in half an hour. On a 90-degree day, the temperature inside can reach 110 degrees within 90 seconds, and 130 degrees in ten minutes. An animal trapped inside will suffer heatstroke at 110 degrees and may collapse and die.

In a car parked in the shade, with windows partially open, the temperature may not rise quite so fast, but the heat can go high enough to kill any living thing inside. Also, people seem to forget that the sun moves, and that the car they parked in the shade can be in the sun minutes later.

Remember that a dog's normal body temperature is between 100 and 102 degrees. The animal cannot withstand a body temperature of 107 without suffering permanent brain damage and will die very soon.

Yet, as every city dweller knows, a dog peering out the rolled-up window of a parked car is a common sight. Dog owners are risking a terrible death for their pets every time they leave them in the car even for a very short time. Why do they do it? With all the warnings that have been issued on this subject by animal shelters, animal hospitals, veterinarians, and other concerned sources and widely publicized by the media, you'd think by now everyone would know better. Yet apparently many folks still haven't got the message, or have chosen to ignore it, because heatstroke is a common killer of dogs. For information on what to do in case your dog suffers heatstroke, see below.

A dog can get into other kinds of trouble in a locked car. I heard about a German Shepherd whose owner left it locked in the car for a short time one winter night when he ran out of gas and walked to a filling station to get help. The dog apparently went crazy with anxiety, for it chewed up a considerable amount of the seat upholstery before its owner returned. The upholstery contained metal springs. Fortunately, the owner got his pet to a veterinarian in time to save its life. But it took quite a bit of fancy surgery to remove the fabric and twists of metal from the animal's stomach.

Bear in mind that a dog can be stolen from a parked car, even a locked parked car, since—as every car owner knows well—locked cars can easily be broken into. Gentle, friendly dogs are the most vulnerable.

For suggestions on safe ways to take your dog with you when you drive, see Chapter 12.

Hot Weather Hazards

(If you've skipped over the previous section, The Dog Left in a Parked Car, please read it now.)

When the temperature soars in the city, dogs especially feel it because they lack that cooling mechanism that our human bodies are equipped with: the ability to perspire on virtually every surface of our skin. The notion that dogs perspire through their tongues is inaccurate. When a dog pants, it salivates, and the evaporation of this moisture on its tongue does have some cooling effect on its blood and thus on its body. But there's a limit to how much cooling effect panting can have when the animal is exposed to severe heat. This is true of all dogs, but particularly of short-nosed dogs, such as Boston Terriers, Lhasa Apsos, Shih Tzus, and Pekingese, because of their susceptibility to respiratory problems.

Given a choice, most dogs prefer just to lie around and not move much in hot weather, and it's an insensitive owner who will drag his or her pet out for a walk in the heat of the day. If the city has cooled off during the night, an early morning walk will be enjoyable, and if there's a breeze, late night can be a good time. But in the afternoon or early evening, a trip just to the curb should be it. This is especially true for older dogs.

A haircut, such as a puppy cut, offers some relief to long-haired dogs, but a dog should not be shaved in summer. It makes the animal subject to sunburn, insect stings, and more discomfort than it was in with its full coat of hair.

Obviously a scorching sidewalk will burn a dog's feet—that's another reason for keeping a dog indoors during most of the day in sunny hot weather.

A dog with short legs will really feel the heat rising from the sidewalks—not just in the paws, as all dogs do, but in their faces and entire bodies. A neighbor with a Dachshund mentioned this. "For Ludvig, it's like walking on a furnace," he said.

Don't try to transport a small dog in hot weather in one of those carriers with a domed, rigid plastic top. The heat buildup in those things is fast and insidious, and you could arrive at your destination with a dead or dying dog.

Never leave a dog out on a terrace in hot weather. Not only can a terrace become a hotbox if the sun hits it, causing the dog to keel over from heat prostration, but the dog can climb over the side trying to escape the heat.

Be aware of heatstroke symptoms: panting, vomiting, salivating, reddened gums and tongue, racing heartbeat (see First Aid for Heatstroke, below).

Make sure your dog's water bowl is filled, because it may drink more than usual.

Cold Weather Hazards

It always amazes me that a person can put on a sweater, overcoat, hat, scarf, boots, and gloves and sally forth in below-freezing temperatures with his or her short-haired dog wearing nothing but its birthday suit. I've seen dogs tied to lampposts in bitter cold weather, shivering miserably while their owners are in nice warm coffee shops having brunch.

Cold weather is felt especially by dogs that live indoors most of the time, as urban dogs do. Dogs that are unfortunate enough to have to live outdoors year round grow thicker coats as cold weather approaches and, if properly fed, add a layer of fat to their bodies that helps protect them. But the bodies of dogs that spend most of their time indoors do not change very much with the seasons, so going out in winter is, at least for the short-haired dog, somewhat the same as it is for us.

If a short-haired or elderly dog is going to be outdoors for more than a few minutes in severe weather, I think a coat or sweater is a good idea. Also, a raincoat gives good protection in a sleet storm and makes less trouble for you in drying off your dog when you bring it in after a walk in a downpour.

Be sure to dry an animal right away—the legs and stomach as well as the back and head—when you bring it in from snowy or rainy weather. Check the feet for encrusted ice or snow and rinse immediately with water to prevent frostbite.

Dogs, especially young, vigorous ones, need their exercise just as much in winter as at any other time, so their owners should be prepared to tough it out for the sake of their pets. But, like people, dogs can slip and hurt themselves on icy pavement, so pick a non-slippery place for play.

Another big winter problem for a city dog is the chemical salt that's scattered on icy and snowy sidewalks to keep people from breaking their necks. In most urban neighborhoods, the doormen and superintendents are out there with the salt as the first snowflakes begin to drift down. Although helpful to people, this stuff is hell on dogs; it burns their footpads cruelly. I've seen dogs limping, even crying in pain. If traffic permits, you might try to walk in the street, where there's likely to be fresh snow or even slush but no salt.

And that's not the end of it. If you don't wash, not merely wipe, your dog's feet when you come indoors, the animal can get sick from licking them. Chemical salt is poison when ingested.

Dog boots look funny, but in a very snowy city where sidewalk salt is widespread, they may not be a bad idea. Some dogs really hate them, but others seem to get used to them.

Sports With Your Dog

Vigorous play and exercise are good for most dogs, and your pet will think it's great fun to participate in almost any activity with you. But do choose the activity according to what the animal can realistically do and enjoy. Don't try to make a jock or a showoff of your dog.

This applies especially to playing Frisbee with your dog. While some dogs really get into it and will play enthusiastically till they are exhausted, and there are places that hold Frisbee contests for dogs, use common sense about it. This sport is fine for any small or medium-sized dog in good physical condition, according to a veterinary orthopedist at the Animal Medical Center, in New York. But the doctor cautioned that large dogs—Rottweilers, German Shepherds,

Paul Glassner/San Francisco SPCA

Extreme Pepper, a member of the California performance artists Extreme Canines, jumps rope with his handler Chris Perondi (Don't try this at home!)

Retrievers, and the like—are not built to jump and leap. And of course you should never entice an old dog into chasing a Frisbee, even if he or she used to enjoy it.

Jogging: If you like to run, your dog may enjoy going with you, but first, here are a few words of caution:

Bear in mind the animal's footpads. Your dog is not wearing Nikes. This is especially relevant to city people, because you may be running all or most of the way on pavement, in which case it's probably best to leave your dog home. I once heard of a man who was in the habit of walking (not even running) his dog across the Brooklyn Bridge every day. The animal's footpads were torn and bleeding before the owner noticed.

Don't try to make a little short-legged breed jog with you, especially not a short-nosed breed such as a Boston Terrier, Pug, or Bulldog. And never jog with an old dog.

The dog should have good chest capacity and a strong heart. Get it checked out by your veterinarian before taking it jogging, and work it into the exercise very gradually. Once you start taking your pet on regular jogs, be alert to intermittent lameness, which is a sign that the animal is overdoing it.

The dog should be over two years old and under late middle age. Since age is relative to a dog's size and breed, be sure you know what middle age is in terms of your particular pet. For most dogs, except giant breeds, middle age is between five and seven or eight years. The reason a dog should not become a running partner until it is over two years of age is that its bones and joints aren't mature enough. You'd be setting the animal up for serious orthopedic trouble later.

Naturally, an overweight dog should start out very slowly with short, limited runs. Otherwise, your fat pet will collapse.

Don't even think about jogging with your dog off the leash. Everything that I said against walking a dog off the leash applies to running, too.

Some hardy folks can safely run in hot weather, but a dog cannot. The body of a human jogger cools itself by sweating. A dog can only pant, which is inadequate to keep it from overheating while running on a hot day.

If your pet begins to slow down and lag behind while you're jogging, it's trying to tell you that it's overexerting, so you should slow down too or stop and let the animal take a breather.

Don't let your jogging partner gulp huge amounts of water when you arrive home. The animal should drink all it wants—but a little at a time.

Bicycling: After many years of observing people riding their bicycles with their dogs on a leash running alongside, I've come to the conclusion that it is a bad idea. Leaving aside the danger of being hit by a passing car, if the dog veers into the bike, the rider can fall and both can be hurt.

Also, while pedaling and steering, the rider is less able to pay attention to the dog's energy level and therefore may not notice fatigue setting in. The dog really has no choice—it's either keep up or be dragged, the way a person would feel if attached to a moving car. And as in jogging (see above), the dog's footpads can be damaged—the dog is doing distance running on pavement, barefoot.

Swimming and Boating: It is a myth that all dogs can swim instinctively. A dog will move its feet—dog paddle—if it can't touch the bottom, but that doesn't mean it won't panic, choke, become exhausted, and eventually drown. (See Artificial Respiration, below.)

Some people stupidly—and cruelly—toss their dogs overboard from boats as a way of introducing them to the water. You should *never* force a dog into the water. If you go in, let the animal enter the water and follow you if it wishes—in its own time and at its own pace.

Some dogs hate the beach. They are miserable in the heat, sun, and sand and are afraid of the ocean. Let your pet decide how it feels about the beach, lake, or swimming pool. If your dog does love to wade in the surf, by the way, be sure to rinse its coat thoroughly with fresh water afterward.

Garbage

I don't think a dog can be expected not to get into the garbage can. To the dog, the receptacle is filled with appetizing edibles, and when you're not looking, even a dog that has just finished a meal will find it irresistible. Don't be hard on the animal for this—remember that food is just about at the top of its list of instinctive priorities.

Some dogs explore the trash can just for something to do when their owners are out. Puppies do it just out of curiosity, and in play. Most of the time, this habit is objectionable mainly for its nuisance value, since the dog won't clean up the mess it has made.

But sometimes the garbage can will have stuff in it that's dangerous to dogs—bones, for instance, or the string that a roast was wrapped with, or the scouring pads used to clean cooking pans. This sort of thing can play serious havoc with a dog's insides. Bones can stick in the throat and choke an animal. (See First Aid for Choking, below). They can puncture the stomach or intestines, or they can compact and cause intestinal blockage. String can get tangled around an organ or ball up and block a passage. Scouring pads can scour an animal's inner organs.

You can train a dog not to get into the garbage by the same method you use to train it not to lie on the furniture or howl when left alone (see Chapter 4).

Or you can simply get a can with a tight cover, or put the can where the dog can't reach it, or close the kitchen door. Whatever means you use, remember that it is a sensible safety measure to keep your pet out of the garbage at all times.

And don't forget garbage on the street. Many human beings are simply slobs and discard all sorts of stuff on the sidewalks or in the gutter, and no normal dog can resist investigating it just in case it's tasty. Suddenly you look down and your dog is chomping away on heaven knows what. If it swallows before you can get the object out of its mouth, watch your dog carefully for a day or two for signs of illness.

Poisons

You wouldn't believe the kinds of ingested toxins that have sent dogs to veterinary hospitals—or to heaven. The substances are as astonishing and worrisome as the known poisons that little children have consumed when their parents weren't looking. Who would think that a dog would be attracted to detergent, drain cleaner, antifreeze, toilet bowl cleanser, paint, turpentine, roach poison, cigarette butts, matches, cough syrup, boric acid, laxatives, or shampoo? Yet dogs have ingested all of these, and much, much more. So help me, I once heard of a dog that ate its owner's birth control pills.

I have never had a dog that was poisoned, but Dandy once proved to me that under the right circumstances, a dog will consume just about anything. I had gone out with some friends, people she knew and liked, and she apparently took offense at being left behind. When I returned, I discovered that she'd eaten an entire bowl of walnuts that had been on the coffee table—walnuts in the shell. She'd cracked the nuts open with her teeth, scattered the shells about, and eaten the meats. Later, she threw up the mess.

Walnuts, of course, are not poisonous, but the episode convinced me always to cover or put away anything that she or the cats could conceivably get into. I think you can train yourself into the habit of automatically putting edible stuff out of reach, just as you do when there are very young children around.

The following house plants can be poisonous to dogs as well as cats: dieffenbachia, poinsettia, caladium, philodendron, Jerusalem cherry, schefflera, English ivy, and the common decorations mistletoe and bittersweet.

Rather than trying to memorize every single poisonous substance that a dog might ingest, however, it's more practical to assume that your pet (especially a puppy) just might sample anything and everything. Therefore, keep all closets firmly shut, especially under-the-sink cupboards, and don't leave any kind of medicine on a counter or table that the dog could possibly reach. Be sure there are no places in the house where the paint is chipping; for some unknown reason, dogs have been known to eat that, too.

When you're using any paint, thinner, remover, varnish, polish, or wax, keep the lid firmly on except when you're right there on the spot using it. Keep the dog away from any insect poisons you might put around. Empty all ashtrays before you leave a room; nicotine is poisonous to dogs. (I once heard of a dog that sampled the remains of a marijuana butt it found in an ash tray and got high—not funny, since the poor dog of course didn't know what was happening to it and got very upset.)

- Don't let guests offer your dog anything for a lark, such as cocktails, drugs, or coffee.
- At holiday time, be sure to protect a dog from harmful stuff it could chew up—ribbon, tinsel, mistletoe, and other decorations.
- Don't let a dog have any painted toys.

Dogs have been poisoned from chewing their flea collars. If you put a flea collar on your pet, fasten it just tightly enough for you to slip your finger easily between it and the dog's neck. If you leave it too loose, the dog might get its jaw under it and chew on it. Be sure to cut off and throw away out of reach any excess length so that there is no dangling end.

If you have any reason to bring your car's antifreeze into the house, keep it well out of reach. Keep the garage door closed when there's antifreeze in your car. It sounds impossible, but both dogs and cats love the taste of this stuff and will go to great lengths to get at it. Outdoor cats have been known to climb up into the engines of parked cars to lick any antifreeze that has spilled over. Antifreeze (ethylene glycol) is a sure killer.

Sidewalk salt isn't the only poisonous substance that your dog can get on its paws when out for a walk—oil spills in the gutter are dangerous because the animal will try to lick its paws clean later. And if you let your pet run or walk on grass outdoors, be sure that the grass hasn't recently been sprayed with herbicide.

Toys

You'd think that the manufacturers of dog toys would take safety into consideration, but since every pet supply shop is full of toys that are dangerous for dogs, apparently they don't. Among the worst are soft rubber toys and those that squeak. Any dog worth its salt can chew up a soft rubber toy in a matter of hours, swallowing the bits of rubber as it goes along. As for toys that squeak, the squeaker goes down the dog's throat along with the shreds of rubber or fabric the toy is made of. Toys with beads, buttons, bells, or rubber bands attached, and painted toys can be equally harmful (see First Aid for Choking, below).

One safe toy is a hard rubber ball—tennis balls are good. Just be sure to gauge the size of the ball according to the size of the dog's jaws, because a too small ball can choke the animal. Hard nylon and rawhide bones and those tug toys made of rope are okay, too. Some people give their dogs old shoes or socks, which the animals apparently enjoy, but this might encourage them to assume that any shoes and socks are fair game.

The point is that before you give your pet any sort of plaything, bear in mind that it will be chewed as well as tossed about, and examine it for any potential harm it could cause.

Falls

Falling from open windows is such a common type of accident among cats that veterinarians have given it a name: high-rise syndrome. While the majority of high-rise victims are cats, dogs too suffer falls from stairwells, open windows, terraces, fire escapes, and rooftops where their owners have taken them to play.

Every city dweller with pets should have all windows firmly screened. And here's something else to think about: I once lived in a ground-floor apartment where Dandy used to lie against a window and watch for us when we were out. But one day she apparently leaned against it too hard, or bumped it, because I came home to find the pane cracked and a tuft of her fur in the crack. Had she broken the glass, she could have been cut. She also could have escaped and gotten lost had the whole pane gone. So if you have a window seat or any window where your dog likes to look out, be sure the glass is extra heavy; otherwise, put a window gate or screen on the inside.

A puppy will have to be protected from stairwells until it learns to go up and down safely. A baby gate or a special dog gate sold by pet suppliers at the head of the stairs is a good idea.

It's a good practice always to check on a pup's whereabouts before you leave the house, to be sure it isn't shut accidentally in a closet, for example.

Burns and Electric Shock

To a house pet, the kitchen is where the real action is, the most important room in the house, especially when you're there, too. That means that if you have a small kitchen, as many city people do, your dog may frequently be right under your feet.

It's important to keep the handles of pots on the stove turned toward the back, just as you would if there was a small child in the house. (Your dog won't try to reach the handles, but you might accidentally brush against one and spill stuff on the dog.) Your dog can be burned in the same ways the rest of us can, and common-sense measures offer the only protection.

Some dogs, especially puppies, take an interest in electric cords, and the minute your dog shows this tendency, you have a problem. Puppies generally chew cords out of curiosity, or when they're teething, and will lose interest as they grow up. Older dogs may resort to it just for something to do if they're left alone for long periods, or if they're upset and anxious about something—an owner's prolonged absence, for example. An animal that chews on a cord can get not only an electric shock but a burned mouth.

If you have a determined cord chewer, the only solution is to keep an eye on the dog when you're home and either confine it when you go out or disconnect all the lamps and other appliances that have exposed cords—an awful nuisance, but a necessary one if you value your pet's life. (See First Aid for Burns, Electric Shock, below.)

IF YOU LOSE YOUR DOG

If despite your precautions your dog is somehow lost, there are steps you can take that might help you find it. Act immediately. The ASPCA in New York says the first forty-eight hours are crucial.

1. Notify the local animal control agency. This may be the SPCA, humane society, or other agency. If in doubt, ask the police whom to call.
2. Put signs everywhere in the section of town where the dog disappeared, describing the dog, giving your telephone number, and offering a reward. Question neighbors, doormen, supers, tradespeople.
3. Visit all the animal shelters in the city or county, and ask if a pet answering the description of yours has been surrendered. Ask the staff to notify you if one is brought in. Call and visit daily or every few days.
4. Check the lost and found ads in the newspapers. Place your own ad, offering a reward.

I know one young man who visited the animal shelter looking for his lost dog every couple of days for three weeks. Finally, one day there was his little mutt, looking at him as if to say, "What took you so long?"

FIRST AID

If you should find yourself and your dog in one of the situations described in this chapter, try to keep cool. It's natural to get very upset when your dog is in a serious emergency, but if you lose your head, you could do the wrong thing and make matters worse. Also, because the animal is sensitive to your feelings, if you go to pieces, you'll be unable to give it the reassurance it needs. In addition to the first aid, the will to live can make the difference with your pet.

I'll give you information on how to cope with those extreme situations, just in case. If you ever do have to save your dog's life, you should know how.

First Aid for Bite

If your dog is bitten by another animal, clip the hair around the wound and flush it out with hydrogen peroxide or betadine solution.

Then take the dog to a veterinarian. Even if the bite looks okay now, it may need stitches, and the dog should receive antibiotics and probably a rabies vaccine booster if the animal that bit it is not owned or if its vaccination history is unclear.

First Aid for Bleeding

Blood pouring out of a wound can be very scary, and if the animal loses a lot of blood it can go into shock, so you should stop the bleeding if possible before you start for the veterinarian. Press a clean dressing on the wound and hold it in place for a few minutes. Don't take it off to see if the bleeding has stopped, because if the blood has formed a protective clot you don't want to disturb it. If the wound bleeds through the dressing, add more on top of the first. If necessary, keep pressing firmly with your hand to stop the bleeding. Apply a bandage over the dressing and get the dog to a vet.

If the bleeding is at a limb or the tail and doesn't stop, you might have to apply a tourniquet. Use a bandage, tie, handkerchief, or belt about one inch wide (don't under any circumstances use string, rope, or wire, which could cut the flesh). Tie it around the limb or tail above the wound, then tie a pen, stick, or spoon to the knot and twist it in such a way that it tightens the bandage or whatever you have wrapped around the affected limb or tail, just enough to stop the bleeding.

Release the tourniquet for a few moments every fifteen minutes, then retighten, until you reach the veterinarian.

First Aid for Burns

A dog can have a serious burn that you can't see because hair covers it, so carefully clip the hair around the area of skin to examine the extent of the burn. If the burn looks only minor—red and sore—apply cold water or an ice pack gently to the reddened area.

However, if the dog's skin is blistered or charred, don't touch it. Get the animal to a veterinarian at once, making sure that nothing comes in contact with the burn. Be on the lookout for shock (see below), a serious complication that can be caused by a bad burn.

First Aid for Choking

A dog choking on something will gag, salivate, and paw at its mouth, and if the obstruction blocks the windpipe, the dog will lose consciousness. First look in the dog's mouth (this is not easy, for the animal will be frantic, and even a normally gentle pet might bite you; if you have a pair of gloves handy, put them on). If you can see what it's choking on, try to remove it with your fingers. Face the fact that you will undoubtedly get bitten, but that's better than losing your dog.

If that doesn't work, you'll have to get the animal to a veterinarian fast. Its breathing or heart may stop, so you might have to administer artificial respiration or CPR on the way (see below).

First Aid for Convulsion or Seizure

A convulsion is a symptom rather than a condition in itself. It can be caused by high fever, heatstroke, liver disease, a blow to the head, brain disease, or poisoning, as well as epilepsy. The dog may fall down and twitch violently; it may stiffen, froth at the mouth, urinate or defecate, and lose consciousness. Or it may run around bumping into things and barking wildly, a state of frenzy in which it is unable to stop and unable to respond to you.

How to treat a dog having a convulsion depends in part on the cause. If it is suffering from heatstroke, you have to concentrate on first aid for that (see below). If it has been poisoned, that calls for a different sort of first aid (see below). But if there is no apparent life-endangering cause, then treat the convulsion by wrapping the dog in a blanket, keeping it from hurting itself, and getting it to a veterinarian immediately.

Convulsions can last from thirty seconds to about three minutes. But the animal should be taken to a vet, even when the seizure stops.

Contrary to popular belief, the dog cannot possibly swallow its tongue. Don't put your hand in the dog's mouth—that won't help and you might get bitten.

First Aid for Electric Shock

If the dog has received a shock and is thrown away from the cord, it will probably go into cardiac arrest, so you should begin CPR immediately and get it to a veterinarian.

However, and this is important, if the dog still has the cord in its mouth, don't touch it or you might get electrocuted yourself. Disconnect the plug from the outlet. Then start CPR and rush the animal to a vet.

One effect of electric shock—pulmonary edema—can develop as late as twenty-four hours afterward, so the veterinarian may want to x-ray the dog's chest and hospitalize it for observation. He or she will also check for burns around the dog's mouth.

First Aid for Eye Injury

If you notice your dog squinting and pawing at its eye, the first thing you want to do is prevent it from injuring itself by further pawing and rubbing its face on the floor.

Flush the eye with water. You may notice that a sort of extra eyelid has moved out from the inner corner of the eye and partly covered the eye; don't be alarmed by that—it's normal. But you do want your veterinarian to see if the eye has been injured and to clip the dog's nails to prevent further injury if the dog paws at itself.

Dogs with pop eyes—Pekingese, Boston Terriers, Shih Tzus, Pugs, and the like—are subject to alarming emergencies in which an eye actually comes out of its socket. Cover the eye with a sterile dressing that has been soaked in a solution of sugar and water (add enough sugar to make the solution cloudy) and keep the eye covered with that while you rush the animal to the veterinarian. The sugar solution will keep the eye from swelling, which would make it impossible for the vet to get the eye back in its socket.

First Aid for Heatstroke

A dog with heatstroke will drool, pant, collapse, vomit, and, if not rescued in time, have convulsions. Its temperature can reach 107 degrees.

You must immerse the animal immediately in cool water and keep it there for some thirty minutes. Then put an ice pack on its head while you get it to a veterinarian.

First Aid for Poisoning

This is a scary crisis, but you must keep calm and act quickly. The signs the dog will show depend on the type of poison it has swallowed. The animal could be vomiting, twitching, drooling, trembling, and crying out in pain, or it could be comatose or having convulsions. You must act promptly.

The first thing to do is to find out what your pet has swallowed. This is crucial because there are two different courses of action to take, and what works for one kind of poison is wrong for the other. If you can't reach your veterinarian for instructions immediately, call the twenty-four-hour ASPCA Animal Poison Control Center (1-888-426-4435)—better yet, get someone else to call for you while you administer first aid, because time is of the essence. (You'll also need your credit card—$45 per case.)

Put that number in your personal telephone book, and check out the website (www.napcc.aspca.org) now while there's no emergency. In fact, there are other Animal Poison Control Centers listed on the Internet as well; just be sure you have the number of one in a handy place.

Until you get professional help, here's what to do: If the substance swallowed is a corrosive acid or alkali, or a petroleum-based product (such as detergent, cleanser, drain or oven cleaner, lye, plaster, paint, paint solvent, or floor wax), or if the dog is comatose, do not induce vomiting. Hold the dog's head downward and flush out the mouth with water, then get it to swallow olive or vegetable oil, milk or cream, egg white, or milk of magnesia—a tablespoonful at a time. Be sure the dog swallows. When the dog seems somewhat relieved, rush it to a veterinarian. Take the container of what the dog ate with you.

If you are absolutely certain that the substance swallowed is a non-corrosive poison (for example, plants, medicine, vitamins, shampoo, insecticide), induce vomiting. Give the dog an emetic, such as hydrogen peroxide mixed half-and-half with water, or prepared mustard mixed with water, or table salt mixed with water—a tablespoonful at a time until the dog vomits. Or, if you have ipecac syrup on hand, that's also good—one and a half teaspoons for a little dog or a puppy, two teaspoons for medium-sized dogs, three teaspoons for a big dog. As soon as the animal vomits, get it to a veterinarian, taking the vomitus and the container of whatever the dog ate with you.

First Aid for Shock

More dogs die of shock following an accident than from the injury itself, so if your pet gets seriously hurt or burned, you want to be alert for signs of shock and treat the animal for that as well as attend to the injury.

Any serious trauma, burn, or loss of blood can cause shock. The animal will have a fast heartbeat (maybe even 150 beats per minute), rapid breathing, and white or very pale gums. Wrap the dog very warmly in blankets or coats (if the dog has been badly burned, avoid touching the burned area of skin). Lower its head, and keep it in that position while you rush it to a veterinarian. If it is bleeding, do whatever you can to stop it (see First Aid for Bleeding, above).

ARTIFICIAL RESPIRATION and
CARDIOPULMONARY RESUSCITATION (CPR)

Even though you will probably never need this information, I suggest you commit the instructions to memory. If an emergency should ever arise in which your pet needs this kind of first aid, you won't want to waste time in reading directions.

Dr. Audrey Hayes, formerly of the Animal Medical Center in New York City, points out that either procedure is exhausting for one person alone, so if you can yell for help while administering to your dog, do so. These emergencies really call for you to do three things simultaneously: keep your pet alive by giving artificial respiration or CPR, get someone to help you, and get the dog to a veterinarian without delay.

Artificial respiration is for an emergency in which the dog has stopped breathing but the heart is still beating. (If the heart also has stopped, CPR is required; see below.) To determine for certain if the dog is breathing, hold a mirror up to its nose to see whether the mirror mists over.

Place the dog on its side with its neck extended. Clear its mouth of any blood or mucus. Now hold its mouth closed, place your mouth over its nose, take a deep breath, and blow into the nostrils for three or four seconds. If the dog is a puppy, blow in quick puffs.

Repeat ten or twelve times, then stop and look to see whether the animal is breathing on its own. If not, keep it up until the dog is breathing—otherwise its heart will stop. You must get the dog to a veterinarian fast; if it still hasn't begun breathing, continue giving artificial respiration en route, any way you can.

Cardiopulmonary resuscitation (CPR), if administered within a few minutes after a dog's heart has stopped, may save the animal.

Give artificial respiration for two or three seconds. Now, if the dog is small, place it on its back, put your hands on its chest, fingers clasped over the breastbone, and compress your palms quickly and firmly, once every second for ten to twenty seconds. Then give artificial respiration again for two or three seconds. Repeat. Keep alternately pumping the chest and blowing into the nostrils, stopping every few minutes to check for breathing and heartbeat. To check for heartbeat, feel the heart at the left center of the chest, under the front leg, or in the groin where a hind leg meets the body.

If the dog is medium-sized or big, after giving artificial respiration for two or three seconds, lay the dog on its side and place your hand just below the rib cage. Press quickly and firmly, down and a little forward, once every second for ten to twenty seconds. Then give artificial respiration for two or three seconds. Keep alternately pumping the chest and blowing in the nostrils, stopping every couple of minutes to check for heartbeat.

Keep giving CPR while transporting the dog to a veterinarian, stopping only when the heart resumes beating. If the heart starts but the dog still isn't breathing, continue artificial respiration.

Note: You might want to have this 109-page book on hand: *Pets and First Aid: Cats and Dogs*, produced by the Humane Society of the United States and the American Red Cross (GR 3244, $12.95, from HSUS, 2100 L Street NW, Washington, D.C, 20037).

CARRYING AN INJURED DOG

Since many of us who live in cities don't have cars, since taxi drivers often refuse to take dogs, and since dog ambulances may not be immediately available, you may find yourself facing the problem of how to get your sick or injured dog to a veterinarian. A little dog, of course, you can just pick up in your arms; it's the medium-sized and large dogs we have to worry about. The best way to carry a medium-sized dog is feet down, broadside against your chest, with one arm wrapped around its chest, the other around its rump.

But first, if the dog is in pain, it might try to bite you, so wear heavy gloves in handling it and muzzle it with a scarf, dish towel, large handkerchief, or nylon stocking or panty hose. (But don't try to muzzle a dog that is vomiting, gagging, or choking.) To make a muzzle, tie the dog's mouth shut with the cloth, knotting it under the dog's chin, and then bring the ends to the back of its neck and tie them. Don't make the muzzle so tight the dog can't breathe, especially if it's a short-nosed dog, but tie the muzzle tight enough so that it stays on.

To transport a dog when you have another person to help you, you should improvise a stretcher. Ideally, the stretcher should be rigid and flat like a board, but how many of us have such a thing in our city homes or apartments? An ironing board might serve, if you have one with no folding legs, or can secure the legs closed somehow so they're not getting in the way. Next best is a blanket or coat. Roll the dog gently onto it and immobilize the animal by tying it to the stretcher with a belt so it can't fall, especially if it is thrashing about.

Another very useful means of transport is a child's wagon. Lay the dog in it and fasten it with a belt so it can't roll off.

However, if you can't get help and can't get a wagon, you can carry the dog across your shoulders. (Be sure it's muzzled before you try this.) Lay the dog on its side with its legs facing you, and grasp its front legs with one hand and its hind legs with your other hand. Now kneel down and slide your head under the animal's middle while pulling it over your shoulders by the legs as you stand up. Unless the animal is unconscious, better hang on tight, because if it struggles you might drop it or lose your balance. Still, this is a much better way to support a big dog's weight than trying to clutch it in your arms across your chest.

BEING PREPARED FOR A DISASTER

After September 11, 2001, the magazine of Best Friends Animal Sanctuary ran a fine article entitled "Animals at Ground Zero," about rescuing and caring for the pets that were left behind in buildings that were evacuated, some of whom had owners who never returned. The article included a list of steps to take to safeguard your pets in the event of an emergency.

Especially for those of us who live in large cities, I am repeating it here, with the permission of Best Friends:

1. Make sure all pets wear ID tags at all times, including the phone number of a trusted friend or relative in another part of town.
2. Keep a sturdy carrier for each of your cats.
3. Have an evacuation plan, and make sure you have rehearsed it with your pets.

4. Put "Fireman Alert" notices on your front and rear windows, indicating how many animals live in your home.

5. Keep a good photo of your pet, along with a list of local shelters, rescue groups, and emergency veterinarians. Keep one at home and a duplicate somewhere else.

6. Two tips when searching for lost pets: When they panic, dogs tend to run as far as they can; cats tend to run for cover to the nearest hiding place.

7. Chain-link fencing holds up better than block wall in the backyard. Frightened cats will jump through broken windows, but not so easily through aluminum mesh screening.

8. After an earthquake, dogs can be terrified by aftershocks. If they're used to car rides, try putting them in the car, since they associate cars with being bumped around.

You may also wish to consult a booklet entitled *Pets and Disasters: Get Prepared*, produced by the Humane Society of the United States and the American Red Cross (PM 2161, sold in batches of 25, $4.25, from HSUS, 2100 L Street NW, Washington, D.C. 20037).

8. GROOMING

Keeping Your City Dog Looking Good

W hen the wild dog first took up with human beings long ago, probably nobody noticed or cared that it was not an especially fastidious animal. Hygiene had not yet been invented, so most likely the people weren't too fussy about the dog's condition, though they might have made it sleep outside their dwelling when it had been rolling in carrion.

From what I've read of history, we human beings were a long time in cleaning ourselves up, let alone our domestic animals, but somewhere in the course of centuries, many of us began to be offended by unreasonable amounts of dirt. Cleanliness became a virtue, and one day a dog owner must have looked at his or her pet and said, "Rover, you need a bath. You also need to be combed and brushed and to have your ears cleaned out, and your breath is pretty smelly, too—let's have a look at your teeth." Dog grooming was born.

By grooming, I don't mean have a dog's coat trimmed in the latest haircut and its nails polished as if for the show ring. I mean having a clean, well-kept, healthy-looking animal that is a credit to itself and its owner. Like it or not, a dog's appearance speaks volumes about its owner.

A dog makes a stab at its own upkeep. It will try to remove mats, burrs, and parasites from its coat with its teeth; it may wipe its mouth on the rug after eating; it will scoot along on its bottom if it feels bothersome stuff clinging to it after defecation. But for the most part, it is dependent on its owner for its grooming, just as it is for food, shelter, protection, and love. When you see a pitiful, filthy stray, bear in mind that living in human dirt and lacking human care are what have reduced the animal to that condition.

Regular grooming sessions accomplish other worthwhile objectives besides keeping your dog looking good. They help strengthen the bond between the two of you. Even if your dog initially doesn't like to be brushed, it will grow to appreciate and enjoy your undivided attention, especially if you talk to it.

Also, in the routine of checking on your pet's body, especially its coat, ears, teeth, and eyes, you notice health problems that need veterinary attention. You'll spot sores, rashes, cuts, lumps under the skin, inflamed areas, and ear, tooth, and gum problems before you might otherwise notice them and before they begin to threaten the dog seriously. Professional dog groomers say that quite often in the course of their work they discover and alert clients to conditions in their dogs that should have veterinary attention.

Get a puppy accustomed to grooming while it's still very young. Hold it on a table, not on your lap, but put a rubber mat or something non-skid under its feet to give it a firm footing. Go over its body with your hands, open its mouth and check the teeth, and look in its ears and under the tail. Examine its feet, separating the toes. Brush it all over. The pup will learn to like the experience, or at least to tolerate it. Adult dogs that aren't used to being groomed can view it as an ordeal and even become hysterical at a professional groomer's. Conditioning a dog early in life can make routine care a lot easier for both of you.

The best time to groom your pet is right after a walk, when the animal has relieved itself and is ready to relax.

Every dog owner should have a few basic tools: a comb and brush appropriate for your particular dog's coat, a pair of nail clippers (the kind especially designed for dogs), and a good tearless dog shampoo. Below, you'll read how to use them.

BRUSHING YOUR DOG

The city dog's coat needs regular care. It won't collect external parasites to the extent that it probably would if it lived in the suburbs or country, but its coat brings in dust and dirt from the street. It sheds—year-round. Heating and air conditioning tend to dry it out.

Brushing serves to remove dead hair, which reduces shedding; it stimulates the natural oils of the skin, giving the coat a healthy sheen; and it gets rid of dirt the dog has picked up. Obviously, long-haired dogs need more brushing and combing than short-haired dogs, but every dog will benefit from at least a quick once-over with a comb and brush, daily or every few days. Combing is even more important than brushing; dog owners would do well to comb their dogs' coats thoroughly at least twice a week.

Dogs with long, silky coats tend to mat badly, and you have to keep ahead of this tendency or the mats will get out of hand. A coat full of mats and tangles looks unsightly, and because mats pull and irritate the skin, they are probably extremely uncomfortable. Brushing and combing should be a pleasant experience for a dog, so be very gentle with the tangles and talk soothingly all the while. Then the animal will learn to put up with having its tangles and mats removed because it will feel cared for.

It's a good idea to take your dog's collar off indoors, at least at night. With a long-haired dog, this helps prevent matting of the hair around the neck, and a short-haired dog won't have that band around its neck where hair has been rubbed thin by the collar.

Don't forget to comb out or clip off any dried matter under the tail. Dogs with furry rumps sometimes can't help getting stuff stuck on their bottoms.

Shedding is regulated by nature according to temperature and daylight; it increases in spring, and also in fall to make way for a new, denser coat. However, when a dog lives in an environment that is heated, cooled, and lighted artificially, this natural regulation is not needed. Consequently, although your dog may shed somewhat more in spring and fall, it will normally lose hair more or less year round.

Some dogs, particularly if they live in very warm houses or apartments, tend to get dandruff. If your pet has this problem, you have to brush unstintingly, but don't bathe—frequent bathing can make dandruff worse. Ask your veterinarian about the dog's diet—maybe it's not getting enough of certain vitamins or fatty acids. I've heard that brewer's yeast is good for dry skin, and you might try adding half a teaspoon of it to your dog's food daily; it can't hurt. Or try a fatty acid supplement, such as Linatone or Lipoderm.

The type of comb and brush you use will depend on your particular dog. Short-coated dogs, such as Dachshunds, Basset Hounds, Beagles, and mixed breeds with similar short, smooth coats, need a fine-tooth metal comb and a medium-soft, short-bristle brush or a grooming glove. Brush gently but firmly with the grain of the hair and wipe off any loose hair afterward with a soft cloth.

Medium-coated dogs, such as Golden Retrievers, spaniels, setters, and mixed-breed dogs with similar coats, need a wide-tooth metal comb and a wire or firm-bristle brush. Comb first, then brush with the grain of the hair, giving special attention to the ears, chest, rear end, and base of the tail, where the hair is especially thick.

Long-haired dogs, such as Lhasa Apsos, Shih Tzus, Wheaten Terriers, and long-haired mixed breeds, need a wide-tooth metal comb (a fine-tooth comb will tear the hair) and a brush with long, stiff bristles. First, gently work out the tangles and mats with your fingers and the comb. Mats form at the roots of the hair, so be sure you really separate the strands. Brush one section of hair at a time, with the grain of the hair.

Double-coated dogs, such as German Shepherds, Siberian Huskies, and other dogs with shortish, dense coats, need a wide-tooth metal comb and a brush with long, stiff bristles. These dogs have a topcoat of coarse hair over an undercoat of soft, dense hair. Give them a light combing, then brush from the skin out, against the grain of the hair.

Dogs with curly, wavy, or woolly hair, such as Poodles, Miniature Schnauzers, and mixed breeds with similar coats need a wide-tooth metal comb and a short-bristle wire brush. These dogs need professional haircuts every six or eight weeks, but you can keep them in good shape in between. Comb lightly, then brush. One Standard Poodle I knew, named Chopin, wore what's called a "sporting clip" (short on the body, longer on the legs and the top of the head), which his owner brushed against the grain, daily, after combing his ears and topknot. Coco, the Miniature Poodle of a friend of mine, had a "lamb cut" and got the same care almost as often, plus a bath every two or three months.

Remember, if a dog is not getting the proper balance of nutrients, with enough fat, its coat will be dull and dry no matter how much regular brushing it gets. Also, the coat is one important barometer of a dog's health. If the coat is in truly poor condition, this may be a symptom of illness, and the dog should be checked by a veterinarian.

BATHING YOUR DOG

Baths take on special importance to city dog owners, because nobody likes living in the same house or apartment with a dirty pet. In relatively close quarters, you're much more apt to notice when your dog begins to get a bit overripe. Also, the air pollution of most cities makes bathing necessary more often.

How often? You'll probably find that your dog will need a bath at least every couple of months. Even a monthly bath will not deplete the natural oils in the dog's skin, and some people bathe their pets more often than that with no undesirable consequences. The coat itself will tell you by its looks whether or not you're bathing it too often. For city people, bathing a dog usually means the bathtub, though a little dog might fit in the basin or the kitchen sink. Put a lot of newspapers or towels around, because, even if no water gets spilled during the bathing and rinsing, the dog will shake itself mightily during, or at least after, the bath. Most dogs hate getting a bath and have to be dragged to it looking reproachful and martyred.

A puppy shouldn't be bathed until it is at least six months old. Don't bathe a dog right after it has eaten. And never bathe a dog when it isn't feeling well, or within a week of its having shots. Don't bathe it until a month after an operation or stitches for a wound.

Don't use soap or people shampoo on a dog; most are too strong for a dog's skin. Use a good, tearless dog shampoo.

Here's what you'll need to do:

1. Walk the dog so it can empty its bladder and bowels.
2. Comb and brush the dog's coat, removing all tangles and excess undercoat.
3. Spread towels and thick newspapers around the bathroom and lay out several clean towels for drying the dog.
4. Set out a sponge or washcloth and a large plastic pitcher or a nose attachment for the faucet, and put a non-skid mat in the bottom of the tub. (The tub mat is important because if the poor animal loses its footing and falls, getting its head under water, it will panic and thrash about and possibly escape, and all you need is to be struggling to maneuver a frightened, sopping wet, soapy dog back into the tub.)
5. Put a rolled-up bathmat or an old cushion at the side of the tub for you to kneel on, because the floor will get awfully hard under your knees before you're through.
6. Put on old clothes that you won't mind getting soaked.
7. Draw a tub of warm, not hot, water—about the temperature you'd use for a baby. The water should be deep enough to cover the dog's belly when it's standing up. Don't try to put the dog in when the water is running; some are frightened of the noise.

Steve Seebold

Neither rain nor snow keeps this trio from the
swift completion of the evening walk

8. Now search out your pet, who is probably under the bed.
   Use the leash to lead it to the bathroom if you have to. Close
   the bathroom door. Lift the dog gently into the tub, with
   lots of reassuring talk and praise.
9. Stuff cotton in the dog's ears to keep the water out. If for
   some reason you're not using a tearless shampoo, put a drop
   of mineral oil or a tiny bit of petroleum jelly in each eye.
10. Wet the animal thoroughly and then soap it, working
    from neck to back, leaving the face till last so that it will
    be wet and soapy for only a short time. Use a washcloth or
    sponge on the face, avoiding the eyes. Unless the dog is
    unusually dirty, one thorough all-over soaping should be
    enough.

11. Rinse thoroughly. This is where a hose is handy, but don't just sprinkle the water on—hold the nozzle close to the skin so the clean water gets right in there. If you don't have a hose, you'll have to risk scaring the dog by running the water to fill the pitcher many times with clean water, because just rinsing in the bathwater is not enough; you have to get all the soap completely out, and the bathwater will be soapy by this time. If you don't get all the soap out, the dog's skin will be irritated and the coat dull and sticky. Let the water run out of the tub while you rinse with clear water so that by the time you're all through, the dog is standing in an empty tub.

12. Towel the dog down while it's still in the empty tub, because it will shake itself several times, spraying water. When you lift it out, or let it climb out, it will shake itself some more, but at least you'll have gotten some of the water out of its coat.

13. Keep toweling the dog until it is as dry as you can get it. If your pet will tolerate the hair dryer, use it, directing it on one area at a time and brushing as you dry. It's important not to direct the hair dryer on one spot for more than a few seconds—keep it moving. If you have a long-haired dog, combing will prevent tangles and hasten the drying process, but be careful not to hurt the animal by pulling hard on tangled strands. Use a wide-tooth comb and work gently.

14. Tell the dog how gorgeous it looks. Give it a dog biscuit or other treat.

15. Keep the dog in a warm, draft-free room for several hours. Make sure it doesn't lie in a direct draft from an air conditioner. And don't take it outside until it's thoroughly dry, not only because it might catch cold but because the damp coat will attract dirt and dust from the street.

If you have a white-coated dog, you might want to give it dry shampoos of cornstarch, baby powder, or commercial dry dog shampoo between baths. Stand the dog on newspaper and work the substance into the coat, then brush thoroughly. If you don't brush all the powder out, the dog will trail it all over the house. Dry shampoo is also good for puppies too young to be bathed, and for old dogs who live in a very cool or cold house.

A good bath removes grime, irritants, and bacteria from a dog's coat, but shampoo and water are not effective against tar, car oil, paint, chewing gum, and other comparable substances a dog occasionally gets in its coat. Don't use any dry cleaning fluid—it will burn the dog's skin and is highly toxic! You have to use a solvent like turpentine to remove paint; nail polish remover works on chewing gum; and baby oil or vegetable oil might soften tar and motor oil enough for you to comb them out. Don't get turpentine or nail polish remover near the dog's eyes, ears, genitals, anus, or any cut or scratch. After you've got the offending substance off the dog, including the equally offending stuff you used to remove it, wash the area with soap and water, rinsing well.

If you take your dog on holiday with you and it swims in the ocean or a pool, be sure you rinse the salt or chlorine out of its coat after each dip. In fact, the rinse should be supplemented with a real bath at the end of the vacation, to assure that the salt and chemicals are totally out of the coat.

If you take your dog to the country and it has a confrontation with a skunk (and city dogs, being unsophisticated about wildlife, may provoke one), you'll want to act quickly for your own sake as well as the dog's. The traditional anti-skunk shampoo is tomato juice, but a vinegar-and-water or baking-soda-and-water solution might work, too. If the dog's eyes and ears are affected, wipe them with a soothing ointment. Whatever you use, it will take a lot of bathing to get rid of the smell to the point where you can live with the dog. The dog will be confused and upset, so give it a lot of reassurance and don't make it feel more humiliated than it does already.

YOUR DOG'S EARS

Part of every routine grooming session should be an ear check. A dog's ears can get dirty just from being outside, rolling on the rug, lying under the bed, or simply existing in polluted city air. That being the case, you'd think that a dog with hang-down ears would be better off than one with stick-up ears. But a dog's ears need air circulation to remain healthy, and dogs with floppy ears are more susceptible than others to ear infections.

You can clean a dog's ears with a washcloth or cotton-tipped swab dipped in mineral oil, baby oil, or vegetable oil—not alcohol or any substance that will sting. (Don't use peroxide, either, because the dog might not like the fizzle it makes in its ear.) Gently wipe all the crevices, going downward as far as you can go in the ear. A dog's ear canal is designed so that it goes downward for a short distance, then makes a sharp horizontal turn toward the eardrum, so as long as you only clean downward, you won't injure the eardrum. Don't under any circumstances use a syringe to clean the dog's ears—then you could really damage the eardrums. Don't clean every day unless the dog's ears are dirty—a normal amount of wax is needed to protect the skin.

Be sure to check your dog's ears after it has been running in a park or through bushes, or rolling in the grass—it could have picked up burrs, seeds, or other foreign matter. Remove these with a cotton-tipped swab dipped in mineral, baby, or vegetable oil. And be sure to check the ears if your dog has been in a dog fight, even a play fight, because serum and blood make a good medium for bacteria.

If your dog has a lot of hair growing at the entrance of its ears, you probably should keep that trimmed. A groomer sometimes plucks excess hair out of a dog's ears—this is fine as long as he or she puts an antibiotic on the plucked spot afterward to prevent infection.

When a dog has an ear infection, it's likely to hold its head on one side or rub its head on the floor. The ear will be tender and is usually red and swollen. There may be a bad smell and dark brown wax or a discharge. This condition calls for immediate veterinary attention.

Foreign bodies such as ear mites or ticks can damage a dog's ears. While adult dogs rarely get ear mites, puppies are susceptible. Ear mites are microscopic, cause intense itching, and are very contagious to other animals. The puppy will scratch and shake its head and is usually pretty uncomfortable. You can't see the mites except under a microscope, but you'll see a brown or black waxlike substance in the ears. The pup should be taken to the vet for diagnosis and medication—and be sure to go the whole way with the medication for as long as the veterinarian instructs; even if the puppy seems to experience quick relief and the ears look okay, do not stop the treatment ahead of schedule.

You can usually get rid of ticks yourself, if they're in a part of the ear that you can reach easily. First, use a cotton-tipped swab to put a drop—just a drop—of alcohol (whiskey will do) right on the tick, and then use your fingers or tweezers to grasp it and pull it out. If the head remains in the skin, the spot may be inflamed for a few days but will rarely cause infection (see External Parasites, Chapter 6).

ROUTINE EYE CARE

For most dogs, routine eye care means only wiping dirt or normal discharge from the corners of the eyes with a tissue or cotton ball moistened with water or mild boric acid solution. Be sure to wipe only at the inner corners, next to the nose, and don't draw the wiper across the lids.

Tearing is a problem of old dogs; their eyes might have to be wiped several times a day. Dogs with white faces don't produce more tears than other dogs, but the tear stains show up more, so they need more frequent wiping just to look good.

Dogs with protruding eyes, such as Pekingese, Lhasa Apsos, Pugs, and Boston Terriers, are subject to eye injuries, so owners of such breeds should examine their pets' eyes daily. Also, dogs that have a lot of hair hanging over their eyes need special attention, because overlong facial hair can scratch the eyeballs. It's a good idea to keep the hair over the eyes clipped.

Cloudiness of the eyes in an old dog is normal and does not impair the animal's vision. But redness, inflammation, a yellow color, or discharge in the eyes of any dog should be called to the attention of a veterinarian.

FOOT CARE

Every routine grooming session should include a quick check of your dog's footpads. You'll want to look for cuts, scrapes, and deep cracks or fissures that are prone to infection. Check between the toes for mats and disentangle them before they cause discomfort.

You'd think that dogs who walk on pavement would wear their toenails down enough not to need trimming, but this doesn't seem to be the case. While your dog's regular home grooming sessions won't include nail trimming, you should check the length of the nails frequently and trim them when they grow overlong. The nails should just clear the floor when the dog is standing upright. Otherwise they can cause the toes to spread in an abnormal fashion, and the dog will be uncomfortable, walk funny, and eventually limp and become lame. Unless a dog is heavy and is walked a lot on pavement, its nails should be trimmed every two months.

Be sure to use clippers specially designed for dogs. If you try to use your own nail clippers, you'll hurt the dog, because its nails are too tough for anything but the right tools. Work in a good light and speak quietly and reassuringly to your dog when you trim its nails. Trim only the tips. If you cut too much off and hit the quick (the pink line coming down into the nail from the foot), you'll hurt the dog and the nail will bleed. Some dogs have black toenails in which you can't see the pink quick; with those, you obviously have to be very cautious. Cut almost to the groove on the underside or just to where the nail starts to curve downward. Don't forget to trim the dewclaws—those useless nails on the legs just above the feet. If they become too long, they can curl and cut into the flesh.

Have peroxide and styptic powder or pencil on hand when you trim your dog's toenails, because if you accidentally cut too much

Louie and Elmo, two well-kept, well-indulged city dogs

and the nail bleeds, you should disinfect it with peroxide and then apply the styptic to stop the bleeding. If the bleeding is excessive, you may have to apply cold wet compresses for ten minutes or so, before the peroxide and styptic. Also soothe and stroke the dog, because it will be very upset.

Dogs hate to have their feet touched—that's why it's a good idea to get a puppy used to it early. I often wished Dandy had been conditioned to having her feet handled when she was a puppy. My gentle, passive pet turned into a thrashing, bucking, hysterical beast on whom I had to get a stranglehold while Jim Stewart, her groomer, with all the patience in the world, managed to do the job. Yet Susannah tolerates it with long-suffering silence.

If your dog is still patient by the time you finish trimming its nails, smooth the tips with a nail file or emery board.

Dogs sometimes tear their nails in playing or running around. A nail catches on a rug, floorboard, or some protrusion and begins to bleed. First aid consists of pressing cold compresses on the spot, but if the nail is really torn, the dog must be taken to the vet.

Paul Glassner/San Francisco SPCA

A San Francisco SPCA groomer makes sure that a dog for adoption looks good

With a long-haired dog, it's a good idea to keep the hair on the feet clipped fairly short. Otherwise the dog will be forever tracking dirt, mud, snow, and ice into the house.

If the grooming work I've described sounds time-consuming, let me add that it will go fast once you get into the routine. And this kind of care will pay off in better health and comfort for your dog and lower veterinary bills, in addition to keeping your pet looking good.

PROFESSIONAL GROOMERS

Some breeds with stand-out, long, or wiry coats need professional haircuts once in a while, not to look fashionable but simply to look neat. If you've ever noticed a Bichon Frisé, Poodle, or Miniature Schnauzer whose coat has gone to seed, you'll see what I mean.

I'd be the last to suggest some of the weird hairdos I've seen on certain show dogs. The trim that makes a Poodle a walking ball of fur from neck to waist but leaves its hindquarters naked is grotesque, in my opinion. The dog can't be comfortable with a burden of hair around its front half and exposed around its flanks. But a Poodle with a nice basic "lamb cut," which requires professional attention only every six to eight weeks, looks adorable.

Also, dogs with thick hair that live in hot climates or where the summers are intense are probably more comfortable if their coats are trimmed and thinned. A "puppy cut" seems to help these dogs through hot weather.

If you have a puppy of a breed that will be getting a professional trim regularly or even once in a while, it's advisable to get it used to the grooming parlor early, so it feels comfortable there. Leave the pup in a cage at the groomer's for an hour or so from time to time and just let it watch. Then, when its turn eventually arrives, it won't be scared.

How to judge a groomer? By asking friends whose judgment you trust, as I suggested in choosing a veterinarian. Some dogs have very definite preferences for being groomed by women instead of men, or vice versa. Also, look for a person who really likes dogs, and check on how the dogs that are being worked on are behaving. It's reassuring to be able to see the grooming shop in action; if the groomer does his or her work in a basement or back room where the client is not allowed, that's a bad sign.

Some working people drop their dogs off at the groomer's on their way to work and pick them up in the evening. This is fine for dogs that are comfortable at the groomer's. When they're not being worked on themselves, they watch the others, or sleep. But if your pet feels unhappy and anxious at the groomer's, you might try to book a time when it can be taken as soon as you bring it in. Ask how long your dog will be there and pick it up as soon as it's ready.

In big cities like New York, there are many groomers who will make house calls. You'll have some cleaning up to do afterward, but the pet will have the comforting advantage of being in its own home. Also, you'll be spared taking it to the groomer's and picking it up. But go by your animal's reactions. Some dogs may regard the experience as an invasion of the sanctity of their own home.

One friend told me that her dog developed an eye irritation that her veterinarian recognized at once as "groomer's eye," caused by irritating soap. If your dog's eyes are red and sore after a bath in a grooming parlor, call it to the groomer's attention—or change groomers.

Some groomers routinely give dogs tranquilizers before they work on them, to reduce anxiety and make them calm and tractable. Jim Stewart believed that this kind of groomer should be avoided unless he or she works for a veterinarian, right in the clinic. Not all dogs tolerate tranquilizers equally, and drugs should be used only with medical advice and supervision.

One thing a professional groomer will do is empty a dog's anal sacs, which are on each side of the base of the rectum. It's a good idea, because if the anal glands become blocked, this can lead to discomfort and possibly infection. Normally, the sacs are emptied every time the dog defecates, but sometimes they can become impacted. Groomers and veterinarians know how to empty a dog's anal sacs by pressing on them. I personally don't recommend that dog owners attempt to do this themselves unless they have been taught by a professional.

9. TWO'S COMPANY

A Friend for Your Dog

Dedicated dog lovers sometimes have a hard time stopping at just one. You hear of a dog that desperately needs a home, you find one on the street, you pass a pet shop, or you see a dog on TV that's up for adoption from an animal shelter, and you melt. These are all good reasons for taking in a second or third dog. There are so many millions of dogs needing homes in this world that it's almost a moral obligation to have as many as you can realistically care for.

There's another, very sound, humane motive for acquiring a second dog—or perhaps a cat. If nobody's home at your house during the day and sometimes in the evening, a single dog can get very lonely. As we discussed in Chapter 4, a dog can be taught not to bark and howl when it's left alone, but often just the presence of another creature is a good solution to the problem of a pet's separation anxiety. It seems to me that giving your dog a buddy to keep it company is a loving thing to do for it anyway.

You might think that two pets would be twice as much trouble as one. Actually, in some ways they are less trouble. When you have to work late, for example, or decide to go to dinner directly from the office, or are having fun somewhere and wish to stay longer, the disturbing image of your pet waiting at home alone can make you very uncomfortable. This can put a damper on good times and be distracting during business obligations, and with good reason, because for a single pet, you're It—you're all it has in the way of regular companionship. But knowing that there are two or more social animals at home to while away the time together can make you feel a lot less concerned and guilty.

Also, it is definitely mean to leave a single dog alone over a weekend, even if a sitter comes in daily to tend to its needs. But two or more animals, given daily care by a sitter, can keep one another company till you return. As one who has often been a sitter for absent friends' pets, I can tell you that there is a huge difference in behavior between the single animal and the pair, trio, or more. The solo dog or cat exhibits far greater anxiety.

Many dog owners firmly believe that their pet would be outraged if another animal were brought into the household. Some have even tried it and been convinced by the incumbent's initial reaction that it would never work. This may be true in rare cases in which either the resident or the incoming animal is highly aggressive or insecure. But it is hardly ever the case among normally sociable, neutered pets. While not all will welcome another with open paws immediately, and some may grumble for weeks, nearly all dogs will adjust to a newcomer eventually, and most will be much happier having a friend. And in fact, even if the animals never learn to love each other, they nevertheless seem to get some satisfaction just from the other's presence.

One tip in introducing a second pet, whether it is a dog or a cat: Never force the two animals on each other. Some pet owners mistakenly drag the two creatures right up to one another, make them touch noses, and restrain them in close contact. Instead, you should respect each animal's space and let the initial contact be more natural. If either takes one look and wants to run and hide, let it, and allow them to meet each other in their own time.

Another tip: Whether you adopt a cat or another dog, don't treat them like Siamese twins, but reserve some time every day for a one-

Dog friends—Nutmeg and Susannah

on-one relationship with each. A pet needs to have you all to itself sometimes, even for just a little while. Susannah, as my only dog, gets plenty of my time alone, but each of the cats seeks me out alone at certain times, and for the moment I treat it as if it were my only cat.

BRINGING IN A SECOND DOG

I once heard a wonderful, true story about a woman who had an elegant purebred Standard Poodle that she walked in Central Park. One day, her spayed female pet met up with a pitiful, scruffy-looking stray, obviously down on his luck. The Poodle apparently decided that the stray was the greatest dog she'd ever met, and the two cavorted around together in as many games as the Poodle's leash would allow. If dogs can fall in love, these two did. When the lady and her dog headed for home, the stray followed.

"Peaches kept looking at me as if to say, 'Please, Mom, can't we keep him?'" the Poodle's owner related. "I simply didn't have the heart to drive the dog away, so he came on home with us, and I figured I'd call the ASPCA later to come and pick him up. Of course, it never happened. The change in Peaches was dramatic. Where

Donna Knipp

Dog friends—Max and Gatsby

before she had been a gentle but rather timid, very dependent dog, crestfallen and often destructive when left alone, she turned into a sunny, exuberant animal, much more affectionate toward us as well as devoted to Buddy, as we named the new dog. And she stopped chewing up things when we were out."

Peaches and Buddy made a somewhat odd couple, the pedigreed apricot Poodle and the ungainly animal who, even after his body filled out and his coat became clean and healthy, was no beauty. But Buddy, neutered and made to feel at home, clearly enriched Peaches' life and cured her of her separation anxiety.

I applaud this tale wholeheartedly. Many dogs will not only choose a friend for themselves but will be perfectly agreeable to your bringing in another. But I do want to add one note of caution: If your pet should select a stray dog for a friend, by all means take it in—but have your veterinarian check it out immediately to be sure it's healthy. A poor dog that's been forced to scrounge for food and shelter is an easy victim for canine diseases, so even if your pet's vaccinations are up to date, you want to protect it from catching anything contagious the stray might have (worms, for instance). And of course you'll want to have the new dog vaccinated and spayed or neutered as soon as possible.

Many dogs that bark when left alone will stop the habit as soon as a companion dog is acquired for them. But Dr. Peter Borchelt, consultant at the Animal Behavior Clinic of the Animal Medical Center in New York City, has warned that if you have a dog that is a confirmed howler or barker when left alone, bringing in a second dog could mean you'll end up with two vocalizing dogs instead of one. Or you could have one dog that's quiet and one that howls. There are no guarantees. But I have known enough dogs that were cured of separation anxiety when another pet entered the household to pass the suggestion on to you as an option to consider seriously.

Let's say you have a normal, well-adjusted dog and wish to bring in another for whatever reason. You want the introduction to go as smoothly as possible. Here are a few suggestions:

Your resident dog will more quickly take to a puppy or younger dog than to one its own age or older.

If you are getting a new puppy, its sex doesn't matter, because your resident dog will be dominant anyway. But if your dog is an adult and you're bringing in an adult, choose one of the opposite sex. And don't inflict a puppy on an old dog who just wants peace and quiet.

Both your resident dog and the new one of course should be spayed or neutered. If for any reason you have not had your pet spayed or neutered, it could be risky to bring in an adult dog of the same sex—you might have one hell of a dogfight on your hands. And you don't want two unspayed or unneutered adult dogs of opposite sexes for obvious reasons.

Unless your dog is extremely mellow and self-confident, it will probably be happier with a new dog that's smaller or of equal size.

Have someone else bring the new dog to your home, or have the two dogs meet on neutral ground and go home together after they've had a chance to check each other out. It could get things off on the wrong foot if you were to walk in on your dog with another dog in tow.

Have both dogs leashed when they meet, but let them explore each other normally. Act natural and calm yourself, and let the dogs know that you don't anticipate any problems between them.

Remember everything you ever knew about introducing a new baby to an older sibling. Give your resident dog lots of affection so it knows it isn't being replaced. If the new dog is a puppy, resist the temptation to cuddle it and fuss over it while ignoring the older dog, and be sure visitors also give the older dog equal time. Be sure to give treats, toys, and attention equally.

On the other hand, don't go to such lengths to lavish attention on the resident dog that it feels the new one doesn't belong, and the new dog feels left out. Make it clear that the newcomer is welcome and has rights of its own.

In very rare instances, an incoming dog will try so hard to make a place for itself that it will bully the resident pet and attempt to dominate it in a threatening way. If the older pet is clearly upset and even frightened, the situation calls for professional advice from a dog trainer or behavior counselor, or—in extreme cases—actually giving up the second dog. If, after a decent trial period and sincere efforts on your part, the two personalities are just not compatible, you should make another arrangement for the new dog, because it isn't fair to your original pet to subject it to continual harassment. Try another, different sort of dog, or a cat, as a companion for your resident dog.

DOGS AND CATS

Sometimes when I mention to people that I have a dog and several cats, they are surprised. "Do they get along?" they'll invariably ask.

It is a firmly established notion that cats and dogs are natural enemies. One explanation is that if they haven't been raised around cats, some dogs—especially certain hunting breeds—chase them because they apparently mistake them for small game. Also, a lot of

Margery Cornwell

A benevolent dog wonders what that silly kitten thinks it's doing

dogs have been taught by stupid, cruel people to attack cats. The redneck way of inculcating cat hatred in a dog is to say "Sic 'em" whenever a cat comes in sight, so the dog gets the message. Cats are often thrown to pit bull terriers to give the dogs a taste of blood in training them for the "sport" of dogfighting.

But the idea that dogs are born to chase cats can be perpetuated even by perfectly nice people so that it becomes a self-fulfilling prophecy. Because dogs pick up and act upon even subtle attitudes in their owners, they can absorb the notion that they're expected to attack every cat they meet just from their owner's body language. If the owner believes that it's the nature of dogs to hate cats, he or she doesn't have to say a word. Just by the tension of the leash and its owner's uncertain behavior, a dog knows that meeting a cat is creating a certain amount of concern. Then the dog may decide the cat is something it must defend its owner against, so it behaves in a hostile manner, thus confirming the owner's original belief.

Sometimes the cat plays a role in the confusion. If a cat has had unpleasant and even life-threatening encounters with dogs, it won't trust them and may take immediate defensive action when it meets one. It may lash out against even perfectly gentle dogs that actually like cats. Naturally, some dogs won't turn the other cheek.

It is not true that dogs and cats are natural enemies. There is no innate or instinctive competition between the species—wild canines and felines have separate hunting preferences and generally ignore each other. It is a great pleasure to have both as pets, to enjoy the beauty, intelligence, affection, and special characteristics of each. So unless you have a confirmed cat-killer, or a dog with a poor track record regarding cats, you shouldn't hesitate to acquire a feline pet. Your dog doesn't have to have a proven liking for cats, just an open mind.

The ideal way to set up a dog-and-cat household is to adopt both animals together when they are very young. Just be careful, if the puppy is big and boisterous, that it doesn't hurt the kitten in playing with it. A hefty three-month-old pup with the most innocent intentions in the world could break a kitten's back, just in fun. Some people recommend that the puppy be old enough to understand basic commands, such as "No."

Both animals should be neutered the minute they are old enough, not only for their individual health but for the benefit of their relationship. No matter how loving they have become toward each other, their friendship could be strained if the behavior of either animal were changed by puberty.

Introducing a Cat to a Resident Dog

If you are introducing a kitten to an adult dog, you also want to protect the kitten from accidental harm if the dog tries to play with it. The kitten should be fourteen to sixteen weeks old, strong enough to run, jump, and climb successfully

Cat therapist and author Carole Wilbourn recommends that you don't adopt a shy cat or kitten if your dog has a high energy level, or impose a bouncing, extroverted cat or kitten on a passive, retiring dog. In other words, try to match their personalities.

According to the Wilbourn method, you should bring the cat into your house in a see-through carrier and leave it where the two animals can observe each other for a while before you let the cat out. Keep the two in different rooms for a few days, preferably separated by a gate or screen so they can watch each other through it. When they finally do meet, don't allow the dog to chase the cat, and be sure the cat can escape to a high piece of furniture if it wants to, where it can contemplate the dog until it feels confident enough to come down. Confine them separately whenever you leave the house until they have become completely accepting and nonchalant about each other.

Keep an eye on them, but just as I advised in introducing two dogs, don't communicate any anxious thoughts you might have. Act relaxed and natural, as if the cat's arrival were the most normal thing in the world.

Wilbourn says you should pretend that you've acquired the cat as a present for the dog. If you act as if you were giving the dog a marvelous gift that it is going to love, the dog might buy it. Make a big fuss over the dog, and mention its name every time you touch the cat for the first week or two, so the dog feels included. This has been known to work.

A couple I once knew had a dog named Samuel Johnson whose best friend was a cat named, appropriately, Hodge. Sam was a Rhodesian Ridgeback, a powerful hound breed originally used for hunting and today known for its aggressive loyalty and superior qualities as a guardian and watchdog. You might think the couple would have had reservations about adopting a cat, but they knew their particular dog, and they knew cats.

Sam was ten months old and weighed nearly eighty pounds when his owners introduced ten-week-old, two-pound Hodge into the household. Sam had seen cats on the street but never up close and was goggle-eyed over the kitten. He was allowed to sniff but not touch at first. Sam's owners made it clear—and I think this was the key factor—that Hodge was somebody they valued, somebody to be protected and nurtured. Gradually, Sam was allowed to come closer and closer, all the while being cautioned firmly that he must be very careful with the small creature. The kitten was afraid of Sam at first but was continually reassured by the owners.

The next day, Hodge was put on the floor and the two animals were allowed to get acquainted under close supervision. Soon Hodge was trailing Sam around, and it was apparent that mutual love was developing. The two slept in Sam's bed—together. Hodge licked the dog's muzzle; Sam in turn groomed the young cat, particularly his face and ears.

So much for your "fight like cats and dogs" stories.

Introducing a Dog to a Resident Cat

You won't have a problem introducing a puppy to a household with a resident kitten as long as you take their relative sizes into consideration and protect the kitten from rough play. It's when you already have an adult cat that you have to take steps to assure that the introduction of a dog or puppy goes smoothly.

I'm assuming your cat is neutered, reasonably well adjusted, and not a confirmed dog-hater that will attack any and all dogs on sight. Even cats that have had terrifying experiences with dogs can learn to trust individuals, but you don't want a new dog harmed by eight pounds of clawing, snarling fury within its first hour in your home.

An adult cat will be thoroughly disgusted by a puppy and needs to be reassured that you haven't lost your mind. It's wise to cuddle and make a fuss over the pup when your cat isn't looking, so you won't hurt its feelings and arouse jealousy. The sex of the puppy is not important.

Trim your cat's nails before bringing in a puppy or dog, and if possible move the cat's litterbox to a spot that will be inaccessible to the dog, to assure its privacy.

If you're adopting an adult dog, be absolutely sure that it has a good attitude toward cats. Ideally, it should be one who has lived with cats before, or at least has learned to respect them.

Carole Wilbourn believes an adult cat will accept an adult dog of the opposite sex more quickly than one of the same sex. This holds true, she says, even though both will be neutered.

And, according to the Wilbourn method, you should have someone your cat doesn't know bring the dog to your home, so the cat won't feel you have betrayed it. Never allow the dog to chase the cat, even in fun.

Just as I suggested about bringing a cat into a household with a resident dog, your own body language will influence the integration process. If you are convinced your darling cat will die of jealousy, you're setting up a situation that is bound to fail. Let your cat know that you love it as much as ever, but that the dog is welcome and has rights of its own.

Be sure to feed the cat somewhere that the dog can't reach—on a table or counter, for example. And Wilbourn says to give the cat a quiet roost to call its own—a box, basket, or pillow on a piece of furniture that's completely inaccessible to the dog.

Unless your cat likes dogs, or at least is used to them, be prepared to put up with a certain amount of hissing and snarling from your cat at first. In all likelihood, this will pass in a few days. It's worth enduring it for the pleasure you will enjoy in having both animals. And don't be surprised if, no matter which pet you had first, the cat becomes the dominant animal. A cat can turn out to be the boss pet, even lording it over gigantic dogs, who don't seem to mind. Both dog and cat will be better off for each other's company—and may grow to love one another.

OTHER PETS

As an urban dweller, you probably won't be acquiring rabbits, ponies, goats, or other wonderful outdoor animals, but you may have birds, and households with children are especially likely to have cute little pet rodents such as hamsters and gerbils. Most of the time, these creatures will be in their cages, so you won't have to worry about their interaction with your dog or with a dog that you wish to introduce into the family. But do use common sense if you let these pets out of their cages to stretch their wings or legs from time to time.

Remember where your dog is coming from. If it is a hunting breed, or a mixed breed with "sporting dog," hound, or terrier ancestry, it will very possibly regard a bird or small mammal as something it is supposed to catch. The first time your parakeet takes wing when your setter, pointer, or retriever is in the room, don't blame the dog if it springs into the air after it. And you can't expect even a well-behaved and gentle hound or terrier to refrain from snapping up that little hamster scampering across the room.

Also keep in mind that large parrots can inflict bodily harm on dogs of most any size, and dogs of hunting breed ancestry could confuse a parrot with a pheasant or mallard. And the sounds parrots make might spook a dog. So it's important to gather all the information you can before you adopt either creature to cohabit with the other. Chances are they'll just ignore each other and be no problem.

Many, many dogs reside in perfect harmony with birds of all sizes—and, in fact, with all other creatures large and small. I once knew a nice Golden Retriever who lived with two parakeets that he seemed to be fond of. They would roost on his head, even on his paws when he was lying down, and he wouldn't even blink. Our dog Benjy never showed any interest in my son's hamsters, even when they ran about on the floor. But we never left him alone with them.

It's best to keep everyone safe by not having unrealistic expectations of a dog. Even if your dog shows no interest in these other species, don't let it out of your sight with an uncaged pet bird or rodent.

As for whether pets of these types can be companions to a dog, I'm inclined to doubt it. I think a dog needs a comparatively social animal like itself—another dog or a cat—for a buddy.

10. THE THERAPEUTIC DOG

How Dogs Help Us

E ver since the primitive dog cast its lot with our ancestors, it has
played many different roles in our lives. Hunting and herding
helper, guardian and protector, companion and playmate, workmate
and guide, child-substitute and source of love—thanks to its infinite
flexibility, the dog has gone along with our demands throughout history. We've relied on its loyalty, willingness, and intelligence and
turned it into whatever kind of animal we needed.

The dog has been so taken for granted that dog lovers now view
with some amusement a phenomenon of recent years: the scientific
interest in this animal and its relationship with us. Researchers have
been investigating what many of us have known in our bones forever—they've discovered that dogs can be beneficial, even essential, to
human health and well-being. Their studies give credibility and
respectability to what we have long intuited.

THE BOND

About twenty years ago, scientific interest in what is now termed the
human/companion-animal bond was sparked by the discovery that
pets may help to extend human life. This was a serendipitous finding. A group of university researchers were investigating people with

coronary artery disease to determine why some lived longer than others. The scientists took in-depth profiles of about one hundred heart attack victims; a year later, they compared the charts of patients still living with those of patients who had died over the year. All variables were examined, including age, occupation, marital status, general health, income, and lifestyle. To the research team's puzzlement, one factor they found consistently was that most of the people still living had pets, while most of those who had died did not.

That raised questions: Is there something in the personalities of people who keep pets that acts as a survival factor? A subsequent study comparing the psychological status of pet owners with that of non-pet owners uncovered no significant differences. So is there something in the relationship between people and their companion animals that in itself may tend to promote health? The evidence from ongoing research suggests that the presence of a loved pet in a person's life can offer emotional and physical benefits.

A group of veterinarians, social workers, psychologists, anthropologists, and other researchers at the University of Pennsylvania were the first to launch an organized investigation into the human/companion-animal bond. An early study revealed that petting a dog or cat lowers blood pressure. It had been known for some time that petting a dog lowers its blood pressure, but until now, no one had thought to measure the blood pressure of the human doing the petting.

Furthermore, it was learned that normally when you talk to another person, or read aloud, you experience a rise in blood pressure. But if you talk to someone, then pet your dog or cat, and then resume speaking, your blood pressure rises less during the second conversation, indicating that the soothing effect lasts a while. Speaking of speaking, the researchers learned that when you talk to your dog or cat (as most pet owners do), the rise in blood pressure doesn't occur. In fact, stutterers don't stutter when they talk to pets. Why might this be?

For one thing, most of us touch our pets as we talk to them, and use a pattern of speech similar to the one we use when we talk to babies—an intimate and affectionate "motherese" that has been associated with lowered blood pressure. Also, because the animal is non-critical and nonjudgmental, there's no reason to worry about how we're coming across. And even though most of us believe that our pets understand at least some of what we say, we can assume they won't give us an argument or think we're fools.

One experiment involved bringing children into a living room, one by one, with a researcher present. At some point during each child's interview, a dog was let into the room. In every case, the child's blood pressure dropped. Just the presence of the dog, without necessarily any tactile involvement of the child, apparently reduced the child's tension. The reason is unknown, but one interpretation might be that on some primitive level, the dog communicated a sort of reassurance.

Another study was conducted in the waiting room of a veterinary clinic, where men and women sat with their pets. Virtually every client fondled his or her pet, either attentively or absentmindedly, whether or not the pet appeared anxious. The behavior of the people seemed to indicate that stroking their dogs and cats was done as much to soothe themselves as to comfort the animals. Just as infants fondle a favorite blanket, or as people in some cultures finger "worry beads" or stones, the very act of touching the familiar creatures seemed to reduce stress.

At a school for very young autistic, developmentally delayed, or emotionally disturbed children, an intervention program of regular visits by volunteers and their dogs is fully supported by the staff. "These children have sensory integration problems and are afraid of many things," says the principal. "I have seen positive results as the children overcome their fear and become willing, even eager, to touch the dogs."

In 1998, a high school student in Oregon shot and killed two and wounded over twenty of his classmates in the school cafeteria. In the anguished days that followed, two young women who with their dogs belong to a service group called Pet Partners were called in by the National Organization for Victims Assistance. Pet Partners—teams of volunteers with their trained and certified dogs—normally visit hospitals, nursing homes, and the like. But in this crisis, these two dogs, a Golden Retriever and a Keeshond, were taken by their partners to the school every day for a week, to help the traumatized students deal with their shock and grief. Besides the students and the staff, the Pet Partners were the only ones allowed in the school. The students fondled the dogs, petted them, wept into their fur, and seemed calmed and reassured by their presence. It was a dramatic example of the healing power of dogs.

THE FAMILY DOG

"Max is a member of the family," a person may say, indicating the canine relative who, for better or worse, is firmly entrenched in the household. Studies of this common attitude indicate that the family dog is regarded as an in-between creature—not quite human, yet more than other non-human animals.

While dogs always need our permission to be in our family and can be forced out suddenly and irreversibly through death or abandonment, many live out their lives as cherished members.

We define a family as a group related by blood, marriage, birth, or adoption, or perhaps just by reciprocal affection, often sharing a home. Many dogs meet the definition of family member, and some qualify as the only family their owner may have.

Family therapist Ann Ottney Cain once stated that a dog may be a barometer of the level of anxiety within its family. "Problems involving human relationships may become apparent in the context of animal-human interaction where they would not be clearly visible otherwise," she said. "Pets can provide important information about how the family system is organized or disorganized." Dr. Cain advised any family therapist to include the pet in an investigation of the way family members interact.

Christmas morning, Bob and Tao

In some families, people may use the dog to help them deal with their intense feelings in a process called triangling. In triangling, one family member gets a message to another not by expressing it directly but through a third person—or a pet. A family member may yell at the dog instead of at the person he or she is really angry with. A spouse may take the pet's side when the other is scolding the animal for some misbehavior, as a way of provoking an argument and bringing out anger over something unrelated to the pet. Needless to say, it can be very confusing and upsetting to an animal to be dragged into human conflicts in this way. Dogs, who are honest about their feelings and anxious to please, don't deserve this.

Children regard the family dog as playmate, confidant, and perhaps protector. The dog is never cross when it wakes up, it's always ready for a game, and it may be the only family member who doesn't scold the kids or tell them what to do.

The dog is waiting when the child comes home from school and, if both parents work, keeps him or her company. The animal may be a reassuring constant in a single-parent family or in one that frequently moves its home base. If the child loves the dog and treats it well, the dog returns the love without qualification. The child can count on it even in the face of a bad report card or other trouble. This positive approval raises a child's sense of self-worth.

The early adolescent period in a youngster's life can be a sort of emotional wasteland in terms of affectionate touching. To a boy or girl too old to be cuddled like a baby but too young for satisfying sexual relationships, the pet may be the only creature he or she can stroke and hug with perfect social and psychological impunity. With the dog, the child feels free to express the very human need for touching. I have seen inner-city teenage boys from a residential treatment school for troubled youth cuddling and caressing two dogs with pleasure and no self-consciousness whatever.

A pet can be a good teaching tool through which parents can help a child develop some of the most civilizing qualities—empathy, self-control, compassion, and awareness of and consideration for the needs and feelings of another creature. If the parents treat the dog with affection and respect, the child will be inclined to follow suit. Some psychologists believe that a child who has learned to take care of a pet is more likely to grow up to be considerate of other people.

One mother in a family with a beloved dog reported putting the children's affection to good use. When her kids become unbearably boisterous, they won't always calm down when she tells them to, but if she says, "Stop that racket, you're upsetting Max," they quiet down immediately.

The relationship of children to companion animals can also be significant in an opposite and ominous way. Studies have shown a correlation between animal abuse on the part of children and eventual criminal behavior. Interviews with criminals serving time for violent crimes have revealed patterns of animal abuse in childhood, leading psychologists to conclude that cruelty to animals by a child is not an innocent, trivial activity that he or she will outgrow. It can be a signal of serious emotional trouble that should never be neg-lected but given full professional attention.

Dogs are common pets among rural and suburban families, but they are especially valuable to urban children, who lack contact with other animate life forms. City children see pigeons and squirrels, perhaps the captive animals of a zoo, but unless they have pets, they have no chance to observe fully and understand a non-human species. Yet increasingly we are forced to recognize that an enlight-ened stewardship of other species and a sharing of the planet with them are essential to our own survival.

THE CHILD-SUBSTITUTE DOG

Conventional wisdom has it that people who make a pet a substitute for a child are a little wacko. This so-called eccentricity receives a good deal of ridicule, especially from folks who offer the opinion that pet owners should instead be lavishing attention, money, and time on fellow human beings. Interestingly, however, persons who make those criticisms are rarely involved, themselves, in doing any-thing for others.

There's also a widely voiced cliché that people who have intense affection for pets have problems relating to other humans. Their pets are presumed to be the object of displaced attachments that normal-ly are reserved for other people. This notion may reflect our cultur-al bias that claims that love for people is the only legitimate one, that affection for pets is sentimental and trivial. It may also result from the observation that sometimes persons who are very shy, disabled, extremely eccentric, or for some reason rejected by other people may indeed turn to companion animals for the love and fellowship they are denied elsewhere.

There is no hard evidence to support the theory that strong love for animals means dislike for people. There is one university study that revealed the opposite, finding that low affection for dogs was accompanied by low affection for people. I have a personal bias that makes it difficult for me to form warm personal relationships with people who dislike animals. Even though intellectually I try to allow for exceptions and tell myself that many kind and decent human beings simply cannot relate to other species, in my heart I am suspicious of them.

"The literature about pets has been encumbered by generalizations without data base which define contact with animals as a kind of inferior substitute for contact with human beings," wrote Dr. Aaron Honori Katcher, a psychiatrist who was one of the pioneers in the study of human-animal relationships. "The relationship with pets has been considered a perversion of human relationships or a substitute for human relationships used by people who cannot obtain the real thing. I think neither of these generalizations is true. On the contrary, the evidence suggests that the companion animal must be looked upon as a kind of relationship which supplements and augments human relationships."

Non-pet owners are perhaps understandably turned off by pet owners who buy jeweled collars and fur coats for their animals. Some dog owners—city folks especially, it seems—do buy needless luxuries for their pets. I once attended an embarrassing display of this at a dog show entitled "Pampered Pets." A Dalmatian dressed in a ruffled red chiffon jacket with matching hat is not my idea of how a dog should look.

But to some people even the spending of money on a legitimate necessity for a pet can seem an outlandish luxury. A special diet, expensive medicine or surgery, or a dependable caregiver for those times when the pet's owner must be absent can look to someone else like a ridiculous indulgence. In between a mink-lined designer raincoat for a dog at one extreme and unconscionable neglect at the other, there's a wide range of care, some of which is bound to seem unnecessary to somebody.

Another advantage of the dog as a child-substitute: While it will grow old, it will never grow up—it can always be its owner's baby. The way I see it, when people regard their pets as child-substitutes, it does the people good, it usually benefits the animals, and it doesn't harm society.

It's fun to have a dog, says
Gladys with Sally and Ed

THE COMPANION DOG

Loneliness has always been a human problem, for we are perhaps the supremely social animals. We know now that loneliness can make us not only unhappy but unwell. While it can afflict persons living in the midst of a large family, loneliness is most prevalent among people who live alone, and it seems to occur in its most poignant form in cities.

A pet, particularly a dog, can be a good defense against loneliness for any single person. Some people claim that just having somebody who's glad to see them when they come home from work is reason enough to keep a dog. A comforting presence at the foot of the bed, a responsive, sentient creature to talk to, somebody to take care of, a companion to go for walks or on trips with, somebody to play games with and laugh at, a warm body to hug—a dog can be all those things and more.

"Our dogs will love and admire the meanest of us, and feed our colossal vanity with their uncritical homage," wrote the American essayist Agnes Repplier—and who among us couldn't use a little uncritical homage now and then? More recently, humorist Dave Barry has noted: "You can say any foolish thing to a dog, and the dog will give you a look that says, 'My God, you're right! I never would've thought of that!'"

A dog is not put off by physical disability or homelessness; it doesn't even notice inadequate education, poor social skills, lack of success. If you're good to your dog, it will never divorce you or leave you for a younger, richer, smarter, sexier, or more successful owner.

It is a truism that walking a dog offers you a chance to meet other people. In my Brooklyn neighborhood, for example, it can take me an hour just to walk Susannah around the block because we meet so many people and dogs we know. On summer evenings, a bunch of us may stand around and talk while our pets socialize.

The late psychiatrist Michael McCulloch pointed out that a dog can be a great social facilitator, especially for shy people. Strangers who strike up a conversation because of a dog are usually on the street or in some other public place where social demands are low and where the conversation can be easily ended. Also, noted Dr. McCulloch, it's the dog who's the focus of attention. A person who lacks poise doesn't feel he or she is being examined.

In a few studies of how people with pets are perceived by strangers, pet owners have come off rather well. In one, psychologist Randall Lockwood showed a group of subjects pictures of people with and without pets and asked them to rate the people in terms of such qualities as friendliness, happiness, dependability, aggressiveness, comfort, and intelligence.

In general, the people pictured with animals—walking, sitting, or playing with them—were rated more positively than those without. A woman walking a dog was perceived as richer and more comfortable; a man walking a dog was viewed as not only wealthier and more at ease but friendlier, more intelligent, more sympathetic, and safer to approach than a man walking alone.

PETS AND THE ELDERLY

I once knew a nice, very elderly gentleman with a sweet but uncommonly homely dog. His dog and my dog always stopped and greeted each other as dogs do, so the man and I made small talk. I never failed to admire his dog, which seemed to please him; in truth, it had a lovely temperament.

He once mentioned to me that he and his dog had shared Thanksgiving dinner together, just the two of them. This brief glimpse of the man's life points up the role a companion animal can fill in the life of an elderly person who lives alone, perhaps without close family or friends.

Many elderly people tell me that they would dearly love to have a pet, but they worry about being able to take care of it. In bad weather, an old person naturally would find it difficult to get out to walk a dog or buy pet food. They also worry about what would happen to their animals if they had to go to the hospital or if they died.

In a more humane world, networks of volunteers, perhaps associated with a senior citizens' center, block association, or even an animal shelter, could serve as supports for the elderly who wished to keep pets. Then, on those occasions when an old person could not walk his or her dog, buy pet food, take the animal to the veterinarian, or whatever, help would be available. No single, older person who wanted a companion animal would be deprived of one for lack of assistance.

"Current concepts of appropriate behavior for the elderly encourage them to give up commitments like the commitment to keeping a pet," Dr. Katcher has written. "This kind of cultural instruction places older people in a trap. The feeling that they are progressively worth less and less to others, that they have nothing to care for, no one who 'needs' them, is a common reason for loss of self-esteem and depression in the aged.

"Companion animals do need their owners, need their care, their attention, and their love. The acts of caring that these animals stimulate may, in the long run, be worth more than an endless series of games and trips that seem to be prescribed for a 'care free' old age."

It has been the practice of SPCAs and humane societies in major cities to conduct "pet therapy" programs, which consist of taking small animals—usually puppies and kittens, sometimes also rabbits, hamsters, and pet birds—to visit patients in nursing homes and hospitals. I have had the opportunity to go along on such visits in cities all over the United States. I've seen the impact of the animals on the patients, whose lives are often cheerless and boring. Anecdotal evidence of the success of these programs is rich and plentiful, and research studies have confirmed it. The benefit the patients derive from holding and petting, even just watching, the small creatures is dramatic.

Once I was with a humane society group on its first visit to a particular nursing home. One old lady immediately clasped a puppy. "I haven't held anything warm and young and alive in my arms in twenty years," she said.

Some of the old people visited talk nostalgically about pets they had when they were young. Often, the surprise to the staff is not what the patients talk about but that they talk at all. It is not unusual for a withdrawn or depressed elderly patient to speak for the first time in months or even years when a pet is placed in his or her arms. "Puppy!" exclaimed one eighty-year-old stroke victim, to the amazement of the nurses. It was his first spoken word in the months he had been in the home.

Occasionally, a patient will burst into tears, as if emotion long unused had surfaced. "I don't know why I'm crying," said one lady in a wheelchair as I helped her cuddle a puppy. "I love dogs!" Even those who are severely disabled respond. Whatever the reason, "pet therapy" helps fill the need to caress and nurture, and confirms the almost mystical connection we have with the companion animals that have shared our lives for thousands of years.

Because of the publicity these therapeutic and appealing programs have received, the recognized benefits to the patients, and the pressure from humane society and nursing home staffs who believe in them, a number of custodial institutions now allow resident pets. Some states have passed laws permitting them. The laws vary from state to state—some limit the number of pets, and all limit the areas within the institutions where the pets are allowed.

A cat named Lisette was donated to a nursing home in Brooklyn by the Humane Society of New York. Lisette lived in the recreation room but made rounds twice a day in the arms of a nurse to bedridden patients and sometimes could be seen strolling down a hall alone on her way to visit a favorite patient by herself. "This animal has brought life to this place!" one patient summed it up.

The animals not only dispense love and amusement and make institutions seem more homelike, but, according to staff members, they sometimes help get patients' minds off themselves. An old lady I met in a nursing home in Boston was very proud of the fact that she was able to take the mascot, a Boston Terrier, for his morning walk.

"Do you take him out even in bad weather?" I asked, for Boston winters can be bitter cold, snowy, and icy—risky for a frail old lady to be out in.

"Oh, it's all right," she replied with a twinkle. "He has a coat."

Just when pets are increasingly allowed to visit and even reside in nursing homes because of their recognized value to human health and morale, it is outrageously heartless that elderly people who live at home (as most do) are so often denied the life-giving companionship of pets because of the no-pet rules in urban housing (see Chapter 11).

As the late Dr. Leo Bustad, veterinarian and author of the book *Animals, Aging, and the Aged*, said, it would be unwise to withhold

Judy Sitz

Peanut is an Australian Cattle Dog, but in his San Francisco
home he rarely has to round up cattle

or withdraw doctor-prescribed medicine from an aged man or
woman; what if that medicine is the companionship of a loved pet?

Animal-assisted activities are now practiced in some six hundred
U.S. hospitals to cheer and divert patients from boredom and suffering. Increasingly, they are being expanded into true animal-assisted therapy, in which dogs are used for specific therapeutic treatment,
such as helping surgical patients respond, even walk, or to calm residents in mental wards.

In time, even HMOs may wake up to such low-tech solutions in
health care as animal-assisted therapy. Many changes need to be
made to make ours a more compassionate society. Guaranteeing the
right to have the companionship of a loved dog or cat in our old age
should be one of them.

11. THE LEGAL DOG

The Rights and Responsibilities of Dog Ownership

Ironically, even with the established awareness of our need for companion animals, and scientific evidence of their importance to human health and happiness, it has become more difficult to keep that quintessential companion animal—the dog—in the place where most of us live—the city. Increasingly, urban rules and legislation are threatening to regulate our dogs right out of our lives.

Not all of the laws that govern the way we live with our urban dogs are wrong. Leash laws, for instance, protect their lives, and clean-up laws make cities a lot nicer to live in for all of us. Animal cruelty laws, inadequate as they are, can sometimes back us up when we speak out at seeing an animal abused. However, one fairly recent type of regulation, which is virtually standard in every city in the United States today, is turning dogs into endangered urban species and denying pets to many would-be dog owners: the no-pet clause in the rules of rental, co-op, and condominium housing.

Below, I'll offer suggestions for dealing with the no-pet clause, and give you some pointers on what you can do about animal cruelty.

CAESAR'S WIFE'S DOG

Down the sidewalk in the early morning sunlight came my neighbor John with his large black dog, Strike. Stopping at a tree, Strike stepped over the low ironwork fence around it and relieved himself copiously on the flowers that someone had carefully planted there. John, an otherwise perfectly nice man, never even noticed.

This is the sort of behavior that gives dogs in the city, and their owners, a bad name. It gives ammunition to dog haters and even makes some dog lovers grind their teeth. In a city environment, a dog should behave as Caesar expected his wife to be—above suspicion.

One way to prevent more laws from being passed against city dogs is to be sure that your pet's behavior, and yours as a dog owner, is impeccable. A country dog can be a noisy, misbehaving roughneck and get away with it because it's less likely to bother other people. But in the city a dog's (and dog owner's) personality traits show up glaringly.

One of the greatest annoyances to neighbors is the dog that barks or whines incessantly when left alone. This can be equally distressing to dog haters and dog lovers. Dog haters would like to throttle the beast, while dog lovers (who may be equally annoyed) worry and feel sorry for it. As discussed in Chapter 4, this habit can and should be stopped with proper training.

Housebreaking should be absolute. Even if your pet behaves okay in the public halls and only has problems in your apartment, sooner or later neighbors, the super, and the landlord will become aware of an unpleasant smell in your place, and though you might not notice it yourself, they will object.

Some housing units limit the number of pets a household can have—in fact, in some cities there are ordinances that limit the number of pets even people in private homes can keep! These laws are muddleheaded, because standards of pet keeping, just like those of housekeeping in general, are highly individual. Some people can keep twenty pets in cleanliness and harmony; other folks can't seem to keep even one pet decently.

The no-pet clause is said by the real estate community to be the result of years of irresponsible behavior on the part of dog owners. While this argument is open to question, it should be stressed that there is no excuse for any of us to keep a pet that's a problem to others. People are frightened by hostile dogs. People are annoyed when someone keeps an inappropriate number of animals in unsanitary and malodorous conditions. People are disgusted by dogs who mess on their property or on public sidewalks. People are irritated by dogs that are permitted to yap or bark on the street late at night.

The first tactic of any of us for stemming the tide against dog ownership in cities is to clean up our act so there is no justification for complaints against us.

LOCAL LAWS

Laws governing dog ownership vary from one locality to the next, but in general your city probably has one or another of these:

Scoop Laws

A paramount objection to urban dogs is, of course, the waste matter on the streets, sidewalks, lawns, and flower beds. It's crucial that every city dog owner observe the clean-up laws faithfully. In my doggy neighborhood, some of us habitually cleaned up after our dogs even before New York City's scoop law went into effect, just to try to reduce the pandemic and unpleasant presence of dog dirt.

Really, cleaning up is no big deal! You can use one of the disposable contraptions on the market. Most folks, however, find it easiest to use a simple plastic bag—just slip it over your hand and pick up the matter (imagine you're picking up sod or mud), turn the bag inside out so the waste is inside, and deposit it in the first public trash can you come to. Another method, if your dog doesn't object, is to slide a folded newspaper under its rear end at the crucial moment, then roll up the paper when the dog is finished and throw it away. This method is especially practical for a dog that has occasional soft stools.

Some dog owners have the offensive habit of being oblivious to where their dogs urinate. I've seen male dogs permitted to lift their legs against people's front steps, bicycles, trees, and flowers. Trees on

Patricia Curtis

Lucy, securely leashed and looking innocent

a city block with a high concentration of dogs may eventually perish from the constant depositing of acidic urine against their bark. Flowers and ivy can be turned brown and killed.

It goes without saying that people should be most vigilant with their dogs in city parks and keep their pets out of playgrounds altogether. At one city playground I know, parents have had to plead with inconsiderate dog owners not to let their animals relieve themselves in the children's sandbox, for heaven's sake. That's an offense that makes all decent dog owners feel ashamed.

Leash Laws

One of the most puzzling practices of dog owners that offends many city people is letting dogs run off the leash. It's puzzling because it not only bothers other people but endangers the dogs.

A common city sight is a dog trotting along the sidewalk apparently quite alone, with no owner evident. All too often, such an owner goes his or her way without paying any attention whatsoever to the pet, expecting the dog to take responsibility for keeping up. Or perhaps this is a way of avoiding the clean-up law; after all, if a person is clear at the other end of the block, he or she won't even notice when the dog relieves itself, leaving passersby in the dark about whose dog the offending animal is.

As I have said, some dog owners mistakenly think they are making their pets happy by giving them off-the-leash freedom, but it can be very stressful for a dog. The crowds, noise, and confusing jumble of scents on a city street make it easy for a pet to lose sight, sound, and smell of its owner.

And how about the rights and feelings of other people on the street? It can be unnerving, even terrifying, to have a strange dog come upon you suddenly, off the leash and uncontrolled. A free-running dog can also upset a dog walker whose pet is on the leash. Sometimes, a confrontation takes place between the two dogs. It can be scary to have to actually beat off an unleashed, hostile dog who dashes up and provokes a quarrel.

A dog off the leash can turn neutral people into dog haters who will be the first to support laws to deprive us of our pets.

License Laws

The attitude that city license laws are merely an unfair tax on dog owners, to be avoided like other taxes, is a mistaken one. An up-to-date dog license gives an owner a fighting chance to retrieve his or her pet if the animal becomes lost. If the dog is picked up by an animal control officer or brought to the police or a shelter by a sympathetic citizen, the license serves as identification.

If an unlicensed dog is injured—say, hit by a car—and brought to a pound or shelter, it may not be given any medical attention. It may just suffer in a cage until its owner comes for it, or it dies or is euthanized. Many shelters that function as the pound, where stray dogs are brought, cannot afford to provide medical care for an injured dog whose owner is unknown and might never turn up to pay the bill.

Even if it is not injured, a lost dog suffers tremendous stress and fear, especially in a city. Look at the panic in the eyes of the next lost dog you come across and ask yourself if you would want your pet to have that expression.

Even if you never walk your dog off the leash and you believe it would never leave your side, no matter what, remember that accidents can happen. Caring and responsible people do lose their dogs sometimes in a variety of unforeseen circumstances. The license alone is no guarantee you will get your dog back safely, but it is one extra, inexpensive protection. A license could reduce considerably the time your dog is separated from you, and might save its life.

Lastly, even if the license you buy every year is never needed to restore your pet to you, the fee supports animal control, which helps other dogs. Whether your local dog pound, or shelter that performs animal control, is a good one or a dump, a dog is better off there than roaming the streets. It is sheltered instead of homeless, fed instead of starving, protected instead of terrorized and possibly tortured—and even if it is eventually euthanized, that death is better than the almost · certain death it would meet from starvation, exposure, disease, accident, or atrocity.

THE NO-PET CLAUSE

A harsh and callous consequence of a tight housing market, the no-pet clause has become a standard fixture in much rental and even cooperative and condominium housing nationwide. It denies the joy, companionship, and protection of pets to possibly several million people. It swells the numbers of pets in animal shelters or abandoned on the streets. And it often forces pet owners who are fortunate enough to live where they can have animals to stay put, even when they can no longer afford the continual rent increases.

Landlords and co-op or condominium boards claim that the no-pet clause is a reaction to irresponsible pet owners who permit their animals to destroy property or annoy other people. They cite cases of dogs who bark all day, cats who mess in public halls, and so on. Even if all their complaints were true, and in isolated cases they may be, the no-pet clauses represent a priori judgments about pet owners.

The assumption is that your pet is automatically and surely going to deface property and offend others. The no-pet clause acts to punish the many for the crimes of the few.

The flaw in this argument is that every standard lease or house rules, in addressing such matters as noise or nuisance or other disturbances, gives all the power necessary, without a no-pet clause, to deal with residents whose pets truly do cause problems. A no-pet clause is not needed for such purposes. The nuisance clause in leases and house rules, and the nuisance laws in every community, assure landlords and co-op or condo boards of the legal means to force residents to control their pets or give them up.

So why, then, the no-pet clause? For one thing, it saves dealing with residents on an individual basis. If nobody is allowed to have a pet, that's one less potential hassle for the landlord or board. Some buildings prohibit families with children for the same reason.

If there is a no-pet clause that is not enforced, it serves as a weapon for landlords and building managers to use to intimidate tenants and keep down complaints, even to punish tenants who demand their rights. If a pet owner has a lease with a no-pet clause that has not been enforced, that tenant is going to think twice before asking for more heat, secure locks, clean hallways, or repairs.

Since city landlords can usually increase the rent every time an apartment is vacated, it is very tempting for them to use every means at their disposal to empty apartments, especially in buildings with limitations on the legal rents.

Some co-op and condo boards allow people who own their apartments to have pets, but deny the right to renters of apartments in the building. The argument offered is that renters care less about the building and would therefore be likely to have a nuisance pet. There is no recorded evidence of this. My careful observation over many years as a city pet owner is that some people are good neighbors and responsible pet owners while some are not, and whether they own or rent is irrelevant.

How to Avoid or Change a No-Pet Clause

Other than by finding one of the comparatively few buildings where pets are permitted, are there ways to avoid a no-pet clause? In rare instances, yes.

Sometimes you can persuade a landlord, board, or building agent to strike the clause from the lease or whatever legal document you are about to sign. This might be possible if you are dealing with friendly and reasonable people, and if you can convince all concerned that you are a responsible pet owner. Perhaps you can provide a letter of recommendation from your previous landlord or board, or neighbors. You might offer to introduce a prospective landlord or board to your pets so everyone can see how quiet and well-behaved they are.

A course of action that's even more likely to work is to offer to pay a security deposit, or even a small monthly fee, in exchange for permission to keep your pets.

If the situation looks promising, it's safest to ask, tactfully, to have such a waiver in writing, especially if you have a dog or dogs. Be extra polite about this, because you don't want to give the impression of being a troublemaker, but if the board or the ownership of the building should change, you might need some proof other than your word that you have permission to have pets. Oral permission is no protection for you, even if there are other pets in the building. Unless a local law says otherwise, a no-pet rule can generally be enforced or not enforced by landlords or boards at will.

The Humane Society of the United States has published a packet of guidelines on the subject of pets in rental housing that includes strategies to help responsible pet owners persuade landlords to change "no-pet" policies (PM 2204, $3, from HSUS, 2100 L St. NW, Washington, D.C. 20037).

It's never advisable to move into a place with a no-pet rule and then smuggle in your pet, or secretly acquire one later. Landlords and boards, like the rest of us, don't like to be deceived and are apt to take revenge against a resident who has lied. It's better to be up-front in your dealings.

If a building you are living in with your pets suddenly decides to prohibit them, a grandfather rule may allow you to keep the ones you have but not to replace them. To head off a no-pet decision, you might do well to take the initiative in trying to persuade the landlord or board to establish firm rules in the building. You could suggest that pet owners be required to keep their pets leashed at all times in the public halls, and to take them out via the freight elevator. You might even suggest a rule that dogs be obedience-trained. Find out if there are specific objections to pets and think of requirements that would address those complaints. It is difficult to get a fair and creative idea put into action where real estate is concerned, but worth the effort.

However, if you are actually threatened with eviction, don't quickly give away your animals or surrender them to the local shelter without exploring your rights. Consider hiring legal counsel. Sometimes a prohibition against your pets can be reversed (see below).

How to Fight a No-Pet Clause

Some pet owners, when faced with eviction from their homes unless they give up their pets, have consulted attorneys and won the right to keep them. It's very important to hire an attorney who has knowledge of no-pet clause litigation—most lawyers have had no experience in this area and are not even aware of the ways and means of defending such cases. However, there is a national organization of lawyers interested in protecting animal rights, and tangentially the rights of pet owners: the Animal Legal Defense Fund (127 Fourth Street, Petaluma, CA 94952; 707/769-7771; Internet: www. aldf.org). This organization can advise you or furnish you with information packets on disputes regarding companion animals, or it can help you find an attorney who is familiar with animal law.

Sometimes there are local laws that protect pet owners. In New York City, for example, no-pet clauses in rental leases were only minimally and selectively enforced by landlords until the real crunch in housing came in the 1970s. (At that time, most city housing was rental rather than co-op or condo.) It became a practice to use the no-pet clause as a means to empty apartments and put them on the market. An overzealous real estate community began to stir up a sluggish market by invoking the no-pet clause, knowing that those people who could would move before they gave up their pets, thereby making their apartments available.

People who had lived openly with their pets for years, pets about whom there had never been any complaints, were suddenly facing eviction unless they gave them up. In many pathetic instances, elderly men and women whose pets were their sole companions were told to get rid of them or move. But move where? They had no place to go, no affordable housing available to them where they could keep their pets.

Tearfully, some of the pet owners began to seek advice from the few attorneys sympathetic to such cases. Some lawyers went to court and argued that their clients needed their pets for physical or emotional reasons, and offered doctors' letters to support it. When enough of these cases were brought to the attention of city lawmakers, hearings were held before the New York City Council. The members became convinced that in reality, many eviction orders had nothing to do with problem pets. The no-pet clauses were being used simply to empty rental apartments.

So, to the intense relief of the city's pet owners, a law was passed—over the real estate community's howls of protest—stating that tenants who had lived openly with their pets for three or more months without complaints could not be forced to give them up, even with a no-pet clause in their leases.

This local law does not challenge the basic premise of a no-pet clause, nor is it any help to pet owners moving into a new building with a lease that forbids pets, or to people who wish to acquire a pet.

Duncan, a pit bull, has never heard that he's supposed to be vicious

It does not help people buying co-ops or condominiums in buildings with no-pet regulations. But it does give some protection to people living in New York City rental housing with existing pets.

In 1983, the U.S. Congress passed bills stating that senior citizens living in or moving into certain types of housing that receive federal subsidy cannot be denied the right to keep pets. This is now technically the law of the land. If you or someone you know needs information about senior citizens' housing and pets, contact the Animal Legal Defense Fund.

Even those of us who are not needful of subsidized housing have a stake in this. Any law that protects the right to own pets recognizes the principle that companion animals are an intrinsic part of human well-being.

Every city pet owner should be aware of, and support, any pending legislation that would limit or abolish the restrictions on responsible pet ownership. You can find out whether any such legislation has been introduced in your city or state by calling your representatives in the city government or state capital.

If there are no such bills, form a committee of fellow pet owners and sympathizers and try to get your lawmakers to sponsor some. Politicians will listen—even if they aren't pet owners themselves, they are aware that animal lovers are a large, often passionate, and important group.

Michelle A. Rivera has written in her book *Hospice Hounds: Animals and Healing at the Borders of Death*, "We don't stand by and allow bias against race, religion, age, sex, or cultural differences, yet we allow bias against our best friends....They deserve to be protected against unfairness just like anyone else. But it is the guardians who must make it so."

As urban dog owners, we have our work cut out for us. First, we have to be unfailingly considerate and law-abiding pet owners ourselves and encourage others to be so, too. Then, we have to change the laws to make it easier for people to have dogs in the city.

ANTICRUELTY LAWS

No discussion of the laws that affect companion animals should omit mention of those that give them some protection against abuse. There have always been some laws to protect some animals from abuse, but they have been largely ignored. Monstrous cruelty to animals—dogs, cats, horses, farm animals, zoo animals, wildlife—was until quite recently public and pandemic, and we have heard about the way animals are still treated in laboratories and slaughterhouses. But public attitudes are gradually changing, and with this consciousness come new and amended laws and more vigorous enforcement of laws already in place. You don't have to feel helpless when you see an animal being abused. All dog owners—in fact, everyone who loves dogs or even cares about justice—should be aware that laws against cruelty to animals exist in every state, and we can use these laws in helping to put a stop to it.

It is impossible to care about animals and not feel a surge of sickening rage at the sight of a neglected or beaten pet. Yet, few people are aware that they can do anything about it. Cases of neglect can sometimes be solved if you speak to the animal owner in a friendly way and point out what he or she is doing that's harmful. But you may be met with just a shrug, and in some cases you may be taking a risk, because people who abuse animals are often violent toward other people as well. Another problem is that the authorities treat cases of animal abuse as a relatively low-priority matter.

Nevertheless, laws are on the books, and the extent to which they will be enforced depends largely on how much the public cares. Lawmakers, district attorneys, animal control officers, SPCAs, and even the police are responsive to pressure from citizens. While anti-cruelty laws are not very stringent, at least we can see that those we do have are enforced and violators punished.

Cruelty to animals is defined two ways: active cruelty, such as beating, shooting, or torturing; and passive cruelty, such as failing to provide proper shelter, medical care, or food. Both are crimes in every state. Even if a person is unintentionally harming an animal, he or she is still generally considered to be breaking the law and can be stopped. This applies especially to "collectors," those kind but unbalanced folks who harbor large numbers of pets in squalid conditions.

A person neglecting or abusing an animal may be warned, or taken to court and fined, and in very rare cases imprisoned. If the neglect or abuse is extreme, the animal may be confiscated by the authorities.

If you know of a case of cruelty, don't hesitate to report it. Where to report it varies from one locality to another, but start with the police. If cruelty investigation is not within their jurisdiction, they will tell you whom to call. That may be the animal control agency, humane society, SPCA, or other animal protection society.

If possible, back up your cruelty complaint with some other complaint, especially one concerning property, which seems to be more sacred in some quarters than animals. For instance, if you know of a dog that is chained up all day and night and barks or whines, add the noise complaint to your objections to the cruelty. Or, if you hear a dog screaming because it is being beaten, insist that the noise bothers you when you register your objection to the treatment of the animal. If someone's half-starved dog gets into your garbage, don't tell the authorities only that the dog is ill fed, but add that it tips over your garbage cans or treads on your flower beds. The object is to help the dog, so use everything you can think of to get the attention of the authorities.

When you make a complaint, give as much accurate, specific information as possible: the name and address of the person abusing the dog, the date the abuse took place (or time period if it's a long-term abuse such as starvation or failure to provide adequate shelter or medical care), description of the animal, the type of object used to cause harm, the license number if a vehicle was involved, the names and addresses of other possible witnesses, and your name, address, and phone number (which will be kept confidential if you request it). Many well-supported urban humane societies or animal control agencies will willingly prosecute cases of animal abuse, and often win, but they do need accurate input from you if you are the instigator of the report.

Once you've made the report, don't just sit back and assume everything will be taken care of. Follow up to see what has been done. If the appropriate agency has failed to act, report this to your district attorney's office. Be pleasant but firm; insist that the situation be corrected.

Don't hesitate to tell the news desk of your local newspapers and TV stations, especially if the law enforcement agency seems to be dragging its feet. The media will usually welcome animal stories, and often the light of publicity—or the threat of it—will inspire authorities to act.

It is always a good idea to join your local humane society, SPCA, or other animal protection society, just on general principles. Then, if you ever do have to report a case of animal cruelty to this agency, you might be more likely to get fast action if you're a member or, even better, an active member. These organizations not only care about the welfare of animals, but depend on the good will of their membership.

12. TRAVEL

Taking or Leaving Your Dog

As a city person, you probably put opportunities to escape fairly high on your list of leisure-time priorities. If you lack your own weekend retreat, you treasure the invitations to those of your friends, or you manage trips to your favorite vacation spots whenever you can. Perhaps you travel on business. And possibly you are contemplating moving to another part of the country.

Where does your dog figure in these plans? In this chapter, the different modes of travel will be examined in terms of taking your pet along. Unfortunately, you're pretty much limited to driving or flying, because most rail lines (such as Amtrak) and bus lines (Greyhound, Trailways) won't allow pets on board at all. Some other train or bus lines may allow small dogs in carriers. Inquire well ahead of time, but don't be disappointed if you're told, "No pets."

For those times when your pet can't go with you, you'll need alternatives for its care while you're away, which will also be explored in this chapter.

BASIC TRAVEL TIPS

Here are a few suggestions that apply no matter how your dog is traveling or what the destination.

A health checkup beforehand is in order, including a heartworm test. A pet that is not in the pink of health shouldn't travel at all, but should wait until it's well.

All immunizations, including rabies, should be up to date. Ask your veterinarian to furnish you with a certificate stating that your dog has had these shots, and take it with you on the trip. If you're flying, be aware that individual airlines have their own health certificate requirements, as do the states or nations you plan to visit, so you'll need to research those well in advance.

Remember to take a supply of any medication your pet needs regularly, enough for the duration. It's also a good idea to take a bottle of Pectolin or Kaopectate, in case it gets an upset stomach.

If your dog is highly nervous or timid, tranquilizers may make it more comfortable. A veterinarian who knows the animal well can advise you. For most dogs, they should not be necessary.

Take familiar things from home, such as your pet's blanket, favorite toys, food, and water dishes.

If you're traveling by air, try to book your flight at mid-week, when traffic in the airport is relatively light.

One thing that is of no use when you are away from home with your pet is, obviously, an identification tag with your home address and telephone number on it. Put a new identification tag on your dog's collar giving the address and phone where you are staying. Of course, that won't help you when you're en route, so have your dog wear a tag on its collar giving the phone number of a trusted, non-traveling friend who has agreed beforehand to take collect phone calls. The tag should read, "Please call collect (area code and number)." Then, if you should lose your dog, alert the friend and keep in continual touch while you're searching the area where it disappeared. Your pet may be lucky enough to be picked up by someone who will contact your friend and leave a name and location where you can reclaim it.

TRAVELING BY CAR

Once, when I was a teenager, I was driving my father's car with my dog Laddie in the back seat. He was looking out the open window and, as it turned out, he was also leaning out. I turned a corner, and out the window he went into the street. Fortunately, I noticed immediately and stopped for him, and he escaped being hit by another car or hurt by the fall, but it was certainly a close shave and I've never forgotten it.

Now that I'm much older and wiser, I know that Laddie shouldn't even have been permitted to ride with his head out the window in the first place—people let their dogs do this all the time, with many resulting eye injuries from dust or cinders or from windburn.

In fact, it was not wise for me to let Laddie ride unconfined in the car with nobody to supervise him. Today, I would put him in a car seat or portable kennel. Well-stocked pet supply stores sell protective devices for traveling pets. If you have a small dog, it might be best to have your pet ride in its carrier. But if the trip will be long, the carrier should be big enough to allow the dog to stand up and to lie down full length.

One of the most thoughtless and dangerous things to do is to have a dog rattling around loose in the back of a pickup truck. I'm sure you've seen dogs riding this way, struggling to keep on their feet or whipped by the wind as they lean over the side. Even if the animal doesn't fall out, it is thrown about and can be injured.

You'd have to be insane to make a dog ride in the trunk, but people have done that, too. A dog can die from heat prostration, asphyxiation, or dehydration, and at the very least can be injured from jolting about.

Don't feed your dog for at least six hours before departure, and unless the weather is hot, withhold water for a couple of hours. Then walk the animal before you leave, and at several stops along the way—always, repeat, *always* on the leash. If it's an all-day trip, the dog should be given water after each walk en route. But never put

Travels of
Trowser

New York

Santa Fe

New Orleans

Boston

Chicago

Washington, D.C.

Photographs by Jonathan Pearl

food or water in the carrier or portable kennel while traveling—it will just spill and make a mess, and no dog should have to sit or lie in that.

Please reread everything I said in Chapter 7 about the dangers of leaving a dog locked in a parked car. Naturally, when you're on the road for any length of time, you have to stop to eat, stretch your legs, go to the bathroom. If you're traveling with another person, one of you should stay with the dog while the other goes in to have a meal or to pick up food. Other options are picnics and drive-ins. If you're driving alone with your dog and have to make a very brief stop, take the dog with you, even into the rest room.

Bear in mind that the greenhouse effect of an overheated car is not the only risk you take in leaving your dog alone—it can be stolen. As you know, there is no such thing as a car that can't be broken into, and dognappers are everywhere. I once met a couple who had left their Poodle locked in their car at night while they went into a restaurant for dinner and found it missing when they returned. Your dog may be a seasoned traveler and enjoy riding in the car with you, but be sure to protect it against heat exhaustion and theft.

Careful planning is essential for overnight trips if you'll be stopping at motels or inns, because you'll need to know in advance whether they accept pets. When you're a guest, keep your dog always leashed except in the room, and if you must leave it alone in the room, keep it in its carrier or portable kennel. And listen outside the door to see if it starts to bark, because if it does, you can't leave it alone.

The best advice I can give anyone planning a motor trip with a pet is to check out *Pets Welcome*, a series of softcover books that list, according to region, inns and motels that accept pets. (These can be ordered through The Humane Catalog for $17 each: 1-800-486-2630; Internet: www.thehumanecatalog.com.)

Some campgrounds permit dogs, if they are kept leashed, but you'll want to find out in advance. The leash law protects dogs from getting lost or injured, or from possibly getting bitten by a wild animal or snake. City dogs do not necessarily take to the wilderness—

and remember that not all dogs are swimmers or even like to go into water.

And here's an extra word of caution: Stay out of the woods during hunting season. Hunting is allowed in all state parks, all national forests, all national parks and, ironically, in most wildlife refuges. Thanks to pro-hunting groups and their powerful lobby, and the silence or lack of awareness of voters on the subject, the number of public lands on which hunting is allowed increases every year. Also, hunters often cross onto private, posted land. Hunting seasons vary from place to place, so find out before you and your pet go traipsing around the countryside, or you could both get shot.

Your dog could also get caught in a trap in places where trapping is allowed—that is, most state parks, all national forests, etc. It is a relatively common occurrence in rural and wilderness areas for unsupervised dogs and cats to lose their legs, or their lives, in traps. City people are the ones most likely to be unaware of hunting and trapping dangers.

TRAVELING BY AIR

The rules and regulations for taking a dog with you on a flight vary considerably.

Let's start with the assumption that you have a small dog and want to take it in the cabin with you on a domestic flight. Forget it, say some airlines; all dogs must go in the cargo hold. But most airlines will allow one or two dogs per cabin—usually one in first class, one in tourist—provided the animals are in sturdy carriers that fit under the seat. If you have a choice of several airlines, shop around first to find out which ones offer the best service in regard to pets.

Don't forget to ask what is required in the way of health certificates for your dog, whether it's going in the cabin with you or in the cargo hold. Also ask about the type of carrier; some airlines have definite regulations, and very few will allow you to use your dog's own carrying case.

You have to make a reservation for your dog at the same time that you make your own, and pay for it, usually at the excess baggage rate. Don't be surprised if there's some screw-up and you arrive at the airport to find they have no record of your dog's reservation. It's a good idea to get to the airport well ahead of time.

At the airport, keep your pet in its carrier. I once saw a frightened little Poodle leap from its owner's arms in a busy airport and flee into the crowd. Fortunately, a quick-thinking bystander intercepted it before it got lost or into trouble. But you might not be so lucky and might never see your dog again.

By the way, your dog doesn't have to go through the x-ray at the gate.

Whatever the rules and regulations, much that applies to traveling with a pet in the cabin seems to depend on the attitudes of the airline personnel on duty at the time you and your pet are flying. For instance, whether or not you can take your pet out and hold it in your lap during the flight may depend on whether the flight attendants, and the passengers near you, like dogs. In any case, it's supposed to stay in its carrier when food is being served.

However, if you have a big dog that won't fit in an under-seat carrier, then the poor animal is relegated to the cargo hold. It must travel in a crate large enough for it to stand up and lie down comfortably in. Some airlines require very specific types of crates. The airline you'll be traveling on will instruct you about the crate and how it should be labeled.

Seems to me a short-haired dog might be uncomfortable on a long flight, because while cargo holds are pressurized, they're not heated, and the air can get awfully cold up in the clouds, even when it's summer on the ground. Nevertheless, dogs do seem to survive in the cargo hold.

Always try to book a direct flight, if possible. But if you must change planes, or if there's a layover or delay along the way, don't assume that your dog will make the connection safely or, for that matter, be comfortable in the cargo hold for very long in hot weather. A few years ago there were occasional horror stories of dogs that died in their crates, which had been unloaded from the planes but left on baggage carts on the airfields in broiling sun and hundred-degree temperatures. For that reason, some airlines serving hot cities will now only fly pets at night.

If you find you're going to be delayed in an airport after your pet has already disappeared behind the scenes along with your luggage, go to the airline desk and ask for your dog so you can keep it with you until loading time. Be polite but firm. Airline employees are busy, but if you make clear your concerns, you can often get their cooperation.

Don't get on the plane until you're sure your pet is being loaded. You don't want to arrive at your destination to discover that the dog was bumped or forgotten. There are no tried-and-true procedures to pass on to you; all I can advise is that you be on top of each situation as it arises and not take anything for granted.

For overseas flights, the airline regulations regarding dogs vary from one airline to the next, and the type of health certificates it will need depends on the country of destination. Some countries also require import permits, visas, and the like. And even before you start to think about those, find out whether or not the place you're flying to will put your dog in quarantine.

Britain's former six-month quarantine law is presently being evaluated and new regulations tested, which may or may not apply to pets entering from the U.S. Check with the consulate or tourist bureau. If you're going to continental Europe, however, I've heard that once you get there, it is in some ways easier to travel with a dog than it is in the United States. Many Europeans travel with their pets, apparently, and railroads and hotels in many European countries are much more lenient than they are here. Check with the consulates and tourist bureaus.

Don't feed your dog for six hours before a flight, and withhold water for about two hours. Walk it as close to departure time as possible. Whether or not you should sedate it depends on its temperament and your veterinarian's advice.

MOVING

Although it's not always possible or advisable to take the dog along on a visit or vacation, taking it when you move is not even debatable. Ask the staff at any animal shelter anywhere in the country what reasons are most frequently given by people surrendering pets. Right up there among the top five is "moving." This excuse is offered as though it were so perfectly understandable that no further explanation is necessary. It's a mystery to me how anyone can abandon a pet, especially for no other reason than the perceived inconvenience of taking it along. I think leaving a pet behind is despicable.

The subject of moving with pets reminds me of my friends Gretchen and Leo Scanlan, lifelong pet owners who naturally took their ten dogs and cats with them when they moved across the country. Because they had so many animals, the most practical thing for them to do was to rent a mobile home for the journey. They planned and plotted the trip carefully, allowing eight days, with stops at campgrounds that they knew permitted pets. They kept their dogs leashed and walked them frequently. Since cats of course are known to be great escape artists, the Scanlans had their six travel in safari cages, two compatible cats per cage, with litter boxes and bedding in each. The entire family made the trip in comfort, with no problems.

People who really care about their pets can work out a way to take them when they move and won't feel inconvenienced or put upon for doing it.

Be prepared to find that most dogs—and even cats—get very upset at the sight of packing cartons and the dismantling of their familiar home. A pet has no idea what is going on and may display anxiety symptoms such as breaking house-training, barking when left alone, or other undesirable traits, even if it has never done so before in its life. Once, when I was getting ready to move, Dandy took to chewing up books and sofa cushions whenever she was left alone. I had to stash her in a local kennel for day care while I was out of the house at my office. As soon as we were ensconced in the new apartment, she settled down and was herself again.

It helps if a dog can be taken to visit its new home as often as possible before moving day. Then the new place won't seem so strange.

A highly territorial dog may take offense at movers who come in to carry out the furniture and household belongings. This type of dog should certainly be parked with a friend or put in a kennel on moving day.

LEAVING A PET WHILE YOU TRAVEL

There are many different types of arrangements you can make for your dog when it can't travel with you, but far and away the best solution is to leave the pet in its own home with a trusted live-in sitter whom it knows and likes. You might know someone who will sit for you out of friendship, but if you have to ask him or her frequently, I think it's better to have a business arrangement. When you pay someone for this valuable service, you feel freer to ask for it when you need it.

Or, if the person you use as sitter also has a pet that your dog likes well enough to live with temporarily, you can have the live-in arrangement on a reciprocal basis. In exchange for sitting with your dog, he or she can count on you and your dog to do the same.

If you have more than one pet, they can be left at home for periods of a few days without a live-in sitter, just as long as someone comes in three times a day to walk, feed, and keep an eye on them. There are people in most cities who offer this service for hire, but this is also a situation in which a reciprocal arrangement works well, especially among people who live in the same apartment building. Several of my neighbors and I dog-walk and pet-feed for one another on a short-term basis.

I do feel sorry for single dogs left alone, even for just a weekend. The nights and days without their owners can seem awfully long to

Susannah has convinced houseguest/pet sitter Jillian that she's allowed on the bed

them. If you have no other pets and are not having a live-in sitter, ask the person who will be coming in to walk and feed your dog if he or she will spend a little time just keeping the animal company.

By the way, if you have a very territorial dog, be sure it has a chance to get to know the sitter before you leave. Otherwise, your pet might not let the person in the door when he or she comes to take care of it.

Another possibility to consider is leaving your dog in someone else's home. If the person with whom you leave your pet is someone you know and trust, and your dog is comfortable in his or her home, that can be almost as satisfactory as having a sitter in your house. In my neighborhood, there's Josephine, who boards dogs in her house. Her canine clients seem to regard Josephine's as Dog Paradise.

However, if there's nobody like that whom you could ask, there are people who advertise, in newspapers or on the bulletin boards of veterinarians' offices, that they will board pets in their homes. These can be just fine, or they may be risky. Visit several of them and check them out. Ask for references and follow up. Ask if there will be other pets in addition to yours, and if so, how many and what kind. Find out if the person's standards and attitudes about dog care are like your own. If the person is fussy about health and wants proof that your dog's vaccinations are in order, that's a good sign.

If all else fails, there are always boarding kennels. I regard them as a last resort not because they are automatically bad places but because I think a dog that lives as a house pet will be unhappy in a kennel, even if the place resembles the Versailles Palace. However, if you do kennel your dog, choose carefully. Try to pick one that your trustworthy, dog-owning friends have used and approve of, or that your veterinarian recommends.

If you don't have any word-of-mouth recommendations and must pick from the Yellow Pages, see if your city has a Better Business Bureau. Such an organization might know if there have been any complaints lodged against any of the kennels listed.

Before you make a final decision, visit the kennel you are considering and check it out for cleanliness, upkeep, ventilation, safety, the attitude of the staff, and the behavior of the dogs that are being boarded when you visit. The sleeping and exercise areas should be of suitable size, with high, strong fences between the runs. At one boarding kennel I heard of, a Cocker Spaniel was killed by two pit bull terriers in the run next to hers. The pit bulls, the breed commonly used in dogfighting, leaped over a six-foot fence to get her. Check the security of the kennel from the outside, also. Although it's unlikely, there's always the possibility that someone might try to vandalize a kennel, including the dogs in it.

Make a reservation well in advance, particularly if you're going to be leaving your dog over a holiday. Some kennels have pick-up and delivery service. When you make your reservation, ask what health certificates are required. Let the kennel know what medication or special food your dog needs, if any. Give the kennel the name and phone number of your veterinarian, and find out what veterinarians the kennel uses in an emergency. Leave your itinerary or a number where you can be reached if necessary and the name and number of a non-traveling friend who could be contacted if an emergency arose in which you couldn't be reached.

It might be wise to leave your dog for one or two short stays in a kennel before you leave it for a long time, especially if it is an only pet and extremely attached to you. Have it spend a weekend or two there before you take off for a two- or three-week period. Take its bed from home and a few favorite toys.

When you drop your dog off at the kennel or turn it over to the person picking it up, be cheerful and relaxed. Don't pass any anxiety or regrets you might have on to your dog—that will only make the separation from you hard for the animal.

There's a useful booklet called *How To Select a Boarding Kennel* that's available for $5.25 from the American Boarding Kennels Association (1702 Pikes Peak Ave., Colorado Springs, CO 80909, 719/667-1600; Internet: www.abka.com; Email: info@abka.com).

13. THE GERIATRIC DOG

Caring for Your Elderly Pet

W hen is a dog old? Despite its popularity, the belief that each year of a dog's age corresponds to seven human years is, as I have said, inaccurate. A one-year-old dog is sexually mature, comparable to a human adolescent. A two-year-old dog is more like a person in his or her mid-twenties. After that, the comparison gap narrows considerably, and you might estimate that a dog's year equals four human years. But, as I pointed out earlier, there's a big difference in the life expectancies of dogs, depending on breed and size.

Giant breeds are lucky to live to eight or nine, big dogs may live to ten or twelve, medium-sized breeds even longer, and little dogs may live to see their seventeenth or eighteenth birthdays. Mixed breeds of course reflect the life expectancies of their parents and ancestors. If a dog comes from a long line of mixed breeds, then you can guess its life span will probably depend on whether it is huge, big, medium-sized, or little.

Therefore, a Great Dane or St. Bernard qualifies as a geriatric dog at about six; a German Shepherd or Labrador Retriever will usually begin to show signs of aging at eight or nine; a dog weighing thirty to perhaps sixty pounds will be entering old age by ten; but a little Poodle or Yorkie won't be considered geriatric until around twelve or older.

These estimates are only rules of thumb. Obviously, a great deal depends on the care a dog gets, its health, and its individual heredity. Among your own canine acquaintances, there are sure to be exceptions both ways. You probably know dogs that are old before their time, as well as those that defy the averages in longevity.

If you are the owner of a geriatric dog, you deserve congratulations and respect, because it indicates that you have given loving care to your pet for many years. The fact is that the lives of most pet animals, dogs and cats alike, are terminated long before they reach old age—through neglect, abuse, or some other form of human intervention. Dogs that are allowed to run loose, dogs that are chained year-round to doghouses in the yard, dogs whose owners are slow to notice signs of illness or injury, and dogs that are abandoned are among those that don't live long enough to grow old.

However, better knowledge of canine health care among dog owners in general, in addition to increased sophistication in small animal veterinary medicine, has given rise to a new class of dog—the geriatric. And city dogs, for all the reasons discussed in the chapters on health and safety tend, on average, to outlive others.

As a dog grows old, the first signs of aging are usually rather subtle—a little gray around the muzzle, a cloudiness of the eyes, slowness of pace, stiffness in the joints, perhaps increased thirst. Unless the animal falls victim to one of the more serious illnesses related to aging, the process is probably gradual, just as it is with people. The changes occur both in physical ability and in personality.

An elderly dog is not only susceptible to the disorders of aging but, if it contracts any of the regular canine diseases, it will probably be affected more severely than a younger dog. Even in good health, it should have regular checkups by a veterinarian every six months. And of course if it does become ill, it needs very close medical monitoring.

SIGHT, HEARING, AND SMELL

Cloudiness of the eyes is not necessarily cataracts (opacity of the lenses) but a normal condition in old dogs and does not interfere with vision. However, dogs do sometimes get cataracts and gradually go blind. Dogs seem to cope better with blindness than human beings do—they don't read, watch television, paint, sew, drive cars, do carpentry work, look at scenery, or go to the movies, for instance, so perhaps they don't feel they're missing as much as people naturally do. Also, of course, they rely a great deal on their sense of smell, so blindness is not as disabling, especially if it occurs gradually. If a visually handicapped dog is kept in familiar surroundings and given a lot of protection and love, it can adjust quite well.

Some dogs develop a slight discharge from the eyes. If your veterinarian finds nothing that requires treatment, just wipe around your dog's eyes gently every day with clean facial tissue or cotton moistened with a little warm water.

Hearing loss is almost inevitable, and for that reason you might want to start teaching your pet hand signals around middle age. And because sight loss may follow, make the signals broad and sweeping enough for the dog to see easily. Instead of just a beckon of the hand for "Come," for example, make a circle toward yourself with your whole arm.

Another way to get the dog's attention is to stamp on the floor. The animal will feel the vibrations of the floorboards.

Partial deafness can disorient a dog—it may vaguely hear a noise, such as a siren on the street, or someone calling its name, but can't tell where the sound is coming from. Now more than ever, you must protect your dog by always keeping it leashed. You may have a very well obedience-trained dog and have always counted on it to obey, but as the dog ages, its deafness could go unnoticed until one day you give it a command on the street that is necessary for its safety and it won't be able to hear you.

A dog's sense of smell seems to be the last to go, but it can happen, and the only problem this might present is that the animal may

Patricia Curtis

Fifteen-year-old Sally wore her sweater in cold weather

lose its appetite as a result. Then you'll want to coax it with favorite foods and hand-feed it if necessary.

TEMPERATURE SENSITIVITY AND EXERCISE NEEDS

An elderly dog might feel the cold more than it did when younger. Even if your pet has long, thick fur and has never worn a coat or sweater, now may be the time to get it one. In very cold weather, a geriatric dog should have protection if it's going to be out any longer than ten minutes.

I'm assuming your city dog has never had to sleep outdoors anyway, so I don't have to tell you that an elderly dog should not, even if it has had to do so all its life. If it sleeps in your room at night and you like your windows open year-round, put a blanket over your short-haired dog or have it sleep in its sweater on very cold nights. Be sure its bed is away from drafts, and—equally important—not too close to a hot radiator, either.

Be sure to dry your dog more thoroughly than ever after a bath. Use a hair dryer if your pet will tolerate it—only don't direct it too long on one spot, because that can cause dry skin. And on a cool or a cold day, wait several hours after a bath before taking the dog outdoors.

An old dog's coat is very susceptible to dry weather, hot or cold, and needs regular, frequent brushing. An overheated house or apartment can dry out the coat of any dog, but as a dog ages, its coat needs your attention even more. If its coat is very dry and flaky, or if your dog seems itchy, talk to your veterinarian about a fatty acid supplement in its diet.

I wouldn't take an old dog out in extremely hot weather at all, except to the curb and back, and then only in the early morning, evening, and night. As I've said, city sidewalks reflect too much heat; an animal close to the ground gets a blast like an open furnace in its face.

An elderly dog should get regular exercise, however, and should not be allowed to lie around all the time. Take it for shorter, slower walks than you did formerly. Let the animal set its own pace. Play quiet indoor games that give it exercise, such as fetching a ball rolled across the floor.

Most dogs like to be where their owners are, so if your aging pet follows you from room to room, encourage it. But it may stumble going up and down stairs and need help. It's not unusual for an old dog to attempt gymnastics that it used to do with ease and fall flat on its face. You want to protect it from overdoing or from actually hurting itself. After Sally fell down a flight of stairs to the loft in my apartment, where I work, I had to prevent her from coming up there with me.

EATING AND DRINKING CHANGES

The best diet for an older dog is outlined in Chapter 5, but I want to caution you again about abrupt changes in the food you feed it. If the store is out of the brand of canned or dry food that you normally give your dog, and you have to buy another, phase it in slowly. An aging dog may have trouble digesting a food that is even only slightly different from what it is used to.

Also, I think giving an old dog two or three small meals a day instead of one big one is a very good idea. That way you never overload its food-processing system.

Your aging pet may very likely drink more water. The line between a normal increase in drinking water and the excessive thirst that signals trouble is a fine one. Many old dogs' kidneys function perfectly well throughout their lives. But you should report increased water consumption to your veterinarian, who will probably want to run a urinalysis and blood test to determine kidney function (see below). If there is real impairment in kidney function, the dog should be put on a prescription diet.

Naturally, increased water consumption will most likely mean the dog has to urinate more frequently. Do not under any circumstances cut back on its water supply in an effort to prevent this. A dog of any age should have access to fresh drinking water at all times. However, if your veterinarian approves, you might try salt-free dog foods (canned and dry), because they may reduce excessive thirst and drinking and lower the dog's urge to urinate.

If you regularly put in long days away from home, it might be a good idea to hire someone to come in to walk your dog, just as with a puppy. However, you can also train an older dog to use newspapers, in addition to going out. When she grew old, Dandy used to try to use the cats' litterbox in emergencies, so I adopted the practice of keeping a layer of papers on the floor next to the box, and if she had to go when I couldn't get her out, she used them. If you have cats, you might try putting newspapers by their box—your dog might get the idea.

Otherwise, put papers in a spot where the dog has made a puddle before, or in some other place you think might inspire the right response. Take some papers with you when you walk the dog, get them a little wet, and put the wet papers with the dog's urine smell on top of a clean layer in the place you want to train the dog to go.

Some very aged dogs become incontinent, unable to control their functions at all. They may urinate in their sleep and wake up in a puddle. If your pet has this problem, try lining its bed with extra-large disposable diapers at night, or put a layer of newspapers on the floor or rug where it likes to sleep. Consult your veterinarian about possible medical treatment for urinary incontinence.

Caring for an elderly dog can require considerable inventiveness and patience. Never reproach or punish it for relieving itself in the house. The dog can't help it and is embarrassed enough as it is.

If you live in an apartment building, you may find that once you have the leash on and are headed for the street, your geriatric animal gets excited, can't wait, and has accidents in the hallway, elevator, or lobby. If so, you might buy one of those belts designed for unspayed, menstruating female dogs, and use it to hold a disposable diaper in place on your dog. Have the dog wear it just to get through the building. Then you can remove it at the curb, throw it away if wet, and walk the dog normally. One creative dog owner I know fitted her geriatric pet with a pair of little boy's jockey shorts, worn backward, tail through the flap, and lined it with a disposable diaper.

You may find your geriatric dog becoming constipated. As I mentioned in Chapter 6, you want to distinguish between intestinal obstruction and occasional constipation. An intestinal obstruction, which is life-threatening, will cause the dog to strain in obvious discomfort, to vomit, and to stop eating. Constipation is characterized by hard or inadequate stools. If your dog occasionally needs a laxative, give it a little milk, a teaspoon of milk of magnesia, or a teaspoon or two, depending on the dog's size, of mineral oil. (Caution: Because mineral oil is easily aspirated, don't pour it down the dog's throat, but mix it in the food.) But the dog should see a veterinarian if the constipation persists, because that might be a symptom of a serious problem, such as a tumor.

DISORDERS OF AGING

An elderly dog can get virtually all the same disorders that were discussed in Chapter 6, but some are more likely to occur in old age and deserve repeating here. I have also added a few that are rare in younger dogs but quite common in seniors. Don't forget to schedule regular twice-yearly veterinary checkups, even if your pet has no overt symptoms of illness.

Arthritis. Just like old people, dogs can develop arthritis, particularly in the hip, shoulder, and knee. The dog will be stiff and lame, with weakness and trembling, and the affected limbs may be misshapen. Stiffness is especially bad in the morning. A dog that had hip dysplasia or patellar luxation when it was young is especially susceptible to arthritis.

Once when Sally was very old I came home from an errand and found her trapped under a chair, whimpering. She had crawled under for some reason and then couldn't bend her stiff legs enough to wiggle out.

Aspirin can help, but your veterinarian should prescribe the dosage. There are also stronger medications for dogs suffering a lot of pain, and natural remedies such as glucosamine/chondroitin mixtures.

By the way, if while reading this book it occurs to you that a bit of aspirin or Tylenol might also help your elderly arthritic cat, don't try it without close veterinary supervision. For some reason, cats are much more susceptible than dogs to aspirin overdose, and a cat could die from a dosage that's appropriate for a dog of the same weight. And never give a cat Tylenol.

Kidney disease. Be on the lookout for this in an older dog, since it is not unusual for kidney function to decline markedly just from the aging process. An old dog that is severely stressed by anxiety or trauma can develop kidney disease quite rapidly. If your dog begins drinking excessive amounts of water and urinating large volumes, your veterinarian should take a urinalysis and blood test to determine how the kidneys are holding up. If the tests indicate abnormal function, the dog will need a prescription diet.

When the kidneys are really in bad shape, the dog will lose its appetite, lose weight, and vomit frequently. By that time, it may be too late to save the dog. You could go the route of aggressive therapy, involving hospitalization, intravenous fluids, and medications to counteract nausea or improve the appetite, but unfortunately, due to the progressive nature of the disease, that's putting the dog through a lot for what probably isn't a long-term solution.

Heart disease. Dogs rarely have heart attacks or sudden cardiac arrest, but valve problems and degeneration of the heart muscle are common in geriatric dogs. Symptoms include coughing (especially at night), breathing difficulties, fatigue, and sometimes decreased appetite. Your veterinarian will want to perform an electrocardiogram and take a chest x-ray, among other tests, and may put the dog on medication and a special diet.

Liver disease. This is usually a secondary infection, caused by a virus, bacteria, or tumor elsewhere in the body. The symptoms include increased water consumption, poor appetite, weight loss, vomiting, and sometimes a yellowing of the whites of the eyes. The dog needs antibiotics, a special diet, and plenty of home nursing.

Tumors. According to veterinary oncologist Dr. Audrey Hayes, the most common tumors found among old dogs are of the skin, bone, and mouth. They may be benign or malignant. Lymphosarcomas (cancer of the lymph nodes) are also common, as are benign or malignant mammary gland tumors in unspayed females or in females spayed after they were a year old. Treatment for tumors is usually surgery or, in the case of malignant tumors, chemotherapy, perhaps in combination with surgery. A large animal hospital or one associated with a veterinary college may offer radiation therapy.

Dr. Hayes suggests that before you automatically euthanize an animal with cancer, ask your veterinarian to refer you to an oncologist for consultation. Even a highly skilled veterinarian in general practice may not be up to date on the latest advances in the specialty of oncology, or may not have the specialized medications and equipment needed for chemotherapy or radiation therapy.

Cushing's disease. An endocrine disease that sometimes affects older dogs, Cushing's disease causes the adrenal glands to overproduce a hormone called cortisol. Symptoms are excessive thirst and urination, increased appetite, weight loss, weakness, hair loss, often a distended belly, and sometimes excessive panting. It is diagnosed by a blood test and can be controlled with medication. Without treatment, the disease is fatal within one to two years.

Diabetes mellitus. Older female dogs are especially susceptible to this disorder. The animal will have increased appetite but lose weight; it will drink more water and have to urinate more frequently. In advanced stages, there may be vomiting, diarrhea, lethargy, and depression. The owner will have to give the dog insulin by injection (anybody can learn to do this for his or her pet).

Tooth problems. Crust and tartar on a dog's teeth are unavoidable but, if neglected, can cause infection in the gums. The dog will have bad breath, eat carefully as if it hurt, drop food from its mouth, and perhaps rub its face with its paws or against the floor. Keep a close eye on an aging dog's teeth, and have your veterinarian examine them regularly.

He or she can show you how to brush your dog's teeth at home (good luck!)—this may slow the accumulation of plaque and tartar. In severe cases, the tartar must be removed while the dog is under anesthesia.

PERSONALITY CHANGES

A geriatric dog needs a lot of tender care and affection. When we ourselves grow old, at least we have some understanding of what's going on with our bodies, but aging can be confusing and stressful to a dog. We don't really know how much self-awareness dogs have; all we can go by, in terms of their psychological needs, is what they tell us in their own ways. Owners of old dogs should be alert to all signals coming from them. Now is the time to be patient and indulgent with them for the years of love and companionship they have given us.

Naturally, an old dog will be less alert, slower to respond, easily confused. It will sleep more than usual and sometimes seem befuddled when it wakes up. It may gaze into space absentmindedly.

Personality changes in elderly dogs are said to take place in one of two ways: The animals either become irritable and crotchety or very dependent. A dog that becomes cranky should be allowed to live a simple life with as few disturbances and discomforts as possible. Be careful not to startle it or wake it suddenly, because it may snap.

Dandy was an example of an old dog who became unusually dependent and habituated. I first noticed it when I took her for a walk one day into a neighborhood that was unfamiliar to her. Instead of being curious and enjoying the adventure, she was miserable. She trembled and glanced around nervously when I took her into a store on an errand. She walked so close to me on the street that she almost tripped me, and she didn't relax until we got back on our block.

An elderly dog is probably most comfortable if kept in familiar surroundings as much as possible.

SAYING GOODBYE

Every owner of an elderly dog, even a healthy one, lives with the knowledge that the pet's days are numbered. You must watch carefully for every change, every sign of discomfort or disease. You should protect, indulge, clean up after, and make allowances for your aging dog. Pour on the affection—it's the least you can do in exchange for the gifts your dog has given you.

Most books on dog care, including this one, will advise you that when the quality of your geriatric dog's life has deteriorated to the point where pain and discomfort outweigh pleasure, you should have the pet euthanized. Your friends and your veterinarian will tell you the same thing. This is easy advice to give, or even accept, in the abstract. But when you actually have a very old dog, a friend who has shared your life and given you joy and companionship for many years, it's an entirely different matter.

Sometimes the moment to euthanize your dog is fairly obvious. In an extreme situation where it's plain to see that your pet is suffering greatly and the veterinarian assures you that nothing more can be done, you can make the decision quickly, and it's over before you have a chance for agonized inner debate as to whether you're doing the right thing.

But in other situations, an old dog may need expensive surgery that could prolong its life but involves much pain, lengthy hospitalization, extensive care, and sizable risk. Or a pet may develop a chronic illness that is not life-threatening but keeps it in permanent discomfort with no hope of relief. When do you decide that enough is enough? There are no easy answers.

The trouble is that with a well cared-for elderly dog, the clear-cut moment when you have only one humane choice rarely arrives. What usually happens instead is that the animal goes downhill slowly. It is confused, arthritic, deaf, blind, and perhaps incontinent, but still eats, still wags its tail and licks your hand. Does it want to go on with its life in this condition, or is it ready to pack it in and is just responding to you out of habit and affection? Has its life become a burden, or does it still enjoy small pleasures? You have always been able to judge with reasonable accuracy how your pet feels, but now the bottom line has arrived and you have no idea.

Your vet can make an educated guess about whether the animal is in pain. But to what degree? Animals have different thresholds of pain, just as we do. There's not a caring dog owner among us who doesn't wish that every aged pet could die peacefully in its sleep, in its own bed at home, instead of continuing a joyless and painful existence.

I wish I could tell you how to recognize the moment for euthanasia when it comes, how to decide in your heart with absolute certainty that you must ease your aged pet into eternity today instead of tomorrow, or next week or next month, if ever. As one who has had

Patricia Curtis

Sally in her senior years

several very old dogs, I can't give you any glib insights. If you have a family, the choices should be discussed and the decision made together, with your older children included. It seems to me inconsiderate for parents to go behind children's backs and spring it on them later, perhaps with some fairy tale about where their pet has gone. Kids should have a chance to say goodbye to the pet.

By the way, don't tell a small child that the dog is going to be "put to sleep." This euphemism can be confusing. Then when the child, or a family member, has to have an operation and is told that it won't hurt because he or she will be put to sleep, the child will understandably react with terror.

Susan Phillips Cohen, a counselor for people whose pets are severely ill or dying at the Animal Medical Center in New York City, and Dr. Carole Fudin, a psychotherapist, presenting a joint paper at a symposium on euthanasia in veterinary medicine, offered some suggestions for helping children deal with the euthanasia of a pet. They suggested that children under five or six years old should be spared the details but can be told that the pet feels very bad, that it can't get well again, and that the euthanasia will help the pet to die painlessly. After age six, they say, the child should have the reasons for and the process of the euthanasia explained to them. If they become angry with the parents or the veterinarian, their feelings should be treated with respect and patience. And they should be permitted to see the dead pet afterward and kiss it goodbye if they want to.

Both counselors say that the way parents handle a pet's death will set an example for children. If the parents act with dignity, compassion, and sensitivity, it will help the children deal with the death of a loved person later on.

Veterinarian Mark Lerman had an episode in his practice in which he was faced with euthanizing the pet of a handicapped child of about thirteen. The dog was brought to him hemorrhaging; it had cancer, but the child was weeping bitterly, certainly not ready to say goodbye to her pet. So Dr. Lerman operated, patched up the dog so it could live comfortably for a few weeks, and spent several sessions with the little girl, explaining her dog's illness and preparing her for its death. In the end, the child was able, at her own request, to hold her dog calmly in her arms when the veterinarian euthanized it.

The Actual Euthanasia

A pet euthanized by a private veterinarian is given a preliminary dose of anesthesia by injection. After the first prick of the needle, the animal feels nothing. Then, when the animal is sound asleep, the fatal injection is administered. If you are present at your dog's euthanasia, don't be alarmed if the dog's body should twitch or its tongue hang out, because it is not suffering. Its eyes do not close when it dies.

Ideally, one should have a veterinarian who will come to the house and euthanize the animal in familiar surroundings. Many dogs are so scared at the veterinarian's that it would be a kindness to spare them their fear at this point. In some cities, there are veterinarians who will make house calls, and you may want to use one for this purpose, even if he or she is not your regular vet.

Whether you have to take your dog to the veterinary clinic for euthanasia or have it done at home, your own behavior can help the dog a lot. Don't communicate your pain to your pet. Have a close, sympathetic friend with you for moral support. Act natural with the animal and be reassuring—this is not the time to throw your arms around the dog's neck and weep. You can fall apart later if you have to, but now is the moment to rise to the occasion.

Veterinarians are divided on whether or not to let a client be present at the euthanasia of a pet. Some encourage it, some won't allow it under any circumstances, but most will permit it if the client requests it (and if the vet thinks the client can handle it). I feel that the owner's presence is comforting to a pet, provided the owner is capable of putting the pet's emotional needs above his or her own at the moment. Many caring dog owners want to stroke and hold their pets, soothing them and letting them know they are loved as they slip into unconsciousness and breathe their last.

Veterinarians are not taught in vet school how to cope with a client's emotions, and I've heard some complain that they feel unequipped to be grief counselors. So don't expect too much from your vet. You may have one who is just naturally empathetic and supportive, but if the expressions of sympathy you need are not forthcoming at this moment, remember that the doctor is focusing primarily on what's best for the animal.

What to do with the body of your dog after it has died is a greater problem for city dwellers than for other dog owners—you can't just bury your pet in the backyard. Even if you have a city garden, there are probably zoning laws against it.

Your veterinarian will dispose of the body or have it cremated for you. If you look in the Yellow Pages of your city, you will probably find pet cemeteries and crematories that will pick up a pet's body from home. Also, some SPCAs and humane societies offer cremation or disposal services. Should you have your pet cremated, you can have the ashes delivered to you if you wish.

Some people derive a lot of comfort from having the pet's body or ashes buried where they can visit the grave. This is why pet cemeteries exist. They are usually beautiful, peaceful places, a testimonial to our bond with our companion animals.

At the symposium on veterinary euthanasia mentioned above, veterinarian Margaret Young told a lovely story about a four-year-old child who insisted on putting the family pet's ashes under the flowers growing on her grandfather's grave. "Now grandpa has someone with him so he won't be lonely," she said.

Coping with Grief

The late psychiatrist Michael McCulloch told of a young teenage boy who was referred to him for possible therapy. This youngster had been sunny and outgoing, a top student, a good athlete, active in school affairs. Suddenly, he had lost interest in his schoolwork and sports and had become unusually withdrawn and quiet. His parents, concerned, had sent him to the family doctor, who couldn't find anything physically wrong with him.

Dr. McCulloch interviewed the boy, who was cooperative but subdued. It wasn't until the second or third time the child was in McCulloch's office that it came out that his dog had died.

"How is it that you never mentioned this to me before?" asked the doctor, suspecting immediately that he was dealing with a classic case of unresolved grief.

"Everyone told me it was too bad but not important," said the boy. "They said Sam was just a dog, and that I should forget about him." The poor kid had been carrying around a huge burden of grief, and nobody had understood or helped him.

The death of a companion animal is still trivialized by society generally. If a man, for example, were to call his office and say he was unable to come to work because a close family member had died, expressions of sympathy would pour forth and no supervisor, department head, or chief executive officer would expect him to show up for a week. But if it was his dog that had died, his need for time off would be regarded as wild eccentricity and treated with puzzlement, amusement, or exasperation—even though the dog may have been his best friend, closer than any family member. In our still quite sexist society, a woman might be treated with more sympathy, because we are allowed to be more "soft" in these matters. Still, she would be wise not to push it.

Some psychiatrists and others in the helping professions believe that the bereavement process after the death of a beloved pet is much like that which follows the loss of a significant person. According to Dr. Herbert Nieburg, author of *Pet Loss: A Thoughtful Guide for Adults and Children*, the degree of grieving is normal in proportion to the affection that the pet owner felt for the animal.

However, the death of a pet under certain conditions can produce a morbid reaction in the owner, depending on what else is going on in his or her life at the time. If a person is suffering from another severe loss—of a mate, parent, child, job, or home, for example—the death or euthanasia of a pet can be catastrophic. This might be the time to seek help from a professional, a group, or some wise and trusted individual—and not to feel ashamed for doing so.

Attitudes toward pet loss and human grief are changing slowly. If your dog should die or have to be euthanized, you can probably expect more understanding on the part of your colleagues, friends, and acquaintances than you could formerly. Above all, don't think there's anything wrong with you if you feel extreme pain and a sense of loss for quite a while.

People vary in the manner and length of bereavement. You may feel like crying for weeks or months, but try to have faith in your normal, human ability to heal.

One nice thing to do that will make you feel better is to make a donation in your dog's name to your favorite animal shelter. In helping the shelter care for dogs that other people have discarded, you honor the species that has given you happiness, and you also strike a blow against human neglect and cruelty to animals.

LOOKING AHEAD

Some people who have loved and lost a dog, especially one that lived with them for many years, and especially one whose euthanasia they presided over, vow "never again." The loss was an experience they prefer not to repeat, so they resolve that the dog that died is also the last dog they'll ever have.

It seems to me that every emotional attachment is full of risk, and whenever you let yourself form strong feelings for a mate, parent, child, or friend, there are no guarantees that you will love or be loved by that person forever. But if you never take the risks, you'll miss the whole ball game.

The human heart has unlimited room for love, enough for any number of dogs. I urge you to get another. Give yourself time for mourning—people vary in the length of time they need. I adopted Dandy ten days after Benjy died because I not only missed him, but was lonely for a dog. I adopted Susannah a month after I gave Lucy to the more suitable home, because I felt I needed a dog. But it may be weeks or months before you're ready, and that is not unusual. Children especially should not be given the impression that the dog who died can be immediately replaced, like a broken toy.

Dogs are not interchangeable—each one is unique in the world. But while you can never duplicate the peerless pet you've lost, dogs fortunately share certain qualities of dogginess. Each one has its own special traits, but they also have characteristics in common. Dog lovers like myself love not only our individual animals but the race in general.

So don't look for a carbon copy of the dog that died. That puts a burden on an unsuspecting new dog of having to live up to a memory, and you may be disappointed in it through no fault of its own. When my neighbor Cathy lost her sedate, gentle Husky, she grieved for a few months, and then, to the delight of the whole neighbor-

Paul Glassner/San Francisco SPCA

A San Francisco SPCA shelter dog waits for a home

hood, she went to a shelter and adopted. Her new dog was smooth-coated, adolescent, awkward, and exuberant—nothing like the dear departed Volga. But Cathy loved Ruffian just as much.

One point to keep in mind is that it may be many years since you had a puppy, so you may have forgotten how much trouble they can be. Perhaps a grown dog would be more what you are used to—and remember that adult dogs are the ones that most need homes. In fact, there will be one waiting for you at the animal shelter.

Don't let too long a period elapse before you embark on the adventure of getting to know another of these marvelous creatures and of establishing another love affair that could turn out to be just as happy, in its own way, as the one that has ended. Perhaps this book will encourage you. I hope so.

INDEX

In this index the use of *f* indicates a photograph.

Boston Terrier, 19, 38*f*, 146, 150, 160, 177
Boxer, 19
breeders, reputable, 22, 35–38
Brittany, 19
Buddy, 106*f*, 185–186
Bulldog, 150
Bustad, Leo, 207–208

C

Cain, Ann Ottney, 198
Cairn Terrier, 19
cancer/tumors, 245, 245–246
cats
 diet, 91, 98
 and dogs, 29*f*, 44*f*, 184–185, 188–193, 189*f*, 242
 illness/accidents in, 154, 155, 244
 nature of, 51–52, 64
Cavalier King Charles Spaniel, 19
chewing, 40–41, 74–76, 94, 156
Chihuahua, 18, 20
child-substitute dogs, 201–202
children
 babies and dogs, 61
 benefits from dogs, 197, 199–201
 biting of, 15, 58
 choosing a dog for, 13–17, 19, 38–40, 65
 cruelty to animals by, 200–201
 euthanasia explained, 249–250
 as pet sitters, 15–16
 and strange dogs, 58
choosing a dog
 after a death, 254–255
 children and, 13–17, 19, 38–40, 65
 costs involved, 11–12
 gender choice, 12–13
 life expectancy, 12–13
 owner lifestyle in, 5–8, 9
 purebred vs. mixed breed, 20–24, 36
 shelter dogs/strays, 24–26
 space requirements, 8–10
 temperament in, 17–20, 53
 See also puppies
Cleo, 44*f*

clothing for cold/wet weather, 147, 173*f*, 240–241
Cocker Spaniel, 19, 125
Cohen, Susan Phillips, 249
collars, 45, 79, 85–86, 118–119, 154, 169
Collie, Bearded, 19
companionship
 benefits of, 203–205
 child-substitute dogs, 201–202
 for children, 199–201
 to the elderly, 205–208
 family dogs for, 198–201
 puppies need for, 28
 See also friends for your dog
confinement. *See* kennels/crates
Corgi, 19
crates. *See* kennels/crates
cruelty, 31, 36–38, 79, 142, 220–222
crying in puppies, soothing, 46
Cushing's disease, 246

D

Dachshund, 125, 170
Dalmatian, 22
Dandy, 4, 13, 17, 18, 23–24, 23*f*, 65, 77–78, 128, 153, 155, 179, 232–233, 247, 254
day care for dogs, 5–6
death of a pet, 247–254
desensitization techniques, 72, 76–77
destructive behavior, 40–41, 69–70, 74–76
diabetes, 126, 246
diet
 appetite loss and, 108–110
 for coat/skin problems, 170, 171
 commercial food, 91–96, 103
 digestive problems and, 93, 101
 exercise and, 96, 104
 fussy eaters, 93
 how much/when to feed, 96–99, 102, 242
 label reading, 94–96
 prescription foods, 122, 242
 raw food, 94
 treats in, 81, 101, 103, 112